REMEMBERING *the* CAJUN PAST

A VOLUME IN THE SERIES

Public History in Historical Perspective

EDITED BY

Marla R. Miller

MARC DAVID

REMEMBERING *the* CAJUN PAST

MEMORY, RACE, AND THE POLITICS OF PUBLIC HISTORY IN LOUISIANA

University of Massachusetts Press
Amherst and Boston

Printed in the United States of America

ISBN 978-1-62534-919-4 (paper); 920-0 (hardcover)

Designed by Scribe Inc.
Set in Adobe Garamond Pro
Printed and bound by Books International, Inc.

Cover design by adam b. bohannon
Cover photo by unknown photographer, *Viewing the Acadian Memorial*, 2024. Courtesy of the Acadian Memorial Foundation.

Library of Congress Cataloging-in-Publication Data
A catalog record for this book is available from the Library of Congress.

British Library Cataloguing-in-Publication Data
A catalog record for this book is available from the British Library.

In memory of Ronald David

Contents

Preface

In so many words, one of the book's reviewers intimated that this material may be too outdated to publish. As much of the fieldwork dates from two decades ago, what value could it possess today? Isn't the current moment different enough from that one, such that this material offers little insight for the present?

The question is valid, for indeed much has changed. Many forces that led to the Acadian Memorial's emergence have subsided. The economic development strategies promoting heritage tourism and cultural preservation are long gone from Louisiana's strategic development plans. Under the administration of Governor Bobby Jindal, the state's subsidy of the Louisiana Endowment for the Humanities, a key para-statal supporter of the memorial's elaboration, went from millions to zero. Academic research and publishing on Louisiana history continues, but no major public historical initiative concerning Cajuns has launched since 2003. My sense is that, in substantive ways, the time of the memorial's creation has given way to a different moment.

At the same time, the motivation to continue researching and revising toward publication flowed from my conviction that time's passage had not invalidated the study's findings. Some are matters of historical interpretation, which other scholars have not advanced before or since. Others—including those grounded in the fieldwork—seem current, worth circulating for what they might contribute to debates about culture, politics, and public historical practice.

Interviewing the memorial's most enthusiastic visitors during the 2000s, the place of historical truth in their efforts to remake themselves into white ethnic persons with dignity and purpose was immediately apparent to me. My project initially took inspiration from this. From prior research, I intuited that places like the memorial prompted something transformative to happen among people whom I knew and respected. I also surmised that that something involved creative processes of remembering, though their precise contours took years to parse out. Honestly, however, their engagement initially seemed excessive, out of proportion to what a historic site is meant to offer. But that reaction only disclosed the limits of my thinking. With time, conducting more interviews and sifting through grant applications, feasibility studies, and programmatic statements, practitioners' matching aims of subjective transformation, their goal to employ history toward ends of fostering self-governing citizens, became clear. What was entirely too familiar to me—public history's moral, subjectivizing thrust, so entrenched as to be taken for granted—became strange.

Trying to make sense of this alignment, to find a language that could describe its politics, I turned to scholarly literature on history, memory, and relations of power. These also inspired the following analysis. My interpretation of public history's civic politics takes its bearing from work stimulated by Michel Foucault's late lectures, which scholars like Nikolas Rose, Tony Bennett, and others expanded on. Broadly speaking, they identify an abiding gap in analyses of power's operation in spaces like historic sites. A tendency exists to discern politics primarily on the side of external forces that shape a cultural policy space like the public historical sphere. Electoral politics and partisan debates in the public sphere, the social power of class and race, the impact of commercialization, and the like—one searches for power's effects on historical representation in these arenas, as its "inputs." Meanwhile, on public history's policy side—the bureaucratic implementation of programmatic agendas, the design and management of sites, and practitioners' goals for visitors' engagement with them—social relations are cast as technical and apolitical. From this perspective, power does not operate there.

Years ago, James Ferguson's *The Anti-Politics Machine* demonstrated how a politics does indeed exist on this "output" side of governmental activity. Yet his focus on economic development projects in the Global South identified outcomes of exclusion and repression and not much in the way of productive effects on its subjects. To be sure, exclusions and the techno-politics of experts existed in this case. But something else—other relations of power, including ones that make up new kinds of subjects that embrace the truths sites promote—also unfolds in venues like the memorial. *Remembering the Cajun Past* attempts to center and describe that something else on public history's "output" side.

In this regard, the most significant finding I forward is that the politics of public history composed a regime of truth and subjectivity, a civic politics of self-making according to history's truths. As the book illustrates, many social actors, many vectors of relations of power, contributed to the emergence of a novel public history of Cajuns. So the argument is not that, alone or exclusively, these governmental relations of power explain the case. But they were distinct and central to the motivations and objectives that animated this new history's articulation and use, a core nexus that sustained it, irreducible to its other conditions.

While I resist drawing a definitive conclusion about the ultimate political valence of this regime, I insist on its complexity. The elaboration of a new history about Cajuns shifted relations of power in ways multiple and variegated; for the most part, I seek to describe them. Much of the book is structured as a response to the question of how, in historical discourse, various actors first cast Cajuns as a serious problem for the state's governance, followed by others who then transformed them into a kind of model white ethnic group, a "happy minority." I set myself the challenge of illuminating how the latter discourse became instantiated in a complex that now spans the region. Along these lines, the first chapter explains how all manner of authorities vilified Cajuns in pre-civil-rights-era Louisiana. From that perspective, I believe it is a felicitous development that this new history affirms Cajuns' dignity and belonging as citizens instead of perpetuating the prior effects of marginalization and *petite misère*. From my own experience growing up in a Cajun family, in Louisiana towns where most of my age cohort shared similar backgrounds, I knew the ancien régime's pernicious impact. I possessed an innate sense of how it marred individuals' flourishing; I learned much more about this from my interlocutors in St. Martinville, who schooled me with their hard-won lessons.

That said, the new history's effect of enabling Cajuns' full inclusion in the body politic is far from its only political impact. It has endowed apparatuses of the state with influence over historical discourse that did not previously exist, in expert–lay relationships that sometimes possess a hierarchical tenor. It participates in reinscribing class boundaries among people of Acadian descent, aggravating a long-standing social fissure. And it effects a remarkable postsegregation transposition of racial histories, endowing Cajuns with a remote past that renders them heroic victims, while the anti-Black violence of slavery and Jim Crow has yet to find its place in the region's public historical sphere. All these asymmetries also compose its legacy. In addition, the book attempts to foreground a final, consequential effect: the diffusion of a mode of truth-telling about the past that merits interrogation. As Americans, we have constantly been told that historical truths will set us free, so to speak, engendering a more enlightened mode of citizenship if only we would take them to heart. Whether the existing regime of historical representation and public historical practice can deliver on that promise is a question this study seeks to evoke, even if it does not answer it.

A final reason motivates publishing this work so long after it started. As of this writing, the complex I describe remains intact. Decades after its creation, this public history endures, largely unchanged from its original form, continuing as the predominant public historical narrative in the region. Thus, its benefits and limitations, its promise and perils, persist together, posing yet another sociopolitical puzzle for us to problematize and solve.

Acknowledgments

A book project is never a solitary undertaking; one accumulates many debts in the process. An effort that takes decades amasses many more of them.

Though I have not lived there for years, south Louisiana is home to me. My biggest debt is to the many other natives and residents who agreed to answer my clumsy questions and entertain my tentative interpretations. I will always be grateful for their engagement and hospitality, without which this project could not have unfolded. Even in the book's most critical passages, I have tried to convey accurately and fairly their own views of the world.

The research benefited from generous support at crucial junctures. Grants from the National Science Foundation and the Wenner-Gren Foundation funded the dissertation fieldwork that forms the core of the book's ethnography. A fellowship with the Royster Society at UNC-Chapel Hill furthered initial writing and analysis, as did one at the Smithsonian Institution's National Museum for American History. The latter also allowed me to begin exploring federal archives, which proved crucial for the historical interpretations that follow. Faculty research grants at the University of Oklahoma, Metropolitan State University, and St. Olaf College were also key, enabling additional fieldwork and archival research in Washington, DC, and across Louisiana. I am grateful for this extensive support and pleased to finally make good on it.

Many individuals played central roles in the research process. With commitment and insight, Donald Nonini, Catherine Lutz, and Nahum Chandler helped shape the project's initial version in long discussions during coursework and dissertation writing in Chapel Hill. Carl Brasseaux offered liberal amounts of time, encouragement, and institutional support early on. At a pivotal moment, Pete Daniel tendered expert guidance about how to work the archives in Washington. A slew of librarians and archivists tolerated my repeated requests for assistance, including Connie Phelps at the University of New Orleans and Germain Bienvenu at Louisiana State University, as well as staff at the University of Louisiana at Lafayette's Dupré Library. Late in the game, Robert Blythe and Guy Hughes with the National Park Service aided me in important ways.

Over the years, I benefited mightily from the help and company of many assistants. In an early phase, Alana Carmon Bobb, Elista Istre, and the late and beloved Stephen "Etienne" Dugas joined me to conduct interviews and archival research. Abby Purfeest, Laurence Tissot, and their team at INGCO International assisted me with interview transcriptions, as did the late Anne Beard. I coded visitor reception material with Manuela Novoa Villada and, more extensively through support from a St. Olaf undergraduate research grant, with Adriana Sanchez, who performed excellent qualitative data analysis.

I am also indebted to many colleagues and friends who offered counsel, read drafts, and listened to me ramble about the project. If not for the tireless cheerleading and peerless close reading skills of Ron Haas and Robert Scafe, this text would never have seen the light of day. Many others provided insights, encouragement, or assistance over the years, including the late, great Claude Bariteau, Shane Bernard, Chris Chiappari, Vivian Choi, Kristin Dowell, Eric Fure-Slocum, Marc Gonzalez, Dana David Gravot, Gustave Gravot, Thaddeus Guldbransen, Maria Hébert-Leiter, George Henderson, Kamela Heywood-Rotimi, Thomas Pegelow Kaplan, Misha Klein, Thomas Klingler, Christopher Nelson, Joshua Piker, Patricia Sawin, Circe Sturm, Brian Thomas, Matt Thompson, and Margaret Wiener. I received useful feedback during stimulating discussions with audiences that attended talks at Texas State University and Tulane University. The anonymous reviewers for the University of Massachusetts Press made suggestions that considerably improved the manuscript, and editor Matt Becker enthusiastically supported the book from start to finish. The helpful efforts of all these good people notwithstanding, the errors and flaws contained herein are fully attributable to my own limitations and, in a few instances, stubbornness.

Finally, I am grateful to Mary Simon David, who welcomed me back home during many return trips to Louisiana as I did research in between completing household maintenance tasks on her to-do list. Words can hardly express what I owe to my intimate family. Jonah and Marjanne O'Hara-David endured the many absences from family life that such a project entails, yet they made our shared life worth living, generously and with love. And for thirty years now, Danyelle O'Hara's loving support has made everything possible. *Merci mille fois, mes chers.*

St. Paul, Minnesota
July 2025

Note on Names and Cited Material

All names have been changed, except in cases when I cite individuals who spoke at public events reported on elsewhere. To ensure confidentiality, I modified identifying characteristics and, in a handful of instances, used different pseudonyms for the same person.

In official documents, St. Martinville presents itself as a city, a choice undoubtedly inflected by the French meaning of *ville* in its name. But as its population has never exceeded eight thousand residents, I refer to it as a town.

Across the book, I employ different formal modes to convey different speech contexts. In reproducing speech from recorded and transcribed interviews, I cite it verbatim using quotation marks. When I paraphrase or recollect speech reconstructed from detailed field notes, italics are used.

REMEMBERING *the* CAJUN PAST

Introduction

The Happy Minority?

> According to a famous remark by Karl Popper, "The historicist does not recognize that it is we who select and order the facts of history." Popper and [others] do not seem to realize that the problematic element in this assertion is not the constitution of history (who doubts that it is made, not given?) but the nature of the *we*. From the point of view of anthropology, that *we*, the subject of history, cannot be presupposed or left implicit.
>
> Johannes Fabian, *Time and the Other*

Seated on cypress benches inside the Acadian Memorial, we were iced down by the air-conditioning as the conversation heated up. It was a muggy June afternoon in 2001, and I had invited a group of acquaintances, people who acted together in a French-language theater troupe, into this historic site opened five years earlier. None of them were residents of St. Martinville, the town in south Louisiana where the memorial is located, but they knew it well from performing there many times. Each of them loved the place and eagerly wanted to tell me why. It was the kind of animated conversation in which people riff off each other's comments and finish each other's thoughts, almost as if competing to convey the most enthusiastic response to my questions. Halfway through the conversation, Julia Cormier, a middle-aged nurse, gestured toward the large mural painting on the north wall of the memorial space, a striking trompe l'oeil depiction of eighteenth-century Acadian immigrants confidently arriving in Louisiana, and declared,

> For me, probably the biggest message of this mural, and actually of this whole memorial—the thing that I identify with the

> most—is the word "Hope." Because, I mean, even in my personal experience in my family . . . there was at least the hope of things being better. And even when I learned my history—that was the thing, and you know, so much tragedy, so much sadness, so much rejection, so much, you know—like Quentin [another participant] said—this thing about having the drive to continue living and to continue working and being a pioneer culture, especially—it was so hard, I mean, not only was it hard to arrive from Europe into the New World in Acadie, but to arrive here and to be faced with all the challenges of the environment—relearning everything about the environment, dealing with the weather, dealing with the mosquitoes, dealing with the illness [from which] so many of them perished and . . . I mean, the only thing they had was really religion and hope. Because, I mean, there was really no security, and my dad was a rice farmer. There was never anything sure.

Then as now, I found this statement remarkable. Cormier's interweaving of individual recollections with the site's representation of a remote past she had taught herself to claim as her own strikes me as a distinctively creative act. It is part remembrance of difficult personal circumstances, part summary of acquired historical knowledge, and a profound articulation of the two. Notably, a redemptive thrust links the narrative threads: The challenges of colonial life faced by the ancestors and the precarity that Cormier and her family endured are each saved by (seemingly realized) aspirations for a better life. And the whole is suffused with a sense of meaningful discovery, of grasping something essential about herself through the encounter with the site's interpretation of Acadian history.

Cormier's is but one of many similarly intriguing interpretations of the memorial that I heard over the years. In interviews with dozens of local visitors to the site, the intensity of their engagement frequently struck me, including how their descriptions of its significance often elicited personal memories and accounts of how the site connected with personal projects. "It says how during our time, when I was a little girl, that we were presented all the struggles to get here, and we were, they were taking our Cajun heritage, our language from us to make us something different," explained Martha Thibodeaux about her interpretation of the site. "So many people struggled to hold on to what we have, [and] now we are proud," she continued, adding that she had crafted this story of collective triumph over adversity into a song and recorded it. More explicitly than Cormier, Thibodeaux interpreted the site's meaning in relation to her memory of "struggles" during her own lifetime. And rather than presenting it as an ephemeral experience, a one-off visit to a venue that left little abiding impact, she related it to something significant in her life, intimating that she wove its narrative into other important interests and her sense of self.

This is a book about such historical remembering, the historic site that fostered it, and the politics that span, saturate, and shape both. It asks how this emergence of historically informed remembrance happened just like this and why it did at this particular moment. It takes public histories of Cajuns and the Acadian Memorial as its focus because they offer a case in which intriguing aspects of these topics can be explored. One of these is that, for much of the twentieth century, all manner of authorities cast Cajuns as a serious social problem in need of remediation, a kind of white trash blocking Louisiana's social and economic progress. Critics claimed Cajuns' relationship to their past formed the crux of the issue: They were stuck in time, stymied by the trauma of their colonial-era expulsion from what is now Canada, and thus too insulated from the reformative thrust of a modernizing state.

Since the mid-1970s, however, a range of entities across the body politic have opened nine sites related to the Acadian past. Like the Acadian Memorial and its celebratory mural painting, all of them forward the claim that remembering the Acadian past is now important for residents of the region and the country. Somehow, then, forces linked to the public sector (in which the prior vilification of Cajuns also unfolded) and an expanding public historical sphere rehabilitated discourse about them. By following the sudden emergence of this new complex, I contend that we can appreciate a distinct politics—that of social governance and citizen formation under the aegis of the state—that expanded through it. Situating this case with respect to such relations of power will benefit our understanding of both the pragmatics that incited the Acadian Memorial's creation and these animated engagements with it.

The old saw about anthropology is that it seeks to make the strange familiar and the familiar strange. I confess that the latter part of this motto motivates this study to a high degree. Something that scholars and the public often take for granted—that humans remember time beyond their own lifetimes—came to seem odd and complex to me. The longer I reflected on moments like these with Cormier and Thibodeaux and on the raft of new Acadian historic sites, the more a host of questions presented themselves. How could this history of Acadian ancestors, long forgotten and unavailable for use in everyday life or public discourse, become so meaningful, so viscerally salient, in such a short time? How does a site such as the memorial—which, after all, is a collection of texts and objects like the mural, none of which date from the distant past it represents—foster the enthusiasm that Cormier and Thibodeaux displayed? Just as puzzling, until the 1960s, practitioners in many institutions saw it as their responsibility to make Cajuns forget their past because they remembered too much of it. How did so many authorities suddenly decide that celebratory histories like the memorial's should predominate in the region's public historical sphere?

Remembering the Cajun Past draws on Michel Foucault's notion of governmentality as the broad frame for a response, tracing a genealogy of how this formation of Acadian history emerged.[1] I intend to show how the desires of individuals like Cormier and Thibodeaux to redeem their maligned white ethnic selves by remembering the Acadian past came to mesh with the aims of a broad public historical complex seeking to govern Cajuns, Louisiana, and the US through that same history. Both entail relations of power, of influencing the choices and behaviors of others and ourselves, which are often absent from accounts of historical remembrance and discourse. Yet I contend that understanding Cajuns' shifting status across the past half century, from problematic "not quite whites"[2] to a model white ethnic "happy minority," requires foregrounding public history's civic and political aims and uses.[3]

I do not claim these were the only politics that produced this formation. Among other forces, the book situates them against the backdrop of whites' silencing of the Black past during the postsegregation era, a history that, in ongoing struggles in St. Martinville, Black residents persistently evoked. But by placing public history's civic politics alongside more commonly analyzed relations of power like those of racial hierarchy and the effects of commercialization, the perspective I adopt brings into view the power of the state and of its obscured focus on subjective aspects of citizen formation. In the growing realm of public historical practice, history is *for* guiding citizens' conduct. It seeks to generate a conscious, vital relationship between the nation's subjects and historical truths such that they willingly live their lives in alignment with them. These politics are the underappreciated complement to Cormier's and Thibodeaux's enthusiastic remembrance, their material support and the condition for their existence.

THE POLITICS OF GOVERNING THROUGH MEMORY AND HISTORY

HISTORICAL REMEMBRANCE AND THE ETHICS OF SELF-MAKING

To answer my questions, I pursued fieldwork in St. Martinville and across south Louisiana, diving deep into the everyday dynamics of recalling remote pasts, a cultural process that is often taken for granted. Much social theory about historical remembrance buttresses a conventional wisdom that it unfolds organically or that merely assumes its existence.[4] But reactions to the memorial like those of Cormier and Thibodeaux compelled me to become more curious about how and why individuals and groups come to claim a "time out of mind," a distant historical past, as their own. Through reading the scholarly literature as well as from my own experience, I knew that just a generation earlier, self-identified Cajuns rarely articulated this motivated mélange of personal memories and history of the distant colonial past.[5]

In addition to the memorial, St. Martinville also features a charming downtown with many nineteenth-century structures, which forms the basis of its representation as le Petit Paris d'Amerique (the Little Paris of America), a history foregrounding its colonial-era founding by French colonists. But it also sponsors multiple sites that represent Acadian history, including those dedicated to Evangeline, the heroine of Henry Wadsworth Longfellow's popular 1856 poem *Evangeline, a Tale of Acadie*. Commonly defined as present-day descendants of eighteenth-century immigrants from colonial Acadia (now Nova Scotia), Cajuns have lived in this region for over 250 years. Many of the first Acadian exiles who immigrated to Louisiana relocated to homesteads near St. Martinville, and one of the state's largest concentrations of Acadian descendants lives in the area today. If nothing else, this expansive material landscape—structures, plaques, statues, exhibits, and more—presented as a constant provocation to remember distant pasts. I wanted to know how the Acadian Memorial, a new site intended to replace the Evangeline-based history, related to existing practices and spaces of historical remembering. I also sought to understand if and how the memorial garnered uptake from locals.

In anthropology and related disciplines, memory has consistently been theorized as a social process. Following Maurice Halbwachs, scholars posit that "memories are in fact fragmentary and diffuse" and are therefore "made coherent through dialogue with our social surroundings."[6] As groups change, memories are in flux as well. They require grounding in commemorative spaces and activities that stabilize their meaning, giving them the shape, form, and feeling that make them *memorable*.[7] In this light, much research stresses the significance of collective processes—of broad social dynamics and political forces—over those involving the individual per se. Theorists claim that *remembering* unfolds intersubjectively—more an action than a property, something we *do* collectively as opposed to something we *have* individually—and as such is deeply integrated into social practices.[8] In relation to historical remembrance, the argument goes, a stress on whether individuals actually possess memories of remote pasts misses how integrated "memory" can be in the representations and processes of "history" from which analysts erroneously separate it.[9]

In some contexts, I found good reason to doubt whether something as pronounced as "historical memories" unfolded when people referenced distant pasts. With respect to the existing historical landscape of le Petit Paris and the Evangeline sites, they evoked the historical past in ways that were often indeterminate, fleeting, embedded in social activities, or nonexistent rather than something as discrete and conscious as a memory of it. History was notably caught up in projects of economic development and civic renewal. Likewise, in interviews with many individuals who, by conventional criteria, could identify as Cajuns, a broad range of responses emerged, both with respect to whether they identified as white ethnics and in how significant historical remembrance was to them. In these cases, the notion of an explicit consciousness that the concept of historical memory implies—with its connotation of a cognitive, reflexive relation to the past—did not describe the breadth of how history resonated (or not) in the present.[10]

At the same time, I noticed that a historic site like the Acadian Memorial could, through its evocative configuration of space, narratives, and objects, prompt considerable personal investment and individual recollection. One aspect of the politics of such remembering emerged in interviews when individuals expanded upon their own versions of Thibodeaux's mention of her "struggles" against efforts "to make us something different." For much of the twentieth century, authorities cast Cajuns as a serious problem for policy and governance, a group of white ethnics in need of reform by a modernizing state. Many who identified as Cajuns recounted searing "memory tattoos" of contempt and marginalization they endured from the fallout of this widespread derision.[11]

One of my key findings is that memories of these more recent experiences of social hierarchy and state regulation served as fodder for individuals' engagement with the memorial's historical representations. The visitors who reacted most enthusiastically to the site's history described how their personal memories of overcoming those indignities corresponded to its narrative of the Acadian past, using the latter to induct themselves into a relationship to that history.[12] In a performative turn, memory studies increasingly emphasize that remembering collective pasts emerges much like this. It unfolds in dialogue and active engagement with others and with sites themselves, at the interstices between official narratives and individual memories of family or other group belonging, and through the emotion-laden motivations "that bring agents of remembering into and through spaces of remembrance" in the first place.[13]

This kind of memory work among Cajuns and other white ethnics is often interpreted in terms of a politics of nostalgic revival, emerging in the context of a white backlash against the Black movement for civil rights and its aftermath.[14] As Blacks have formed a majority of St. Martinville's residents since the 1970s, the town presented an opportunity to explore how race shaped this articulation of historical remembrance. In the following, I elaborate how many whites' everyday recollections of experiences with their Black neighbors were filled with lapses, denials, and repressions, amounting to a substantial forgetting of the interracial past and present that Black residents frequently evoked. As fraught postsegregation conflicts roiled the town, whites' memories of their relationships with Blacks did indeed shape relations of power in ways large and small.

Another political dimension, however, operated at the memorial, one at least as consequential and arguably more unnoticed. It pertains to the affect and passion that Cormier and Thibodeaux conveyed to me about their experience of the memorial. This involves relations of the self to the self, of an ethics of self-fashioning that, in the contemporary moment, historic sites support as relays of truths about the past. For such visitors, the memorial offered an opportunity to use history to put themselves "in the true." Countering persistent narratives of Cajuns as reprobates, it conveyed positive, archivally based truths about the Acadian past, which in turn furnished a platform to assert abiding truths—profound affirmations and discoveries—*about their selves*. This also involves relations of power, of the part we play in shaping ourselves into the kind of subjects we desire to be through practices of self-making or "techniques of the self."[15] At key moments in the book, I analyze individual and autobiographical recollections in a way that foregrounds these ethical concerns.[16] Adopting Jennifer Cole's notion of "moral projects"—locally predominant meanings of the beneficence, indifference, or malevolence of others toward one's self, experiences of and commitments to fairness and (in)justice, and how these shape and are shaped by individuals striving to achieve them—I attend to how they influenced individuals' historical remembrance.[17]

In turn, the specificity of and investment in moral projects is often where the ethical segues into the political, where "individual concerns and desires [link] to wider sociopolitical formations."[18] In addition to illuminating how the new Acadian history did (and did not) become memorable for locals, such a concept offers critical purchase for discerning how these stances were linked to broader politics. These relations of power have not been foregrounded in research about public history, but they were at the heart of explanations from many memorial visitors concerning how they used it. By adopting their way of seeing the memorial and public history more generally, I explore how an extensive regime of everyday self-fashioning, including involvement in historic preservation, genealogy, travel abroad, and so on, became aligned with the civic goals of public history practitioners, regional formations of race and class, and more.

This is one reason why the *we* of history cannot be assumed, as Johannes Fabian puts it in the epigraph. As the vignettes in the opener intimate, Cormier's and Thibodeaux's historical awareness did not so much precede their arrival at the venue as it unfolded through their visits there. In this sense, the memorial enabled the self-making of historically aware Cajun selves, of an "I" and a "we" who remembered the Acadian past in motivated ways. In presupposing that individuals and groups automatically generate historical memory, many accounts skip this crucial step—that of explaining how and why people acquire it as well as how and why, in many instances, they do not.

PUBLIC HISTORY AND CITIZEN FORMATION: CIVIC TECHNOLOGIES OF MEMORY

Asking questions about the "we" authoring these representations also led me into the archives, which constitute the project's other empirical locus. Explaining this *engouement* for the Acadian past required moving beyond St. Martinville itself to investigate the upswell in Acadian public history that preceded and coincided with the memorial's launch. Between 1974 and 2003,

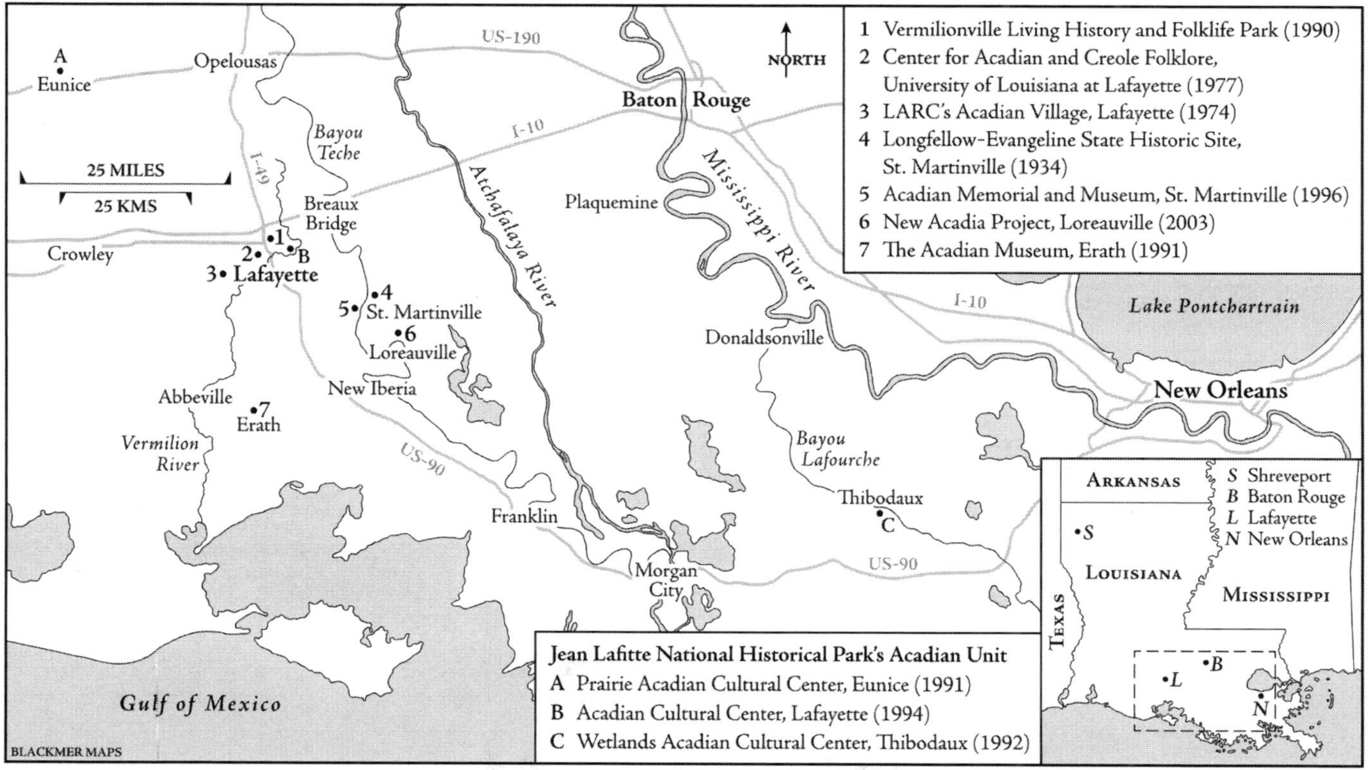

1 Vermilionville Living History and Folklife Park (1990)
2 Center for Acadian and Creole Folklore, University of Louisiana at Lafayette (1977)
3 LARC's Acadian Village, Lafayette (1974)
4 Longfellow-Evangeline State Historic Site, St. Martinville (1934)
5 Acadian Memorial and Museum, St. Martinville (1996)
6 New Acadia Project, Loreauville (2003)
7 The Acadian Museum, Erath (1991)
Jean Lafitte National Historical Park's Acadian Unit
A Prairie Acadian Cultural Center, Eunice (1991)
B Acadian Cultural Center, Lafayette (1994)
C Wetlands Acadian Cultural Center, Thibodaux (1992)
NORTH
25 MILES
25 KMS
Eunice
Opelousas
Crowley
Lafayette
Breaux Bridge
Bayou Teche
St. Martinville
Loreauville
New Iberia
Abbeville
Erath
Vermilion River
Atchafalaya River
Franklin
Morgan City
Plaquemine
Baton Rouge
Mississippi River
Donaldsonville
Bayou Lafourche
Thibodaux
Lake Pontchartrain
New Orleans
US-190
I-10
I-49
US-90
Gulf of Mexico
Arkansas
Louisiana
Mississippi
Texas
S Shreveport
B Baton Rouge
L Lafayette
N New Orleans
BLACKMER MAPS

various local, state, and national entities created nine separate venues focused on Acadian history, including several museums, two historical villages, an archive, and an archaeological site.[19]

In sifting through grant proposals, feasibility studies, and bureaucratic correspondence, I found a remarkable range of civic reasons for this new history. One academic historian asserted that archivally based truths needed to circulate because Cajuns themselves had false historical memories, which led them to sow discord in the region's public sphere. Yet another group of researchers claimed Cajuns formed the backbone of a vibrant regional culture; their history should be represented so that the country might learn from their live-and-let-live ethos, especially as the US needed models of interracial harmony in the wake of the turbulent 1960s and 1970s. And many natives of the region thought Cajuns deserved a positive account of their past, one that would "explain to Cajuns their own mostly forgotten history" and annul the pernicious effects of the negative histories that previously circulated.[20]

Drawing on his theorization of power in democratizing societies, I employ Foucault's concept of governmentality to explore the civic politics of this public history.[21] Foucault used this term to refer to the character of relations of power that have become pervasive in Europe and North America since the eighteenth century. Where previously monarchs ruled the state by requiring obedience to themselves and their laws, governmentality denotes efforts to manage the population and its conduct, seeking to improve its productivity, well-being, and security. Rather than ruling through domination and force, governmentality involves widespread initiatives to shape citizens' "hopes, desires, circumstances, or environment" in preferred directions, influencing their capacity for action by attempting to conduct their conduct.[22]

History is not often theorized as a discourse of power in this way.[23] To be sure, historical knowledge is often deemed necessary for an informed citizenry, the "civic glue" enabling strong commitments to democracy and the rule of law.[24] It teaches lessons that foster patriotism, unity, and more recently, sorely needed tolerance in a heterogeneous society.[25] From more critical perspectives, it is seen as a force peddling myths that obscure inconvenient truths and further the cultural hegemony of elites and other dominant groups.[26] Many criticisms of multiculturalism in its historical mode hold that it functions deceptively, privileging a white, liberal subject in its reimaginings of the nation.[27] One prominent variation on this view finds public history corrupted by commercial influences, which transform it into sentimentalizing kitsch.[28]

I am skeptical about these affirmations as well as these criticisms, though they are illuminating and my argument links to them at key junctures. But I question whether either set of interpretations captures crucial dynamics of power that have made history such an elaborate, technical, and popular complex. For the most part, the formulations summarized previously stress the cognitive character of history's power. Historical narratives instruct, providing lessons about past examples for emulation, or they confuse and misdirect thinking, abetting false consciousness. To paraphrase Margaret Werry's formulation about tourism and state-building, this emphasis risks underestimating history's "material efficacy and complexity."[29] It dissuades us from asking questions about the range of authorities in the US who, for decades, have obsessed over how much (read: little) citizens know their past[30] and about public history practitioners' increasingly elaborate efforts to recreate past worlds and immerse visitors in them.[31] Somehow, these highly curated material infrastructures are meant to create effects that contribute to a polity whose members govern themselves. The link between this thrust to convey historical meaning viscerally and history's micropolitics—the relations of power that circulate in, through, and beyond the "civic laboratories" of sites themselves—is underappreciated and needs further attention.[32]

My study develops this perspective on how history is used to govern. I do consider other forces conventionally invoked in such analyses, such as the politics related to class conflicts and projects. Drawing on research stressing the conflation of class and ethnicity, I note how etiquette has been a predominant idiom for marking class differences among people of Acadian descent, which in turn inflected public histories of them. Also, dynamics in the public history space did not escape those of market forces, whose influence some have stressed. In some ways, the latter were indeed constitutive of the former, exerting an undeniable influence on how its actors interpreted and represented the past. St. Martinville certainly had proponents of the new Acadian history who concentrated on heritage tourism, as local and state leaders pursued it as a strategy for economic development.

Echoing Matthew Frye Jacobson's contention about the influence of the civil rights movement on the white ethnic revival, I also recognize the largely unacknowledged weight of the Voting Rights Act and its ongoing fallout in this context.[33] This transformation had a profound effect on the historical representation of race relations, marking a break with the immediate past. The sporadic efforts of elites to commemorate the Acadian past during the 1950s and 1960s had an assimilationist cast to them.[34] In those narratives, they downplayed the centrality of the Grand Dérangement, the deportation from Acadia in 1755, and avoided describing those ancestors as victims of violence. Meanwhile, Cajuns' happy-go-lucky endurance of discrimination and oppression—with the colonial expulsion as its definitive instance—subsequently became central in historical narratives about them. Journalists, folklorists, historians, and others, in a clear contrast with Blacks, invoked Cajuns' joie de vivre, alongside their apparent unwillingness to indulge in a politics of grievance (even though their past experiences might justify it), to recast them as the "happy minority." Inflected by how racial categories in the US serve to rank groups relative to their worthiness for citizenship and its privileges, this shift has borne political effects through diffuse yet powerful processes of collective cultural memory, which those scholars who downplay individual remembering emphasize.

Yet in its analysis of relations of power, the book centers the politics of the "culture complex," the combination of knowledges (like history), experts and technicians (like historians and curators), and apparatuses (such as historic sites) that are deployed with the goal of shaping citizens' behaviors in profound ways.[35] It highlights how, during the 1960s and 1970s, criticisms of the existing regime of social and cultural policy led practitioners in the public historical sphere to objectify Cajuns in novel ways. Instead of casting them as a group needing to be disciplined, they began to imagine them as members of a community whose ties of belonging required support. In particular, practitioners in federal agencies began to explore ways to promote citizen formation through the more intimate bonds of shared culture that seemingly held sway within ethnic communities.[36]

Similarly, the analysis elevates the role of the minor tradition of historical interpretation, exemplified by Freeman Tilden's influential articulation of it in *Interpreting Our Heritage*. Tilden announced an Emersonian aim to narrate history such that it "provoked" people, leading them to reflect and act on the past's pertinence for the self and the collective.[37] Pointing to Tilden and his impact foregrounds the neglected practical tradition in which he operated, one that seeks to make discourse operate pragmatically and is situated "between academic disciplines, domains of technical expertise, and policymaking."[38] From these perspectives, this new public history can be seen for the political innovation that it is: a discrete, techno-material intervention that seeks to reshape citizens' selves, producing subjective effects that address social problems by aligning their conduct with the truths of the past.

One of the book's key claims, then, is that this comprises another dimension of governing through history. Within a broad swathe of the public historical sphere, a major goal has been not only to represent past worlds *to* citizens but also to use historical representations to produce a certain subjectivity—political and moral sentiments and motivations, along with corresponding behaviors—*within* them. Consequently, *Remembering the Cajun Past* describes the elaboration of the new public history of Acadians as a process that entailed "making up" citizens, enabling Cajun subjects who could recall their Acadian past in the name of pursuing the varied civic goals mentioned earlier.[39]

ST. MARTINVILLE, THE ACADIAN MEMORIAL, AND ME: RESEARCH SITES, METHODOLOGY, AND POSITIONING

An hour's drive from Baton Rouge and 140 miles west of New Orleans, St. Martinville (2020 pop.: 5,379) is a picturesque parish-seat (i.e., county-seat) town on oak-lined Bayou Teche in the south-central part of the state. To my mind, it represented an intriguing place to explore if and when remembering turned historical and how groups and individuals made the remote past matter. Founded during the colonial era, it boasts an enduring culture of historical representation, including the previously mentioned sites that feature Acadian history. I also knew that an academic historian in the region, Carl Brasseaux, had argued that St. Martinville's existing Acadian sites—including Longfellow-Evangeline State Historic Site, a state-sponsored venue inaugurated in 1934—purveyed a decadent "myth" motivated by commercial interests.[40] Thus, pressure from the academy provoked the town's public history, previously the province of nonprofessionals and "amateurs," to change. Apparently, the Acadian Memorial comprised a local response to this critique and piqued my curiosity as to how such a shift unfolded.

My fieldwork began during 2000–2001, when I spent a year doing research in and around the town. Since then, I visited, observed, and conducted interviews there many times, returning for shorter periods in 2002, 2005, each year between 2007 and 2010, and 2019. As a person of Acadian descent, many locals greeted me as an odd yet innocuous presence, a fellow Cajun asking questions about a shared history. But while I grew up about an hour and a half from St. Martinville, I never visited it during my youth and was unfamiliar with the town when I began research. This prompted deep curiosity on my part. Everything about St. Martinville—its history, its economy, the terrain, the social landscape—seemed different from my hometown. Fortunately, some locals indulged my endless questions about this, and many more accepted my requests for shorter moments of exchange.

Yet inquiry itself troubled any simple notion of identification between them and me and of my status as a "native" ethnographer. The very practice of asking people to leave their everyday mode of life and "reflect on [their] own activities and objectify them" creates a distance that comprises one aspect of an ethnographer's professional privilege.[41] In many cases, a fortuitous dialectic of mutual understanding did emerge, a ground of shared experience and interpretation through the cycles of questions and responses. In others, something less auspicious developed. When, during one of our initial exchanges, I explained to an older man my process of circulating and interviewing people, he responded, "Oh, je comprends, t'es manière comme un espion." (Oh, I understand, you're kind of like a spy.) He and I became friendly, but others undoubtedly shared this reaction with a higher degree of suspicion about my presence.

In some ways, St. Martinville's social composition contributed to this. As mentioned, people of Acadian descent are stratified by class like any group of white ethnics in the contemporary US. Conventionally, the term *Cajun* is described as a simple corruption of Acadian. But for decades, the classification has been bifurcated into *Cajun* and *Acadian*, a distinction often drawn in terms of behaviors and lifestyles that breaks down along class lines. In both ascribed and avowed registers, *Cajun* (and the cruder *coonass*) connotes a certain direct, unpretentious self-presentation, a preference for popular tastes and folk traditions, antielitist sensibilities, and the group's much-noted lust for life, its joie de vivre.[42] *Acadian*, meanwhile, skews middle class: It has been a preferred moniker for those (not least the upwardly mobile) who stress a decorous refinement and is linked to middlebrow preoccupations like writing, literature, language preservation, and historical discourse.[43] Along these lines, the labeling of this new public history as Acadian rather than Cajun did not only stem from a desire to depict deep continuity between current residents and their ancestors from colonial *Acadie*. It was also a matter of avoiding *Cajun*'s "base" connotations.[44] Some insisted on the distinction between themselves and Cajuns, using public history to underscore this difference even as they sought to deploy it for the latter's uplift. Accordingly, I do not follow the convention that *Acadian* and *Cajun* are synonyms; in some contexts, they were used differently, at times with antagonistic connotations.

And St. Martinville's social heterogeneity did not end there. Some locals warned me not to infer from the prominence of Acadian public history that St. Martinville is "a Cajun town." Instead, they explained, it belonged to the white Creoles or "aristocratic French" who first settled it before the Acadians' arrival. Today, *Creole* largely signifies as a social classification for people of color, the descendants of free people of color (*gens de couleur libres*), who, to a great degree in antebellum Louisiana, were of mixed Black-white ancestry. Yet for much of the past three centuries, *Creole* predominantly signified as a label referring to whites, especially wealthier descendants of early European settlers. In addition to how it was used to maintain boundaries between Blacks and whites, the classification also marked a difference between whites identifying as Creole or French and those who identified as Cajun.[45]

At the same time, as part of the sugar plantation belt, the region has been home to a large Black population, both the enslaved and their descendants along with many Creoles of color. Since Blacks became a majority of the town's residents a half century ago, the conflict associated with that shift has arguably been as intense as anywhere in the state. During a racially inflected dispute over town council districts in the 1990s and early 2000s, elections were suspended for a decade.[46] Moreover, like many small towns in rural America, St. Martinville has fallen on hard times. The long decline of agricultural and manufacturing employment undermined economic well-being, and the town's population has steadily dropped since 1980.

Tensions and disputes accompanied these social differences in this setting, which inflected the project's design, my positioning in executing it, and the presentation of its findings in this book. As with research on other racial and class groups, there has been a dearth of studies that take seriously the "relational basis" of Cajun identity and the "cultural continuum along which [social] distinctions operate."[47] In particular, I follow those scholars who develop the perspective that ethnicity exists in a deep, symbiotic relationship with race and class, and especially that it operates to mark certain types of threatening or acceptable difference relative to a white racial norm.[48] In this case, because Cajun identity has been formed in relation to the other social positions that constitute it, I assumed that situating them in terms of their relations with those other groups would offer the most productive angle for studying the formation of their historical memories. In an effort to explore how different social positions and relations might inflect historical remembrance of the Acadian past, I pursued interviews with a range of locals across boundaries of identity and difference.

As one might imagine, at times this approach challenged me. With Cajun interviewees, mention of class cut against the grain of everyday discourse about white ethnicity that often brackets it;[49] my questions sometimes raised eyebrows. Some whites who became aware that I attended public events on the "Black side" of town wondered where my racial "allegiance" lay. In one bar I frequented, a few of its Black patrons assumed I was an undercover narcotics agent, leading to tense exchanges. I faced these challenges as best I could; fortunately, many responded generously to my requests across the decade-plus during which I intermittently pursued fieldwork. Yet given my methodology and despite being a native of the region, I found no easily accessed insider position to occupy, no seamless entrée into deep understanding.

In mere numerical terms, this method met with success; I interviewed dozens of locals across intersecting positions of class, race/ethnicity, and gender. Accordingly, I often frame the mnemonic engagements of individuals and groups in contrast with each other, especially to understand how different whites engaged with distant pasts, both their own and those of their Black neighbors. At the same time, knowledge generated through ethnography is not the mere tallying of collected data. It is intersubjective and situated, the result of interpretations that are negotiated and reflexive. At certain moments in the text, I mention aspects of this co-construction, the challenges it presented, and my attempt to reflexively question my assumptions. With respect to the latter, one crucial instance of this unfolded in relation to the Acadian Memorial itself.

Technically, one might classify the memorial as a commemorative rather than a historic site. Housed in two separate buildings in St. Martinville's downtown, it is composed of a memorial space, featuring the life-size mural painting that depicts "The Arrival of the Acadians" in eighteenth-century Louisiana; bronze plaques with a comprehensive list of Acadian immigrants to the state; and in an adjacent courtyard on the bank of Bayou Teche, a granite altar with an eternal flame. Across a parking lot, the museum contains a small (760 sq. ft.) exhibit glossing the history of the Acadians from the colonial era to the present, added five years after the site opened in 1996. While obviously possessing a commemorative thrust, it stresses its grounding in archival truth. Its interpretation foregrounds that the memorial tells the true story of Acadian history, emphasizing, for instance, that the names collected on the plaques result from painstaking genealogical research.

I initially assumed that alongside abiding racial dynamics—stoked by the desegregation crisis of the 1960s and 1970s—the class dimensions of Cajun ethnicity could be linked to developments in the state's economy, especially the capitalization of its tourist industry, where I situated the impetus for the region's public history boom.[50] Such a conceptualization held the promise of integrating the social power of class and race into the political economy of heritage tourism as an economic development strategy. Ultimately, however, *Remembering the Cajun Past* eschews this perspective.[51]

The main reason is that these conceptual lenses did not seem to illuminate the material at the heart of the matter. The more fieldwork I did, the more archival leads I pursued, and the more I analyzed them, the more the animating core of the Acadian Memorial appeared as an intersecting set of ethico-moral concerns, of mutually shared subject-making goals pursued by both public history's advocates and its subjects. The aims of a broad network of institutional actors in the public history space matched the emotional memories of individuals like Cormier and Thibodeaux. For a host of civic reasons—distinct from if interwoven with social and economic ones—they seemed equally committed to the necessity of inducing citizens into embracing truths about the Acadian past.

Reflecting on these encounters and documents, I eventually concluded I was missing an entire dimension of power: intersecting lines of force generated by diverse movements and institutionalized projects; a robust alignment of actors, techniques, practices, and knowledges; and immersive spatial configurations devoted to making citizens through historical knowledge. A distinct politics unfolded in this complex. Part of my argument is that the memorial reinforces the region's social hierarchies and is inflected by market dynamics related to heritage tourism. But public history does not only subject citizens to dominant interpretations of the past; it also shapes a certain kind of subject, one with aspirations for self-transformation, social status, and freedom. Fully understanding its politics—the education and mobilization it seeks to enable through the diffusion of historical truths—requires centering this axis of subjectivity, truth, and power.

OUTLINE OF THE BOOK

In the next chapter, I review scholarly articles, archival documents, and the popular press from the early twentieth century to the 1960s to show how authorities cast Cajuns as a threat to social order. At the heart of their problematizations sat a historical argument: Cajuns had fixed themselves in a bygone era, clinging to a retrograde sociality and incapable of joining the rest of society in the progressive temporality of the present. Often, these claims were simultaneously racial assertions: Many framed Cajuns as racially suspect whites, their "degenerate" habits threatening to undermine the segregated regime of Jim Crow. Even ostensibly positive attempts to represent their history incorporated such views. Policies accompanying this discourse encompassed a broad biopolitical imperative whereby state and civic institutions sought to regulate Cajun behavior—language, hygiene, education, work habits—to align with national norms of productivity and citizenship. From this angle, it was not surprising that, during interviews featured in subsequent chapters, older Cajuns recounted intense memories of marginalization from that era.

The next three chapters provide an ethnographic account of different aspects of everyday remembering in St. Martinville. Focusing on threads of historical memories that tended toward public history, chapter 2 explores how locals invoked, contested, and mobilized the past for civic and social purposes. It identifies the material and institutional supports for historical memory, including the genealogical societies, historic preservation efforts, and heritage tourism initiatives that underpinned the town's self-promotion as le Petit Paris d'Amérique, a complex of sites and narratives that invoked the colonial past and were sedimented in a faded project of white Creole hegemony. These structures privileged certain memories while bracketing others. Although long implied in previous efforts, local leaders and boosters recently articulated a civic rationale for historical remembering as a discrete dimension of governance: They posited that history could operate as a means of enhancing civic morale. The chapter challenges categorical distinctions between "history" and "memory," suggesting that present-day concerns, whether civic, economic, or personal, motivated both.

Chapter 3 begins with a memory that, in his final act, a Black man lynched during Jim Crow cursed St. Martinville. This narrative frames an analysis illuminating a local politics of memory and forgetting by contrasting Black and white residents' divergent recollections of the past. Many Blacks recalled a continuum of racial oppression—from slavery and de jure segregation to contemporary discrimination—culminating in the belief that unaddressed effects of whites' bigotry indeed cursed the town. Meanwhile, whites' memories often cast Black struggles as moral failings rather than systemic oppression. At the same time, much remembering within both groups unfolded in interrelated fields of moral concern, whereby fostering responsible selves and interracial harmony were shared preoccupations. These concerns shaped therapeutic ideals of reconciliation for a new African American history museum, which, to avoid provoking white discomfort, institutionalized a selective forgetting that sanitized slavery and muffled Black grievances. The chapter demonstrates how public remembrance constituted a moralized battleground for social control in which history, memory, and forgetting were in tension with each other.

Featuring autobiographical remembering among individuals who, by conventional criteria (e.g., Acadian ancestry, French-speaking or francophone heritage), *could* identify as Cajun, chapter 4 situates the experiential ground from which individuals made Acadian history meaningful for themselves. Its goal is to explore how autobiographical memory and moral positioning shaped white ethnic identity among individuals of Acadian descent. I discovered a range of memories and formations of identity: Only one of the three groups I encountered identified as Cajun and associated memories with that label. Distinctive articulations of memory and moral evaluation accompanied each cohort's identitarian stance, suggesting the impact of processes of social differentiation beyond ethnicity, including class, race, and gender. The chapter suggests that memory operates as a moral space, where individuals negotiate identity through ethically charged recollections. Memories were not static but actively shaped social positioning, whether through resistance, accommodation, or critique. Taken together, these chapters demonstrate how local relations of power—civic efforts of citizen formation, postsegregation race relations, moral projects of self-making, and more—motivated and shaped historical remembrance.

The next two chapters concentrate on the diverse forces that intersected to shift public historical discourse about Cajuns as white ethnics and on the lowercase-*p* politics that shaped the Acadian Memorial's emergence. In chapter 5, I offer an account of the new Acadian public history's rise since the 1960s, analyzing how different actors and forces replaced negative accounts of Cajuns' past with one promoting them as a model "happy minority." Proceeding genealogically, I analyze the at times accidental intersection of multiple social projects.[52] These were explicitly governmental in their thrust insofar as they theorized that diffusing Acadian history would address varied problems through the intended effects it would have on citizens. The chapter illuminates how the advent of this new history unfolded not as an inevitability but rather as a contingent, contested product of governance—shaped by electoral strategies, the expansion of professional expertise in public history, and state interventions during a biopolitical turn toward governing through communities.

While others have stressed the influence of commercial forces on the public historical sphere in Louisiana and elsewhere, in chapter 6, I emphasize various civic goals that individuals and institutions articulated in their support of an Acadian public history in general and the memorial in particular. A commitment to historical truth and citizen formation also drove these initiatives. Maintaining my focus on power, I trace how different groups translated their interests across their varied projects, largely through alliance and enrollment but also in the wake of adversarial confrontations. The chapter highlights Foucault's concept of governmentality, showing how state and nonstate actors aligned their agendas—combating historical illiteracy, fostering ethnic pride, and promoting democratic citizenship—through material interventions like the memorial. These negotiated processes were distinctive; they were not uniquely top-down, as local advocates recruited state support for *their* projects. Yet exclusions also marked them; the initiative reinforced inequalities even as it democratized history-making.

In an ethnographic account of visitor reception among Cajuns at the memorial, the final chapter demonstrates how the site operated as a "technology of induction" through which many were prompted and prompted themselves to claim its story as their own. Drawing on varied aspects of their experience, visitors articulated memories, emotions, and personal endeavors to the site's representations. Often, they *discovered* emergent links to the historical past in pursuit of self-fashioning projects, not least the search for social respect denied them elsewhere. This finding supports the larger argument that their subjective investment in the memorial's truths produced an alignment with its architects' citizen-forming goals. Simply put, the site's historical verities induced them to affirm profound truths about themselves. At the same time, many other locals—in absolute terms, perhaps most—abstained from the site's offer, either blocked from it or choosing other memories and spacetimes over the memorial's. While the memorial successfully cultivated historical awareness for some, its reach was limited, exposing fractures in how St. Martinvillers claimed, contested, or ignored this history.

Chapter One

"Like the Dog in the Manger"

History and the Trouble with Cajuns

In the spring of 1906, C. M. Ulrich was angry. On behalf of a group of investors in rice agriculture, the Rice Irrigation and Improvement Association, he wrote a long, rambling letter to the captain of the US Army Corps of Engineers unit in New Orleans about the incident that ignited his ire. In August 1905, the association and the state completed the construction of a dam and lock structure on the Mermentau River near its mouth at the Gulf of Mexico. But no sooner had it begun to operate—keeping the Gulf's salt water out of the river so that irrigation pumps in the Mermentau Basin would draw only fresh water to flood rice fields upstream—than someone demolished it. A dynamite explosion damaged the structure in October, and Ulrich blamed Cajuns for it. In his account, a few Cajun smallholders living on a coastal ridge near the site were the culprits. They blew it up, Ulrich asserted, in their misguided belief that the dam, and not record-setting rains, had inundated their fields. Throughout his letter, Ulrich contrasted "this handful of people with . . . a few patches of corn and sweet potatoes," who had "done nothing" in the century since their arrival in Louisiana, with the considerable investment and commerce associated with rice farming (both in the millions, he claimed) and the prosperous livelihoods of its "thousands of thrifty farmers."[1] Ulrich fumed that this "absurd" act "balk[ed] a great industry" and that "like the proverbial dog in the manger, . . . they do nothing themselves and permit no one else to do anything." Ulrich implied that he expected the Corps' investigation to lead to their criminal prosecution. After all, he asserted, "Every one [of the Cajuns] speaks French and a very bad French at that," and "not one-half can speak English or sign their own names." Thus, "the question," he insisted, was "shall this handful of American-born foreigners be permitted to destroy all this civilization north of them?"[2]

Such disparaging rhetoric proved remarkably durable, lasting for decades. Writing for rural policymakers in the mid-1960s, two sociologists, Alvin Bertrand and Calvin Beale, stressed Cajuns' remarkable insularity; bound by a sociality excessively limited to kin networks, they put little value in education and expressed satisfaction with their poverty-level incomes. Moreover, given that their vernacular was "admittedly . . . not good French," these academics were perplexed that those interviewed believed they should teach their children the language.[3] Since its inferior quality limited its utility for the contemporary world, they skeptically characterized this desire as an unrealistic "nostalgic ideal." Although they detected signs that modernity was making inroads into francophone Louisiana, they advocated renewed effort to break down these traditional attitudes and integrate Cajuns into "the rapidly evolving industrial economy."[4] Continuing the line of analysis present in Ulrich's letter, they posited that Cajuns were too committed to remembering their centuries-old traditions—in so many words, too devoted to preserving their own past rather than entering the nation's present and future. Stymied by the trauma of their colonial-era expulsion from what is now Canada, they were stuck in time and too insulated from the reformative thrust of a modernizing state.

Prior to the Progressive Era, Cajuns were certainly seen as ignorant, lazy, and superstitious in ways that undermined productivity and decorum. However, a qualitatively different discourse emerged from the early twentieth century onward. Authorities increasingly described them as malicious obstacles to the progress that "civilization" demanded. Agriculture, technology, education, civility, hygiene, law: Developments in all these domains increasingly pointed society and the state in a single, unified direction that authorities claimed Cajuns were willfully rejecting. The emergent consensus that society had to rectify Cajuns—their economic habits, to be sure (and, as Ulrich intimated, their respect for the law), but also their language, diet, familial relationships, decorum, patriotism, and more—became something of a force in itself.

This chapter surveys the breadth of these efforts to "do something" about Cajuns' problematic behavior and the rationales that accompanied them. Previous work on this politicization of Cajuns as troubled white ethnics has stressed class relations and status dynamics as determinative influences driving this problematization.[5] Though not inaccurate, they arguably miss something, qualities that Ulrich's letter and Bertrand and Beale's bulletin sharply convey. As multiple projects of democratic governance "[broke] down . . . bodies and modes of conduct into discrete parts," more and more aspects of citizens' subjectivity were found wanting.[6] Rather than one overriding locus of conflicted relations (the workplace) or even two of them (relations of production and of status), many fields emerged in which, in the name of democratic governance, authorities and experts progressively called for Cajuns' comportment to be regulated in order that they be set on the right track toward more productive, healthy, and civically beneficial conduct. This frame of biopolitics—"the attempt to govern a population's health, welfare, and conditions of existence in the framework of political sovereignty"—offers considerable purchase for situating this problematization and disciplining of behavior.[7]

The other dimension of these rationales I foreground is the crucial role of historical discourse in them. Against a tendency to center history in the academy, I join those who see it as a polyvalent, widely circulating discourse. In domains beyond university history departments, narratives about both Cajuns' history and their *historicity*, or the quality of their actions as agents in historical time, formed a key part of justifications for Cajuns' reform. In Ulrich's characterization, for instance, Cajuns' history (i.e., they accomplished nothing since they "were dumped on our shores by the English") was related to their historicity (i.e., they were intrinsically incapable of syncing with society's push toward greater productivity, a historical trend with which Ulrich aligns himself). In stratified social orders, where distinct groups potentially possess their own histories, social actors often use historical narratives to forward their case for contributing to and belonging to the nation *in relation to adversaries*. In such instances, history comprises an agentive, political dimension: It is *for* staking a claim in an antagonistic field, structuring the nation-state's relations of inclusion and exclusion in the process. As I will show, even in the public history proper of Cajuns during this moment, they were a problem to be solved because many labeled them as such, calling out the disjuncture between the country's future and their past. In turn, critics claimed that this bad history shaped Cajuns' troubling culture and subjectivity—including an alleged capacity for racial degeneration—that became an abiding concern animating these efforts.

INIMICAL TO MODERNITY: CAJUNS AS PROBLEMATIC AND NOT QUITE WHITE

As the previous examples suggest, authorities raised Cajuns' economic productivity, or lack thereof, as a predominant issue. A pair of analyses by Walter Kollmorgen and Robert Harrison, a geographer and an economist, respectively, employees of the federal Bureau of Agricultural Economics, can serve as an illuminating case. In the mid-1940s, as a prelude to funding a massive land drainage and reclamation project proposed for an area along the Louisiana-Arkansas border, the two studied the challenges involved with previous initiatives in the lower Mississippi Valley. For decades, large-scale reclamations of marshes along the Louisiana coast were recurring projects; though most proved unsuccessful, proponents were pushing Congress to fund the Louisiana-Arkansas initiative. The authors listed several issues that plagued past projects, noting, for instance, that while developers cited land reclamation in the Netherlands as a successful precedent, their designs rarely included plans to construct the levees necessary to prevent hurricanes from inundating newly drained marshes.[8]

Yet against the backdrop of these failed megaprojects, what most caught the authors' attention was how, despite Cajun farmers' manifest need for access to more land, they had not figured in developers' plans as potential occupants for reclaimed marshes. Instead, for a half century, the state vigorously recruited farmers from elsewhere in the country and the world to expand agriculture, even as Cajun families subdivided smaller and smaller parcels.[9] Harrison and Kollmorgen attributed this conundrum to Cajuns themselves, pointing to their flawed "culture complex": a group "solidarity that is not willfully violated," a "reluctance to migrate or to pioneer in new land areas," and a "lack of . . . managerial ability . . . and efficient work habits."[10] Writing at a moment when tens of thousands of Cajuns farmed, they warned that their "nonchalance . . . should temper over-ambitious or hasty projects designed to sweep all of these people into the fast and rather perilous stream of highly commercialized and competitive agriculture."[11] Instead, they proposed that Cajun youth be directed out of agriculture and into manufacturing work. This solution would be "less expensive and more profitable to society" because, they argued, while extension training failed to reform their faulty customs when it came to farming, those habits would "find little application in [factory] production and hence present no special problem."[12]

Two aspects of this problematization bear emphasizing. First, as is typical of mid-century social analyses, it is saturated with concepts of normal behavior and of a society whose assent toward greater well-being and wealth will be secured as individuals achieve certain types of efficient, productive, and healthy conduct. As governmental agencies and expertise, measurements of all manner of social practices, and techniques for inculcating proper skills proliferated, the norm—the "usual" and the average but also the socially desirable—dominated conceptions of how people should be governed. Though it remains mostly latent in Kollmorgen and Harrison's texts, normativity becomes explicit when they announce a formula—"small farmers must be converted into efficient producers using complex machines and approved agronomic techniques"—which, in their estimation, Cajuns could not achieve.[13]

In such judgments, one can discern a biopolitical imperative and how it problematized Cajuns in a particular way. By the nineteenth century, actors and institutions began to conceptualize governing as a matter of managing basic biological and social dynamics inherent in individuals and groups—their biopower. In their articles, such a focus is evident in Kollmorgen and Harrison's concern with facilitating in Cajuns what, under the influence of the discipline of economics, experts increasingly saw as a highly desirable human motivation: to produce as much as possible in the shortest possible time in pursuit of an ample subsistence. As agencies like the Bureau of Agricultural Economics applied such thinking to farming, the "peasant" habits of Cajuns—for example, staying on a small farm to exploit family labor, as opposed to migrating far away to a larger farm—became suspect. While many accepted this practice a generation or so prior, these emergent norms of efficiency and productivity demonstrated a bias in favor of the individual and a corresponding assumption that group solidarities, like ties to family, should diminish as modernity unfolded.

Under this new regime, then, predilections for small farms and close-knit families became explicitly *abnormal*. Far from being a quaint difference to be appreciated, they posed a problem that required correction. And authorities located the cause of these dubious preferences in Cajuns' entrenched dispositions. As many did, these bureaucrats labeled them as "culture." Although in this context the term has much in common with its current usage, it also has connotations both of opaqueness (as in "inscrutable to the expert observer") and of habits that are deep-seated, even quasi-biological. Both nuances are in play, for instance, when the authors claim that Cajuns' "economic problems . . . are not of recent origin, but date back one or more generations."[14] In this characterization, one hears the hallmark of the racializing discourse that accompanied biopolitical governance; others went further along these lines, as we will see.

Education was another arena in which similar problematizations of Cajuns' culture prevailed. Among pedagogues, journalists, elected officials, and other authorities, Cajuns' resistance to formal schooling emerged as a high-profile dilemma. It would be difficult to overemphasize how, during this period, the acquisition of literacy and numeracy came to be accepted as fundamental to societal well-being.[15] And Cajuns' defiant mistrust of schooling was purportedly robust: During World War II, anthropologist Ruth Landes quotes a local "American" as observing, "[A Cajun boy] wouldn't think of going to school. . . . His father would beat him if he caught him."[16]

Importantly, schooling was not merely focused on enabling the growth of cognitive aptitudes and utilitarian skills. From early in the twentieth century, its advocates understood compulsory education to be "a mechanism . . . to promote social citizenship . . . and the means to produce social civility and social peace."[17] From this perspective, Cajuns needed to be educated not only because they possessed a stubborn ignorance but also because of their misanthropic ways. Marguerite Roman, a white Creole addressing the New Orleans–based Athénée Louisianais in 1924, expressed typical views in this regard. Roman noted that upon immigrating to Louisiana, some Acadians did seek formal education, which allowed them to "become good American citizens who took part in the country's development and fulfilled their civic duties."[18] Meanwhile, Cajuns—in a move that became common, she distinguished these upright residents from a more problematic group by using this different label—avoided education, with the result that they were "opinionated, deceptive, underhanded, defiant," and suspicious of others. These became major concerns animating public support for the compulsory education of Cajuns. Professionals certainly saw education as enabling productive workers, but as Roman stressed, they equally intended it to produce good citizens who fulfilled their "civic duties." And they considered the school—the space itself and the disciplinary techniques practiced there—as the primary means for instilling this civility into Cajun children.

As the century wore on, public officials and other observers became less willing to simply wonder, as Roman did, what would become of Cajuns in a generation, when one would see "what education will have done for them."[19] They replaced this laissez-faire approach with a stronger obligation for all children to attend school. In 1944, the legislature passed Act 239, another comprehensive compulsory attendance law, whose implementation initially targeted locales with high percentages of francophones, including St. Martin Parish.[20] In addition to authorizing sanctions on families who failed to send their children to school, Act 239 launched a "visiting teacher" initiative to address truancy's root causes. The legislation tasked the social worker with "look[ing] for maladjustment in areas of educational, psychological, health, and social needs of children" and then intervening to "bring about adjustments which are educationally and socially sound." They were to visit residences and enforce the law as truancy officers, but according to the local superintendent, rather than focus on punishment, they sought to ensure a child was "happy . . . , healthy . . . , successful . . . , and a social asset [instead of] a social liability."[21] The superintendent assured citizens that this situation required such an invasive approach because the school environment "*determines to a large extent* the type of product a child will be in the years to come" (emphasis added). Since, as Landes reported, some Cajuns were dead set against education for their offspring, the visiting teacher program ostensibly inserted a social worker into familial relations, seeking to overcome parents' resistance and steer children toward a more productive engagement with school and the social world beyond the home.

This development underscores how, in such interventions, Cajuns' relations with and obligations to others multiplied, accentuating their otherness in the process. In an editorial promoting the need for compulsory education, psychologist Paul Young insisted that the foundation of the nation's freedom was also at stake, since "without the ability to read and ponder the printed word, no citizenship can be free from ignorance and dictatorship."[22] Similar to Kollmorgen and Harrison's invocation of "society" to justify their economic proposal, Young foregrounded Cajuns' responsibilities as citizens within the nation-state. In this realm, agents of the state again found Cajuns deficient. In her unpublished ethnography, Landes claims that Cajuns' parochialism was spatially intense, such that "they may never leave the marsh or woods where they were born."[23] Echoing Young's concerns, she outlined its larger civic implications. Because "they [had] no interest in the issues vital to the wider world," Cajuns were "unaware of the meanings in the present war upheavals."[24] Consequently, Landes asserted that "loyalty to anything larger than the marsh was an uncertain concept to them" and that "they [were] found wanting by U.S. Army standards, . . . rejected because of illiteracy and physical deficiencies."[25]

As these texts suggest, literacy and the social skills it promoted were increasingly bound up with obligations to the state and society; the latter were explicitly evoked as entities to which one owed mastery of the former. The schools (like the field or demonstration plot for the agriculture extension agent and the kitchen for the home economics agent) were critical spaces where reformative interventions were meant to strip tradition-bound subjects like Cajuns of their parochial commitments to family and ethnicity, "assimilating" them *as individuals* into a uniform, homogeneous citizenship shared by all Americans.[26] As authorities of all kinds increasingly pointed to these norms as the proper content of social belonging and citizenship, they formed explicit counterpoints to Cajuns' folkways, characterized more and more as benighted through these proliferating relationships and contrasts.

Some were not convinced that, when it came to education, Cajuns' commitments to their ancestral ways were so intractable.[27] But a final striking example of this problematization, one that circulated in a high school textbook, indicates just how adamantly many denounced Cajuns' illiteracy as the reason for Louisiana's underperforming modernization. Noting that the state ranked at the bottom nationally in literacy, sociologists T. Lynn Smith and Homer Hitt laid the blame squarely at Cajuns' feet, asserting that "more than any other factor," the link between their low educational achievement and French language and culture "contributes to Louisiana's poor national standing." They castigated Cajuns as "an unsophisticated agrarian people" who "have clung tenaciously to their old customs and traditions" and "strenuously resist[ed] most encroachments from the outside." As Kollmorgen and Harrison did, Smith and Hitt pointed to Cajuns' culture as the crux of the problem. By "preserv[ing] . . . one of the purest examples of a seventeenth-century folk culture," they resisted mainstream "values and standards."[28] As the post–World War II boom shifted into high gear and modernization theory reached the peak of its influence, attachments to conduct outside of the norm were increasingly disparaged.

In condemning Cajuns for blocking Louisiana's modernization, Smith and Hitt complained that these white ethnics possessed a power that only society should wield: Cajuns assimilated other groups into their own ways. As the authors lamented, so thoroughly had they acculturated the Irish, German, and other immigrants who settled among them that "after two generations, . . . many of them even [lost] the knowledge of their origins and claim[ed] to be pure descendants of the original Acadians who settled Louisiana."[29] Observers previously commented on this acculturating "vitality," but as the stress on a normative subjectivity became all-encompassing, Smith and Hitt cast it as an ominous threat. To resist literacy was one thing, but to assimilate others into illiteracy was to co-opt a key modernizing strategy and transform it into a dark, antisocial force. In Smith and Hitt's view, Cajuns were not a mere problem: They threateningly competed with society and the state as a menacing antimodern adversary.

To be sure, from the late nineteenth century into the 1960s and beyond, numerous observers and commentators—often writers composing travel pieces for national publications—extolled how, in "towns . . . full of charm," Cajuns practiced a "simple, universal, and unaffected hospitality" and spoke a "musical French" that delighted the ear.[30] But little of these views inflected the escalating disciplining of Cajuns' behavior; as a social worker quipped, "The problems readily begin to mask the romance."[31] In addition to the issues mentioned earlier, authorities targeted other Cajun practices for reformist interventions, including marriage between first cousins, a custom whose "appalling results" contributed to "the social problems of the race";[32] lamentable habits of hygiene—"strangely and fatally insanitary ways," like drinking stagnant water, combined with destitution, begging, and mistrust of authorities;[33] and criminality—as Landes frankly put it, "The [Cajun] people are not law-abiding"—their recreational hunting and commercial fishing required increased law enforcement efforts to crack down on poaching. Landes herself admired what she characterized as Cajuns' commendable premodern savoir vivre, but acknowledged that "hustling Americans say angrily that they are worse than 'n-----' when it comes to shiftlessness."[34]

The comparison with Blacks is significant, and I will return to it later. First, it bears stressing that these behaviors could be contextualized in relation to other actors and changing circumstances, with Cajuns' comportment as but one aspect of the social landscape. Like others, Vincentian sociologist Father Edward Kammer cast the low literacy of the many Cajun marsh dwellers who were the subject of his research as a social problem. But he situated the challenges of literacy and subsistence in a much broader tableau, noting that illiteracy was also problematic *for* Cajuns because it put them "at the mercy of unscrupulous associates" who swindled them out of land ownership.[35] He also noted that the enclosure of the tidal marshes, long treated as a kind of commons, forced trappers to pay rents that further impoverished them and that antiunion forces thwarted their collective attempts to manage coastal fisheries and increase their incomes.[36]

In other words, one could, as Kammer did, situate Cajuns and their "backward" folkways in the context of a social formation riven by conflicts and populated by other actors whose efforts could also be critiqued. Instead, in both the popular press and academic studies, authorities simply assumed the normativity of "mass society" and "modernity" as desirable and inevitable. Thus, the explanatory stress fell on Cajuns alone: on their extreme isolation from the world, their inflexible resistance to new ways of thinking and acting, their dogged commitment to outdated habits, and their profound ignorance, which gradually became a matter of open ridicule.[37] Through these many analyses and observations, a whole complex of Cajuns' problematic comportments came into view, which not only served as justification for their regulation but also signified behaviors observers condemned as immoral. In exhibiting so many negative traits toward others—they were "tactless, . . . impulsive, impetuous, highly inflammable, ultra-sensitive, unrelenting in hatreds"—Cajun dispositions became a moral problem.[38] Tenaciously and incorrigibly, they were not simply out of sync with modernity but rather stupid, wrong, and bad.

Across all this commentary and analysis, a historical argument about Cajuns—one that glossed both their remote past and their *historicity*, their quality of being actors in history—featured prominently. From the perspective of authorities and experts, few aspects of Cajun lifeways were appropriate for the modern world. Their dispositions, their traditions, their antisocial behaviors: they needed to slough it all off, as did other white ethnics and indeed members of any group who held commitments other than those to the nation and the market. Given that they did not or could not, some went so far as to posit that Cajuns' particular historical trajectory had created a sort of deep-seated psychological shock that explained their tenacious antimodernism. A version of these claims from two rural sociologists stands out as the most elaborate. As T. Lynn Smith and Vernon Parenton phrased it, their colonial encounter with the British in Acadia resulted in a "harsh and cruel fate" that "so reacted on the entire *Gestalt* of this group as to make them cling all the more tenaciously to their mode of living, irrespective of the consequences."[39] Accentuating the interiorizing thrust of behavioral analyses cited earlier, they cast Cajuns as literally stuck in the past, incapable of moving beyond a centuries-old trauma. And in contrast to contemporary thinking that ethnic and national histories can be productively woven together, the governing paradigm was exactly the opposite. Cajuns' harrowing history apparently formed the fulcrum of what kept them from entering modernity. In this view, teaching Cajuns about their past or heritage had no or even negative value. These were the crux of the problem.

Finally, it is relative to comments like these that one might situate how Cajuns and their deplorable habits were linked to racial discourse. Most obviously, other whites constantly used Cajuns as a foil to make normative and "successful" forms of whiteness visible and, to a certain degree, taken for granted. During the early twentieth century, authors often took care to distinguish Cajuns from other whites; in a master's thesis, Marguerite Pecot insisted that Cajuns "must not be confused with the more cultured and aristocratic progeny of French-Spanish ancestry, the [white] Creoles. . . . who have enjoyed all the advantages accruing from the march of progress."[40] As the century wore on, the comparisons became implicit, as when Kollmorgen and Harrison merely referenced "efficient producers using complex machines and approved agronomic techniques" in contrast to Cajuns' fecklessness.[41]

In either case, the anxiety and scorn that many whites expressed in relation to Cajuns were both different from and linked to that reserved for Blacks. In terms of the social order that white Louisianans worked to construct, Cajuns were, to put it simply, "inside" the state and civil society that they pursued, while Blacks largely remained "outside" of them. That is, as problematic as they might be, Cajuns were classified as fellow whites. As such, they were considered capable of improvement and worthy of the numerous efforts that schools, extension agencies, civic groups, and others expended on them. With few exceptions, meanwhile, Louisiana whites placed African Americans in a separate category. Because, as the discourse went, evolution had endowed the Black race with so little intellectual and moral potential and because so many whites concentrated on fostering only their docility and subservience, they did not target Blacks with the same intensity when it came to governing them and ameliorating their capacities.[42]

Such a characterization is cursory but suffices to undergird this assertion: For some whites, part of the problem with Cajuns—and an especially unnerving concern at that—turned on how they gave the lie, so to speak, to the very premise of Jim Crow. The notion that whites were naturally superior to Blacks served as the cornerstone of de jure segregation; the latter's inferior, fixed evolutionary inheritances made this an immutable fact. In their persistent inability to modernize and adopt mainstream habits, however, the tens of thousands of Cajuns scattered across south Louisiana amounted to an immense and (through the proliferation of studies, censuses, and maps) increasingly visible counterfactual to those claims. Early in the century, when the vivid fear that races could degenerate as well as progress animated eugenic policies, people worried about which direction Cajuns were headed. Social worker Homer Borst noted that together with the "hereditary qualities" of their "French peasant stock," Cajuns' "intimate contact with another race in which the spirit of the tropics is personified" engendered a "decidedly difficult cultural problem." Borst highlighted with concern statistics showing that Cajuns were concentrated in regions with significant Black populations and frequented "colored midwives" and "Negro 'voo doo' doctors." In concluding with the question "Will social work become a permanent institution in these [Acadian] parishes?" he clearly meant to provide an argument justifying its necessity, in no small part to combat this threat of racial decay.[43]

Through these observations, Borst essentially posed the question, Would Cajuns develop their full racial potential as whites, or would they regress toward the rank of Blacks, whose habits their ways disturbingly resembled? In the "anger" of Landes's informant, claiming that Cajuns were more "shiftless" than Blacks, and in Smith and Hitt's more polished textbook denunciation, which stressed their underperformance *as whites*, one discerns similar preoccupations.[44] Under a political regime based on whites' putative natural superiority, Cajuns made one doubt this principle and thus were also *racially* problematic in a profound way.

Taken together, these varied concerns suggest that others did not merely stigmatize Cajuns, in the sense of subjecting them to an inferior identity in a status hierarchy or castigating them as poor workers. Rather, in the many flaws that authorities identified and their various efforts to address them, they cast Cajuns as a menace internal to society, an enemy within whose skewed proclivities threatened to undermine its stability and well-being on numerous fronts. This is how Michel Foucault describes the racializing impulse that emerged in the nineteenth century as biopolitical concerns with regulating populations became prominent.[45] Obviously, Cajuns' classification as whites led to a fundamentally different kind of problematization when compared to that of Blacks. But in the examples presented, one discerns the tendency to identify and assess social abnormality, as so many deemed Cajuns incapable of becoming the kind of individuated subjects, responsible and incorporated into a uniform citizenship, that progressive and then New Deal politics of social welfare required.[46] Instead, experts located the causes of this "failure" in faulty, deep-seated biohistorical dynamics and proposed solutions in the name of defending the social body from danger—hallmarks of the era's racial discourse. In this overview of the predicament that Cajuns posed for society, we glimpse the effort involved in governmental and civic as well as status politics and how Cajuns were problematized, racially and historically, as a perilous challenge to them.

EVANGELINE MADE UP: FAKELORE, EXHIBITION, AND BIFURCATED PATHS OF "REMEMBRANCE"

A similar lens—one centering how governmental interventions sought to shape citizens' conduct in pursuit of a particular sociopolitical order—can be applied to the public history of Acadians during this period. Most prominently, this involves the sites devoted to Evangeline, which became central to St. Martinville's public culture. Henry Wadsworth Longfellow's poem of the same name, *Evangeline, a Tale of Acadie*, was an immensely popular epic about the protagonist's expulsion from Acadia and subsequent wanderings across North America. The poem's influence spread across many countries and lasted well into the twentieth century; as the site of the Evangeline Oak and Longfellow-Evangeline State Park, St. Martinville was arguably ground zero for such effects in the US. Yet even though these initiatives ostensibly told the story of Acadians' immigration to Louisiana, practitioners again identified Cajuns, amid these efforts, as a problem needing attention. At this moment, there were distinct civic aims particular to the realm of public history and specific ways in which living Cajuns troubled them.

Perhaps the most intriguing aspect of Evangeline's use in St. Martinville concerns its renarration as local history. A white Creole jurist, Felix Voorhies, published a serialized account, later circulated in book form as *Acadian Reminiscences*, claiming that his maternal grandmother's memories had formed the basis for Longfellow's poem.[47] Voorhies asserted that the British military's deportation of Acadians from Nova Scotia separated two real-life lovers, Emmeline Labiche and Louis Arceneaux, who, like Longfellow's Evangeline and Gabriel, were fatefully reunited years later under an oak tree on the banks of Bayou Teche. Alongside Voorhies's account arose the legend that a particular oak tree near the center of town was the actual site of Emmeline (Evangeline) and Louis (Gabriel)'s reunion. Later, during the 1920s and 1930s, Susan (Mrs. A. A.) Anding, a civic booster and highway construction advocate, joined forces with local amateur historian Andre Olivier and newspaper publisher C. T. Bienvenu to lobby for the establishment of a memorial park to the poet and his female protagonist. This led to the founding of Longfellow-Evangeline State Park, Louisiana's first state-sponsored historic site. And during the decade-long push to inaugurate the park, boosters struck a bronze statue of Evangeline—in the likeness of actress Dolores Del Rio, who played the heroine in a 1927 Hollywood adaptation of the poem—and placed it behind the Catholic Church in the town's main square. The statue purportedly marked Labiche's gravesite.

To date, two principal lines of interpretation have emerged about this public history. In his book *In Search of Evangeline*, historian Carl Brasseaux challenged the entire St. Martinville–Evangeline complex as commercially motivated "fakelore."[48] Brasseaux plausibly argued that Felix Voorhies had not narrated actual family lore and thus that Anding, Olivier, and their successors recounted a false history of Labiche and Arceneaux. Since these figures were fabrications, Brasseaux concluded, the profit that tourism might generate had motivated those who set up the historic sites.

There is much to support this view. In a diary entry from 1892, Wilbur Blackman, a circuit court judge visiting St. Martinville, recounted, "Every year, I was informed, from fifty to sixty tourists from the north [to] go over to St. Martin to look at the scenes and country made immortal by Longfellow's poem."[49] Thus, before locals designated an Evangeline Oak, tourists apparently sought out such a tree, inspired by Longfellow's accounts of the lovers' ill-fated reunion. By the turn of the century, St. Martinville competed with other towns in the region as the site of the "real" Evangeline Oak.[50] Longfellow's mention of "St. Martin" gave local boosters a leg up in this competition, but as Voorhies's effort makes clear, they were not content to stop there. In reading the archive associated with the park's emergence, the disputes, competing factions, and fabrication of historical representation from whole cloth are indeed striking, all seemingly associated with self-interest and jockeying for tourists' money. Creating the historic park unfolded in a long and acrimonious process; at one point, defending her management of public funds to establish the Longfellow-Evangeline site, Anding complained to the legislature that in St. Martinville, "nothing can be done to develop the Park because there is no co-operation. Most people of the town will not have anything to do with it because it is so and so's project, and it's no use to work and have the other fellow get the credit."[51] In Anding's papers, there is a photograph of Andre Olivier, dated "Jan[uary] 1926," in which he stands next to shrubs and tall weeds at the back of the church, with an arrow pointing into them and the words "Here lies what is immortal of—Evangeline—Emmerline [*sic*] Labiche" written on the back.[52] Ostensibly, Anding, Olivier, and their allies picked this spot as Labiche's/Evangeline's resting place, conveniently locating it in the center of town, near the Evangeline Oak—and most businesses. From the siting of the Evangeline Oak to the inauguration of the state park, it seems that the desire to capitalize on the economic benefits from *Evangeline*'s immense popularity drove these projects.

But in dismissing Evangeline as fakelore, Brasseaux overlooks the way historical representation operated at the time, especially the theory and practice of how historical objects and narratives should circulate and the civic effects they might have in doing so. In proposing a particular content for Longfellow-Evangeline, some of its promoters intended the "National Memorial Park" to function as a "place for remembering" to shape the public's historical awareness. In an essay that Anding circulated to justify the park, she explained that she advanced it mainly as a tribute to Longfellow and his fictional heroine: The "great American poet" was a "lasting historian" because he "translate[d] life's experiences, its potencies and passions, into poetry and art."[53] She promoted casting a bronze statue representing the two, since Longfellow had "so nobly expressed the beauty of a woman's devotion." And she specified that there would be a museum exhibit of Acadian artifacts and records to remember the Acadians "who were among the first revolutionists [*sic*] for freedom and liberty on the American continent" and "who played a prominent part in the late World War." In the other prominent analysis of Evangeline-based history, W. Fitzhugh Brundage suggests that the significance of Anding's efforts lies in how they "encouraged Acadians and others to acknowledge . . . [their] traditions [of family, community, and heritage]."[54] But this was not the gist of Anding's proposal. Rather than drawing citizens' attention to the local and the ethnic, it sought to connect them to historical events of *national* significance and prominent achievements in literature and the beaux arts. Anding's vision thus aligned with the dominant practice of the time: Individuals and groups needed to be bound together to the nation. From that perspective, the local merited remembrance only inasmuch as it linked citizens to key events in the country's past and to an emerging American high-cultural canon.

Anding's remarks align with more elaborate statements from experts concerning how history affected citizens and contributed to order and progress. In a report from the mid-1930s, the curators of the Louisiana State Museum wrote, "The welfare of society demands that its fundamental principles be understood and appreciated. The eye imparts to the mind the sensation of learning faster than the ear, hence exhibits in museums well arranged and attractive are primal educational forces. . . . Museums show the way to the future by occult demonstrations of past occurrences and thereby encourage the young, and restore confidence to the older generations. The Museum appeals to direct experience and is concerned with the reality of the past and that the future offers little to those who do not know their way."[55] In museum practice, this stress on educating the public in the "fundamental principles" of past experience through a sensually engaging display of objects constituted an emergent yet widely shared premise. As Tony Bennett details, nineteenth-century Romantic theory posited that contact with high art ennobled viewers. Influenced by Immanuel Kant's philosophy of aesthetics, this notion enabled a "reconceptualization of the space of the art museum as one of self-formation," whereby, through acts of judgment about the beauty and excellence of artistic form, the public would work to form themselves in a self-governing way.[56] Similarly, authorities in museums and memorials began to theorize that positive civic and political habits could be generated from well-designed historical exhibits. Once its advocates succeeded in gaining stable institutional support for Longfellow-Evangeline, the Office of State Parks collected and displayed artifacts at a restored plantation house, featuring exhibits whose "ancientness" was "so well proportioned and honestly executed" that it generated a site of "incomparable and picturesque fascination."[57] The success of governing society depended on such an approach, because, as the Louisiana State Museum curators spell out, basic values needed to be "understood and appreciated" in order for people to "know their way" and secure society's welfare.

These pragmatics of historical exhibition were based on logics of imitation and emulation. Visitors needed to see representations of great acts (to have "fundamental principles" from the past "imparted" to them) to pursue proper conduct in the present. As Bennett contends, historical and anthropological exhibits during this period also sought to generate a desire in visitors to strive and contribute to social progress. Adding the notion that citizens' imagination and motivation needed to be activated, this approach envisioned spurring visitors to measure themselves against great exploits of the past; in finding themselves wanting, they would endeavor to do more. Echoing this goal of active inspiration, park administrators boasted that once "natives" visited Longfellow-Evangeline, they were moved with "the pride . . . [to] keep alive and relive the exploits of their ancestors."[58] While motivated by tourism, the effort to create an Evangeline site cannot be reduced to it; it also attempted to assemble narratives, objects, and practices of spectatorship in ways that would productively shape citizens and their conduct.

In this regard, however, there are good reasons to believe that Anding and others intended for Evangeline history to operate in different ways for different audiences. On the one hand, many of Anding's associates were, like Olivier and Voorhies, descendants of white Creole aristocrats whose families had intermarried with Acadians or members of wealthy Acadian clans. Displaying great history and art was meant to provide a worthy model for their emulation, one made accessible through their secure acquisition of literacy and exposure to the beaux arts. On the other hand, as previously discussed, most people of Acadian descent could not read, and so Evangeline history would not work to shape their conduct in this way. Along these lines, the local appropriation of Longfellow's poetry as historical narrative had a perverse effect on how many came to view Acadians and their historical trajectory. Taking *Evangeline*'s portrayal of Acadians as an accurate history, they contrasted the "picturesque," "quaint," and "charming" Acadians before the Civil War with the "lazy, . . . decadent . . . poor-whites" they "became" by the twentieth, concluding that the Acadian "race" had degenerated.[59] This echoes Borst's fears of racial regression, a surprisingly enduring notion in the region's public history. From this perspective, Evangeline history either was entirely beyond their ken or needed to awaken in Cajuns—again, a label used to distinguish rural farmers and fisherfolk from wealthier "genteel Acadians"—a spark of recognition of their faded excellence. Thus, Acadian history would govern these groups differently: For one, it reinforced and stimulated their propriety and intelligence, while for the other, it would have to jar them out of severe social decline.

This intersects with another reason why the boosters, history buffs, and officials who promoted Evangeline-based history meant for it to work differently on the Cajun masses. The local retelling of the Evangeline story overlapped with their enduring vision of how to best achieve social order in Louisiana. While inscribed within nineteenth-century tropes about gender, Longfellow's Evangeline nevertheless possessed an intriguing degree of agency. The heroine moves from the passivity of the deportation to an extensive search (in Louisiana and elsewhere) for her lost love and then to aiding the indigent in a Philadelphia poorhouse. In narrating his grandmother's memory of Emmeline Labiche as the "real" Evangeline, Voorhies circumscribed that agency considerably: When Emmeline meets Louis Arceneaux (or Gabriel) in St. Martinville and learns he has remarried, she loses her mind and must be cared for by an elderly white Creole matron, Madame Bordas, until she dies of a broken heart.

Regardless of whether this aspect of his tale is historically accurate, Voorhies's narrative aligns with a common fictional subgenre of the time, one that had clear civic aspirations. During the late nineteenth century, one of the foci of works by local writers such as George Washington Cable and Sidonie de la Houssaye involved the then-current anxieties and tensions over relations between white Creoles and Cajuns. Often at issue was whether an uncouth, ill-mannered, and/or indolent Cajun would accept tutelage from (or even marriage to) a Creole aristocrat, under what conditions, and with what results. As Bonnie James Shaker argues about Kate Chopin's contributions to this subgenre, such narratives "circulated as behavioral manuals" in a hierarchical social order, whereby "upper orders were responsible for those below" and "lower orders were to respect their superiors."[60] For Cajuns, these stories offered the moral that they would best contribute to the postbellum social order by following the lead of their more sophisticated Creole cousins—for men, by adopting the latter's "correct attitudes toward work" and "bourgeois morality and comfort," and for women, by accepting their codes of "social and sexual mores."[61] Thus, a widespread local trope infantilized Cajuns as dependents in need of their social betters' guidance, and St. Martinville's particular version of Evangeline dovetailed with this vision of order and propriety.

In so many words, Cajuns could learn what Evangeline might teach them by receiving it secondhand from their mentors. In politician Dudley LeBlanc's Evangeline-themed pilgrimages to and from the Canadian Maritime provinces, one can readily discern such a practice. LeBlanc was something of an ethnic politico, who campaigned in French and wrote a history of the Acadian deportation. He timed his highly publicized trips to Canada to coincide with his campaigns for office and included bevies of young women dressed in costumes as Evangeline (for a return to their homeland, as it were). But in addition to Acadian heritage and campaign publicity, at least one of the pilgrimages managed to weave in a measure of uplift for the less sophisticated. During this trip, he paired young Louisiana women from rural areas with more literate peers from Canadian towns and cities, with the purpose of stimulating the former to adopt the latter's progressive practices, not least their bilingualism. Since some "Acadian mothers and fathers have not learned the value of education,"

LeBlanc explained, "we felt that by bringing to [rural women] those who spoke the same language, they might be inspired . . . to learn to speak English."[62] Brundage views this as evidence of LeBlanc's "condescending attitudes toward the very culture that his association purportedly preserved," but as with his interpretation of Anding, such a reading projects late-twentieth-century white ethnic identity politics into this mid-century context.[63] As I outlined, many (including some who, like LeBlanc, were descended from Acadians) shared a widespread consensus that Cajuns presented serious challenges to social governance. In the context of public history, this notion prevailed as well, though the technique employed here—using bilingual Acadians to lure their disinclined peers toward English—suggests an attempt to entice them into modernity instead of disciplining them into it. Regardless, remembering Evangeline offered another occasion to reform Cajuns.

"THERE ARE NO CAJUNS, WE ARE ACADIANS": WHEN ST. MARTINVILLE (ALMOST) BECAME THE CAJUN CAPITAL OF THE WORLD

In the late 1960s, a debate occurred in St. Martinville that illuminates much about social governance and historical discourse as postwar white ethnic identity politics in south Louisiana began to shift. Although it involved a failed proposal to name St. Martinville "the Cajun Capital of the World," the dispute is especially notable for the arguments marshaled against the project. In them, claims about Cajuns' fecklessness persisted, even as some began to imagine a different articulation between Cajuns and the body politic. In its defeat—which a few locals remembered and commented on, mostly in irony, during my fieldwork—the unsuccessful bid suggests how reconfiguring Cajuns as agents of civic virtue required elaborate discursive work.

In hindsight, the proposal seems innocuous. The local chapter of the civic organization the Junior Chamber, or Jaycees, suggested that the town add Cajun-themed activities to its July 4th celebration. Jaycee president Paul Hardy (who would go on to become the state's lieutenant governor) proposed activities such as naming a "worthy, respectable businessman who best exemplifies a successful Cajun" as "Mr. Cajun."[64] Influenced by the popularity of nearby Breaux Bridge's annual Crawfish Festival, the proposal's backers could imagine such an affirmation in light of two basic developments. First, while

"Cajun" circulated publicly as a slur, some white francophones of working- and middle-class status used the label self-avowedly, as a term of endearment among themselves. Also, like other white ethnics, many Cajuns were caught up in the thriving postwar economy, becoming upwardly mobile as they benefited from both expanding public subsidies (such as the GI Bill and Federal Housing Administration loans) and the Gulf Coast's booming petroleum sector. As they became wealthier and more literate, not all of them identified with the Evangeline-based history as the Jaycees' proposal implies.[65] Along with the Mr. Cajun award, they proposed an official declaration of St. Martinville's status as Cajun Capital of the World. In the fall of 1968, they aggressively lined up local political support, including that of the mayor, the town council, and the prestigious Rotary Club chapter.

The proposal seemed set to prevail when it met a vehement response. For weeks after the town's *Teche News* reported the police jury's (i.e., county commission's) unanimous support for the measure, letters—many adversarial—rolled in, and an organized campaign to reverse the endorsements coalesced.[66] Opposition became so stiff that local officials took the unusual step of calling for a public poll on the matter. Despite the evidence to which the Jaycees pointed—for example, that the label evoked many positive qualities and that the vast majority of its members would accept being named "Mr. Cajun"—the survey results were overwhelmingly negative.[67] In mid-March 1969, the council withdrew its support, and the project collapsed.

While an ethnic "man of the year" prize isn't inherently historical, the context—specifically, the Evangeline sites and their tight association with the label *Acadian*—made it so. Letter writers made this link clear. Longfellow's account "softens every [negative] connotation of the word 'Cajun,'" wrote Mrs. Ed Bulliard, who further claimed it was "Evangeline who gives St. Martinville a gentle and distinct importance." According to Verne Maraist Bienvenu, "[St. Martinville] is perfect the way it is—old, historical, the home of Evangeline. To change it to 'Cajun Capital of the World' would be historically incorrect, and rather ridiculous, wouldn't it?" Others argued that since French and Spanish "noblemen" first settled the area, their descendants should maintain pride of place in its history, and they certainly "[did] not deserve to be called 'cajuns.'" Several writers referenced the royalist French émigrés and their refinement, encapsulated in St. Martinville's unofficial moniker as the "Little Paris of America," and made it clear that "Cajun" was incompatible with such a "proud cultural past."[68]

Other efforts to promote a history and a culture explicitly labeled Cajun were launching, some of which seemed to promise sweeping change vis-à-vis the past (see chapter 5). But some publicly opposed such proposals, and in that regard, this situation is particularly noteworthy insofar as citizens mobilized to dispute the value of such a move and to demand that public bodies rescind their support for it. In part, this can be attributed to the town's singular features and how Acadian history was articulated to its sociology and economy. As previously suggested, elites in St. Martinville, who largely did not identify as either Acadian or Cajun, managed Evangeline history as one element of a broader historical narrative about themselves and the region, which, in turn, was tied through tourism to the local economy. In other ways, however, it clearly connects to important dynamics identified thus far and clarifies how they intersected with public history during this moment.

One such dimension involved how Cajuns' impropriety marked a significant difference within whiteness. As we saw, assertions about their problematic behavior were integral to many governmental initiatives; here again, in the domain of history and cultural policy, those concerns remained, again deployed to problematize them. Opponents insisted, for instance, on an explicit distinction between Acadians and Cajuns. The latter, Mrs. Bulliard explained, were "web-footed, backwards, illiterate people, suspicious of change and new ways, content to babble in a corrupted 17th-century dialect, . . . indolent and lazy." Conversely, she said, "our Acadians" were "simple" yet possessed "qualities of hardiness, endurance, and solidarity," who sought to "speak their native tongue and be understood, to have access to the sacraments in [their] religion . . . , to again own a piece of land . . . and once more experience the . . . hope of harvesting [it]."[69] These characterizations make explicit reference to class (e.g., property ownership) but go well beyond a focus on occupation or status per se. As mentioned earlier, such language also has racializing overtones in that differences between Cajuns and Acadians are quasi-naturalized, especially through the focus on defective Cajun bodies, including the attribution of subhuman ("web-footed") traits.

With respect to these different labels, the moral dimension of the comparison is striking: Drawn almost entirely in terms of virtuous Acadian conduct and dispositions in comparison to debased Cajun ones, the contrast between good and bad behavior could hardly be blunter. Perhaps most remarkably, Bulliard brought these depictions of collective virtue and vice to bear as the crux of determining who and what should be represented as local history.

Given that Cajuns' trajectory "ends [in the present] with the degradation of their identity" (again, the assertion of Cajun degeneration), she affirmed that "our national image should remain the 'Home of Evangeline.'"[70]

Again, this stress on proper conduct was related to the purpose of historical representation as a civic activity. If public history needed to offer symbols and objects to guide behavior, then Cajuns' corrupt comportment could scarcely achieve such a goal. Andre Mouton, a self-identified Acadian who joined Bulliard in opposing the Jaycees, made precisely this point. "Don't try to debase us by using the word Cajun," Mouton stipulated, "because that name always pertained to ignorant people . . . as repugnant to all good and noble Acadians . . . as the word 'N-----' is to . . . a black American." Like Bulliard, Mouton insisted on distinguishing between Cajuns and Acadians, who he claimed had immigrated to Louisiana "because they wanted to be free men." To "do justice" to this "beautiful heritage," Mouton suggested the town be proclaimed the *Acadian* capital. Though he frames it more polemically, Mouton largely recapitulates the logic articulated by the state museum curators decades earlier, intimating how commitments to this vision of shaping conduct through public history had become widespread. To promote the common good and form competent citizens, history should foreground commendable past acts (a "beautiful heritage") and enable the current generation's willingness (or "pride") to replicate them. Cajuns, however, utterly lacked such a "usable" past. And since only Acadians possessed a history of which citizens could be proud, Mouton concluded, "There are no cajuns, we are Acadians."[71]

As previously described, Bulliard's and Mouton's claims were not unusual. Preoccupations about Cajuns' indecorum were pervasive, and the notion that *Cajun* and *Acadian* referred to distinct social groups was common. But in this context, these critics made the evaluations of conduct that formed the boundary between them categorically pertinent in matters of public history. This brings to mind John Kasson's contention that "manners are [not] merely empty formalities" but instead "are inextricably tied to larger political, social, and cultural contexts," with "ramifications [that] extend deep into human relations."[72] Though my reference to behavior covers wider ground than Kasson's manners, its gist—that we overlook a far-reaching concern with conduct—is analogous. The Cajun Capital debate underscores that in a civic context, institutions and actors positioned the shaping of comportment at the center of what they hoped history could "do," of what they thought it was "for."

Along these lines, the dispute suggests that as what some refer to as the "Cajun renaissance" began to take shape, many people were ambivalent about, if not hostile to, Cajuns and their history as subjects of representation. They doubted that Cajun historicity, with all its negative connotations, could enter the public realm and serve a redeeming civic purpose. Following the modernization theory undergirding many initiatives, they continued to hold that Cajuns should forget their past. For this stance to be reversed, not only did their arguments need to be overcome, but new ways of thinking about the social world, the problems it presented, and the relationship of Cajuns to those challenges needed to be developed. Existing projects in which Cajuns and their past were thoroughly problematized had to be displaced, their hold on the public imagination decentered. That this did happen was the outcome of novel initiatives and elaborate discursive scaffolding that transformed Cajuns from a problem into a solution. It is this emergence that I will explore in chapter 5.

CONCLUSION

In discussing how prose casts time and space as context and ground for human agency, Mikhail Bakhtin suggested that a number of recognizable and stable configurations, which he called chronotopes, recur in European fiction.[73] Applying that notion to the texts reviewed in this chapter, one might say that a recurrent chronotope emerged in Louisiana across the twentieth century. In it, time moves inexorably forward toward the realization of a telos of progress, aided by agents and institutions acting in concert with its underlying logic. In this setting, however, resides a collective actor who is out of step with this unfolding reality, and whose agency, whether by volition or accident, runs consistently at counterpurposes to the paths that all are meant to follow. Within these parameters, the plot, so to speak, often involves the efforts of more enlightened forces to correct that group's problematic actions and set them on *le bon chemin*.

These are the chronotopic dimensions of the persistent narrative about Cajuns I have described, which emerged from analyses and debates accompanying a range of social projects, including that of spreading knowledge of Acadian history. To be sure, this discourse never achieved the totalizing dimensions attributed to Blackness, whereby, in all domains, authorities cast African Americans as threatening society's very survival, necessitating decisive, far-reaching, even violent action. And it is no longer the dominant chronotope. Nevertheless, it took a stable form, with consistent features, a regular cast of characters, and predictable plotlines. Significantly, while acknowledged as having European heritage, the chronotope operated to separate Cajuns from other whites, singling them out as different and troubled. From C. M. Ulrich's angry denunciation to Andre Mouton's insulted dismissal, Cajuns' whiteness was consistently suspect and in need of correction and reform.

Crucially, these accounts were more than fictional narratives. They were embedded in efforts to reconfigure the social world. They were discursive in Foucault's terms: authorized speech linked to policies, technical programs, and sites of intervention seeking to govern the population. From this perspective, Cajuns' problematic whiteness emerged with—was produced by—the expansion of capitalism and biopolitical norms that characterized twentieth-century public policy through the mid-century. The classroom, the agriculture demonstration plot, the kitchen or living room and porch (where the home economics extension agent and social worker intervened, respectively): In each of them, specialized knowledge and techniques, trained agents of the state, and novel products and practices were brought to bear to change Cajuns. To appreciate Cajuns' profile as a white ethnic group requires bringing into view these goals and policies that made them so.

History—narratives about the flow and direction of collective time and how Cajuns contravened it—featured prominently in these efforts. The many moments when authorities evoked it in these texts, including through references to civilization, progress, culture, degeneracy, and so on, carried considerable explanatory weight. They are not often considered public history, but perhaps they should be.

Some scholars stress that across the twentieth century, many worked both within and outside the academy to transform historical discourse into a neutral, objective, technocratic discourse, to separate it from political uses like these.[74] But as Michel-Rolph Trouillot contends, these understandings of historical narratives "grossly underestimate the size, the relevance, and the complexity of the overlapping sites where history is produced." It "has many hearths"—emanating from "ethnic and religious leaders, political appointees, journalists, and various associations within civil society as well as independent citizens"—and academics are not its predominant keepers.[75] They also overlook history's abiding use as a discourse of power. As Carol Greenhouse suggests in her cross-cultural study of the politics of time, temporal narratives are primarily "'about' agency and its availability as grist for political self-legitimation."[76] The preceding accounts made this explicit. Experts like Borst and Kollmorgen and Harrison spoke on behalf of the nation-state and its teleological history of progress, positioning themselves as its avatars as they called out Cajuns for their deformed habits and warped history. Within the nation-state, one mode of wielding power has been through this kind of management of competing histories and their claims to political prominence. Historical narratives have been *for* ranking the kinds of acts and agents that matter in the spacetime of a given polity. In this sense, they create social order by constructing a temporal order.

An important consequence of this politics bears stressing for the rest of the book's argument. In *Cajuns on the Bayous*, a lighthearted travelogue published in the mid-1950s, writer Carolyn Ramsey relates her encounters with Andre Olivier, the amateur historian who helped establish Evangeline as local history in St. Martinville. Framing her account as a search for Evangeline's descendants, she bookends the text with two moments of dialogue with Olivier. In the first, he tells her that defining "the Acadian" is a "difficult question" and that in her search for them across the state, she will "find them everywhere . . . and yet, . . . nowhere."[77] Ultimately, Ramsey concludes that while she indeed met many Acadians, "to find a single man who called himself Cajun . . . was an impossible thing." Ever the raconteur, Olivier cast this as a great secret, that Cajuns were "a myth of their own making."[78] But Ramsey slips in a sociological aside that in her travels, a Cajun was "always the other fellow," and this chapter explains why.[79] Charged with the disdain and loathing described earlier, Cajun became an epithet, a fighting word roughly equivalent to "white trash."[80] As a loaded and widely used classification, *Cajun* mobilized many to act *on* those so labeled. But as Mouton claimed, few if any desired, as Matt Wray puts it, to "coalesce around [this] ascribed identity"—to inhabit it as a subject position.[81] As a result, through the 1950s, little group formation unfolded under its banner. And a broad spectrum of authorities intended this. They proposed that Cajuns should cease to exist by transforming themselves, shedding the stupidity, bad French, deviance, and mistrust of authority that blocked society's forward movement. They were meant to forget their past—all of it.

Chapter Two

The Past as a Civic Force

Historical Remembrance in St. Martinville

On an overcast Friday afternoon in November 2000, St. Martinville's municipal government sponsored a dedication of the newly renovated Duchamp Opera House. Situated at one corner of the main square downtown, the brick structure held a special place in the local imaginary that belied its modest size. During the nineteenth century, its open second floor was the site of performances, including those of visiting opera troupes from New Orleans, from whence its name. More than any other building, it evoked the cultural sophistication to which the town's elites once aspired, offering material proof that St. Martinville merited its nickname of le Petit Paris d'Amérique. Unsurprisingly, several speakers stressed this aspect of the site's past.

But most of the ceremony involved the recognition of the Bienvenu family, which was tied to the structure's more recent history. Descended from colonial-era settlers, three siblings, Willie, Zerben, and Reuben, operated Bienvenu Brothers Department Store in the building during most of the twentieth century, where they offered inter alia hand-tailored suits from New Orleans. After the store closed in the late 1990s, the brothers' children donated the edifice to the town, and officials highlighted that generous act during this event. They unveiled a plaque commemorating the family's donation, during which, in a touching moment, one Bienvenu descendant was moved to tears. Now a landmark, the site's new name foregrounded its distant past, but in the ceremony itself, it was the Bienvenus' standing as entrepreneurs and civic benefactors that locals recalled. The editor of the local *Teche News* amplified this, writing of his "vivid memory" of how Reuben Bienvenu's "very special service" in the clothing store made him "feel like a VIP."[1]

As this intimates, a prominent part of the town's public culture involved invoking memories of the past. As I began fieldwork in St. Martinville, moments like these were common. Municipal authorities inaugurated three new historic sites during a five-year period, and a venue's rollout sometimes comprised several such events. One aspect of this ceremony foregrounded to a great degree an intriguing feature that was present in all of them I attended. In the opera house dedication ceremony and the *Teche News*'s commentary, the focus centered on recollections of the Bienvenu Brothers store and their descendants' donation, while the building's more remote history as the opera house was secondary. Though chronologically prior, its nineteenth-century iteration served as a backdrop for recalling remarkable events that occurred *within living memory*. Thus, the pursuit of historical meaning took remembered experience and contemporary concerns as its starting points. It centered remembered time: the ongoing significance of the Bienvenu family and its multigenerational legacy of achievement and beneficence. As such, the ceremony's participants constructed a link to a more distant past *through* current preoccupations and recollections from their own lives.

This hybrid dimension of historical remembering—as an intertwining of experience-near recollections with sites, objects, commemorative activities, and conventional narratives tied to distant pasts—arguably constitutes it. As his starting point for conceptualizing historical memories, Maurice Halbwachs suggested that they are derived from both an intergenerational transmission of experience (e.g., the "living bond" of grandparents recollecting their lives with their grandchildren) and the "reconstruction" of the past acquired through written history (e.g., as learned in school from teachers and textbooks).[2] He stresses that to be remembered (with its connotations of personally meaningful and tinged with affect), historical remnants must engender a sense of "filiation" with the past; through practice, traces of ancestors and their deeds are articulated to and made relevant to experience, bridging the distance that separates individuals from time out of mind.

The way that remembering remote pasts possesses this constructed character led me to approach its public manifestations from a particular angle. As this chapter and the next two will suggest, if one starts not from the common affirmation that St. Martinville possesses a history but instead from what people remembered and stressed about the past, no widely shared, consensual historical *memory* of such a thing existed. The history of St. Martinville instantiated by the opera house, its evocation of Little Paris's cultural refinement, was significant for some but not others. Retiree Sam Benoit remembered how, as a young man, one of the Bienvenu brothers had denied him credit. He wanted to purchase clothes for a wedding he was serving in, he recalled, but "he [the store's owner] refused to let me have them, because that was the Bienvenus, and I was a Benoit." Sitting in his dining room, he continued indignantly, "I never went back in that store. . . . And my mother had shopped at that store [*taps table for emphasis*] *all of her life*." Benoit did not attend the dedication ceremony.

The difference between the *Teche News* editor's memory of shopping at the store and Benoit's relates to one of the inherently problematic tensions in the very notion of historical remembering. As Paul Ricoeur notes in his reading of *The Collective Memory*, Halbwachs recognizes that history is often unitary, recounted in the singular (e.g., "*the* history of St. Martinville"). Meanwhile, as Halbwachs mentions but does not stress, memories of any collectivity are multiple, refracted through dynamics of belonging and exclusion across the social body.[3] The centrifugal qualities of memories across a group—how two St. Martinvillers remembered Bienvenu Brothers Department Store in divergent ways—can be obscured by accepting the notion that, like conventional historical narratives, recollections across collectivities are unified and homogeneous.

I start from this insight: that under stratified conditions, remembrance manifests heterogeneously across the social body. From this angle, what needs to be explained is how a subset of recollections and narratives about the distant past achieves coherence, salience, and predominance. Assuming this dispersed character of *remembering* in practice, I explore how and for what purposes a centripetal historical *memory*—like that of St. Martinville as le Petit Paris—held sway. As a lens for conceptualizing this, the following sketches out a landscape of historical memory in St. Martinville. This spatial metaphor refers to the conventions and institutions that privilege recollection of specific events, enabling them to become socialized. To illustrate this, Laurence Kirmayer noted the difference between memories of the Holocaust among its survivors and those of victims of childhood sexual abuse.[4] Where the former suffer from intrusive memories, the latter tend to dissociate from the past and "forget" their abuse. Rather than attribute this variation to psychology, Kirmayer claims that it is social. The two groups have occupied distinct landscapes of memory—configurations of "social practices, the larger context of social meaning, and the way that these converge to create a virtual space of recounting"—one fostering recall, the other disabling it.[5] From this perspective, any sustained remembering unfolds due to material and social landmarks that support it; without these, memories wither and fade. Transposed into the context of St. Martinville, I posit that historical remembrance of the town as le Petit Paris rested on scaffolded terrain, like the renovation of the opera house and its dedication ceremony. An elaborate material and symbolic infrastructure—a landscape of spaces, practices, stratification, tropes, and projects—highlighted certain aspects of the remote past and enabled their remembrance. The rest of the chapter outlines some of the principal markers of this terrain.

Along with historical remembrance's hybrid character, this intrinsic requirement for social supports opens onto another of its basic cultural features. In acts of historical remembering, people were often *doing something as they recalled historical time.*[6] In honoring the Bienvenu family for their actions, the dedication ceremony had a social and pragmatic focus: It affirmed them as exemplary citizens, thereby promoting a particular social order in the present. While invoking the distant past had many aims and motivations in St. Martinville, a recurrent one was putting it to use like this, as a force capable of shaping behavior and civic belonging. Many other locals similarly focused on mobilizing history's motivational potential, rendering it a resource for normative sociality and civic pride. Intending for such remembrance to inflect others' conduct, they sought to make historical accounts circulate such that they would stick in people's memories. Thus, historical remembrance was implicated in matters of influence, citizen formation, and self-making—in relations of power. As I will argue in subsequent chapters, this does not differ categorically from how practitioners in the public history space operated.

THE LANDSCAPE OF HISTORICAL MEMORY IN LE PETIT PARIS D'AMÉRIQUE

When, during fieldwork, others asked about my interests, I first replied I was interested in "local history." Responses to this varied; frequently, individuals begged off any knowledge of the topic and suggested I talk to someone else. Invariably, these residents recommended locals more educated than themselves, alluding to one of history's connotations. Discourse marked as historical was often associated with higher levels of education and status. The opera house dedication underscored this, highlighting certain types of achievements and virtues. The architect's distinctive design, its location on the town square and use as a venue for highbrow activities, the Bienvenu brothers' commercial success, their heirs' munificent donation—all of these instantiated a history that was middle class as well as white and masculine.

This skew had material dimensions, correlated with unevenly distributed intellectual skills. As the area's oldest town, St. Martinville not only possessed a core of older structures that evoked the past (about which more in the next section) but was also a place of ongoing recourse to archival and legal records. Under most conditions, this work enabled only a utilitarian historical memory, circumscribed by the limited aims of their use. As an act of recollection, the tracing of property ownership as part of a secession remained diffuse and chronological; it did not congeal into a collective representation. Yet these archives patently influenced a broader historical memory.

A comparison with nearby Breaux Bridge suggests one reason for this consequential effect. In the late 1950s, the latter town celebrated its centennial, and the event was so successful that officials decided to repeat it as an annual festival. In doing so, however, they quickly transformed its focus. Where the centennial had historical themes—contests for best period costume, displays of antiques, an edition of the local newspaper recounting the town's past—its successor shed them and morphed into a popular event, with crawfish eating and peeling contests, beauty pageants, and performances of contemporary music.[7] While evoking the historical past as the crux of commemoration proved to be short-lived in Breaux Bridge, it had much deeper grounding in St. Martinville. A key condition of this was material: The longevity and thickness of local record-keeping meant that as repositories of records, the courthouse, library, and churches operated as centers of calculation for historical knowledge.[8] In amassing and concentrating material traces of past events and lives, these collections enabled locals to access a wide range of historical documents—a feat not easily replicated in Breaux Bridge—and thereby compose extensive narratives. And St. Martinville had a tradition of residents working the archives to produce such accounts. Over the years, they mined the sacramental registries, conveyance records, plat books, periodicals, photographic collections, and vertical files, crafting brochures, inventories, proposals, and historics that circulated to varying degrees.[9] Not surprisingly, its most text-savvy residents—teachers, lawyers, docents, journalists, and both amateur and professional genealogists and historians—composed them.

This inflection permeated everyday historical awareness in mundane ways. Suspecting that I might draw the wrong conclusion from the town's extensive

Acadian history-making, *one resident bluntly informed me, "St. Martinville is* not *an Acadian town." Instead, he explained, "It's more an aristocratic French town," where descendants of those early settlers from the continent continued to set the tone, socially and politically.* To outsiders, this situation has seemed confusing, even contradictory: Why would descendants of aristocratic French settlers, non-Acadians, represent the town as the self-proclaimed "Birthplace of Acadiana"?[10] As chapter 1 intimated, historical memories were embedded in various aims, and not only that of straightforward self-representation. This response hinted at another connotation of history and another of its goals. "St. Martinville *is* an aristocratic French town": The predicate suggested a claim about belonging to, even possessing, the place—an assertion of privilege in the present based on a claim about the past.

These social labels remained salient markers of difference, classifications in which history was intertwined with class divisions and an everyday politics of status. Some have followed geographer Cécyle Trépanier in positing a late twentieth-century "Cajunization" of south Louisiana—that is, the adoption of a Cajun identity and cultural affiliations by all residents of francophone descent.[11] Yet as others pointed out, this shift always involved holdouts. A significant percentage of white St. Martinvillers qualified among the latter, maintaining a strong sense of a distinct identity, of French but not Acadian descent.[12] Like the New Orleanians studied by Virginia Domínguez, they previously referred to themselves as white Creoles, which marked their Latin (as opposed to Anglo-Saxon) origins as well as their distance from mixed-race free people of color.[13] But as the twentieth century wore on, they abandoned this label for a variety of terms—aristocratic French, *Français de la France*, Euro-French, or simply French—all of which they invoked in opposition to Cajun or Acadian.[14] Even newcomers became aware that these categories mattered. "'Oh no, I'm not Cajun, I'm French': Until [my neighbor] went to the nursing home, she used to say that," recounted a recent arrival. "She made a real point of saying that to me." The transplant characterized relations between the two groups as marked by "tension."[15]

These labels could be rendered as a matter of geographical provenance. But these St. Martinvillers did not stress that meaning. Instead, their use signified behavior differences and evoked memories of the boundary-making that characterized their relations with Cajuns. Their efforts to create distance had spatial dimensions (e.g., assembling in distinct neighborhoods) and associational ones (patterns of exclusive socializing, including strictures against dating and marriage). Kevin Richelieu defined Cajuns as "people with their heads bowed, and just going along, nose to tail, wandering all over the world, with no place to live." He described how his family insisted on maintaining a physical distance from Cajuns, for example, by preventing him from playing with the "kids . . . that grew up on the back street." Recalling the middle-class milieu of his upbringing, Richelieu, an accountant, singled out his upwardly mobile mother, who was adamant about not being identified with the stratum she was trying to leave behind. "No . . . I'm not a Cajun," he imagined his mother saying, pointing toward others. "*They're* Cajuns!" Many acknowledged that social relations were shifting in St. Martinville such that constraints limiting contact between the two groups were losing their force. Nonetheless, the negative connotations of Cajun continued to resonate, inflecting behavior in the present.

Enmeshed in everyday practices of inclusion and exclusion, *French* and *Cajun* remained potent labels signifying ranked differences in taste and conduct. When the World Acadian Congress was held in Louisiana in 1999, Richelieu accepted an invitation to attend commemorative activities that St. Martinville hosted. Yet he specified that, while an avid tennis player, he "wouldn't take [his] racket to Lafayette and play in something called the Cajun Tennis Club." Its connotations were popular and coarse and thus misaligned with the activity's upscale cachet. As Richelieu's comments intimate, this status politics also shaped historical remembering. Those who identified as French and saw their behaviors as more refined felt similarly about their past. It was more distinctive, more definitive of the town's identity, more worthy of recollection.

Some locals furthered this kind of historical awareness through genealogical research. Circulating among St. Martinvillers, I encountered many who pursued it, alone or with others, as a hobby. As a civil parish and district court seat since the state's inception, St. Martinville has been home to numerous lawyers, judges, and politicians, as well as other professionals, some achieving a certain renown.[16] It is perhaps unique in this respect; only a handful of Louisiana towns of its size possess such a profile. Moreover, progeny of the first European settlers continued to live in St. Martinville. Occupying influential positions—as elected officials, business owners, senior civil servants, and civic boosters—their lives unfolded in their ancestors' wake, so to speak, of which many seemed well aware. Certain families foregrounded this publicly. A group of those with origins among French nobility agreed to the display of their coats of arms in a historic building downtown, and a genealogist published their family trees, stressing their prominence, for example, as founders of the oldest Catholic parish.[17]

Interest in genealogy served more formally as the status-based focus of social activities as well: In the Friends of the Maison Duchamp and the regional chapter of the Daughters of the American Revolution (DAR), more affluent St. Martinvillers together pursued their familial histories. Participation in these groups traced a well-worn path into developing awareness of the town's past, forming another prominent strand of historical consciousness. From one perspective, these groups could be characterized as "workshops" of historical memory in a Halbwachsian sense, since they enabled individuals to foster strong affect toward their ancestors. Yet group members did not merely extend genealogical knowledge but also linked their predecessors to events of widely recognized significance. The DAR's premise illustrates this, requiring potential members to document descendance from a Revolutionary War soldier. By establishing an archival link between a forebear and the Revolution, the quality of the heroic agent and the patriotic virtue associated with that event devolved to that ancestor—and to the individual and her family. In a text from the 1970s, a DAR member, after summarizing the record of her ancestor's military service, concluded with a flourish that he "contribut[ed] his part towards securing the freedom of the American colonies and the establishment of our great country."[18] Every time the *Teche News* ran announcements for DAR meetings and highlighted locals who served in leadership roles, it confirmed this significance.

In addition to the notion of a genealogically transmitted historical inheritance, an associated idea of a broader sociocultural one existed, covering an accumulated legacy of habit, disposition, and conduct active in those who shared it. That is, locals acted on the assumption that public historical memories were *for* enabling the behaviors depicted therein—for spreading certain types of conduct. To be sure, in practice, the genealogical and the cultural were intertwined, especially where members of a family succeeded in publicly commemorating their ancestors' memorable acts. Yet they forwarded those memories not merely as an exclusive familial inheritance but also as commendable acts meant to impact others. Past events that St. Martinvillers promoted to public relevance, like Felix Voorhies's recasting of Evangeline as local history, were exemplary achievements intended to be appreciated, even emulated, by the public. Thus, while affirming a certain prestige for themselves, those who successfully commemorated their ancestors simultaneously upheld their forebears' excellence for others' inspiration.

Such aims could be subtle, but they were concrete. Accounts of the Durand spiderweb wedding exemplify this. Though centered on what seems like an embellished fable, they relate to a consequential project that sought to edify the public. The legend goes that on his antebellum plantation, planter Charles Durand sponsored a lavish wedding celebration for two of his daughters. With the aid of thousands of imported spiders, Durand draped the treelined alley leading to the main house in webs that were then covered with gold and silver dust, creating a spectacular setting for the ceremony. An exhibit at Le Petit Paris Museum on the town's main square featured a costumed interpretation of the event from a Rotary Club ball in 1984. As the Duchamp Opera House dedication suggests, these counted among the most elaborate and cherished representations of the town's past.

In Harnett Kane's mid-twentieth-century retelling of the legend, the ostentatious élan of white Creole elites like Durand referenced their long-standing claims to preeminence rather than an odd behavioral quirk. Kane's version juxtaposed Durand's Creole penchant for indulgent affluence with the clever calculations of a successful Irish American neighbor, evoking distinctions that became keenly relevant in the state's public culture.[19] After Louisiana's entry into the Union and faced with waves of anglophone immigration, elites like Durand, who were Creoles in the root sense—that is, descended from French and Spanish continentals but native to the New World—felt threatened. As Anglo Louisianans rose in prominence, they asserted that their contributions to building Louisiana earned them the right to continue participating in governing the state.

Among these qualities, they cited their genteel comportment, which they compared favorably to the coarseness and utilitarian single-mindedness of Anglo-Americans. To paraphrase historian John Kasson's argument about civility, the assertion of a cultured savoir vivre in this context was about more than hosting gaudy weddings: It referenced a vision of how to establish authority and order. One's capacity to perform propriety and taste indexed that for self-governance; cultured refinement served as evidence of a discerning, self-controlling subject. Moreover, elites posited the cultivation and display of mannered subjectivity as a basis for *social* order; for those not born into practices of seeking the good and the proper in all things, "rules of etiquette would extend the laws and teach each individual his social duties."[20]

White Creoles explicitly forwarded this argument, making it through retelling such stories of their ancestors' refinement.[21]

As such, this project of white Creole social hegemony, outlined in the previous chapter, had waned. In interviews, no one situated the wedding in relation to it, and the Petit Paris Museum exhibit mentioned Kane's version of it only in passing. Yet its vision of historical remembrance's purpose—as a practice through which those of higher social standing might model proper behavior for their inferiors—remained deeply sedimented in more recent efforts, underscoring how recollecting the remote past was embedded in social hierarchy. After the Acadian Memorial's opening in 1996, one of its sponsors claimed, "It allows [Cajuns] to have something beautiful, something nice. It's not a Saturday night dance or a *boucherie* [hog butchering]. It's *the first time they are associated with something beautiful*" (emphasis added).[22] The butchering undoubtedly refers to a local festival, La Grande Boucherie des Cajuns, during which participants roasted a slaughtered hog amid craft vendors and music performances. In this remark, the speaker ostensibly promotes an effort of self-improvement and social uplift: The memorial would redirect locals from less sophisticated pastimes and introduce them to a novel experience of beauty and refinement.[23] Though history had more than these status-inflected accents, they were among its most pronounced.

EVANGELINE FADE: LOCAL HISTORY MEETS ACADEMIC EXPERTISE

The extended moment during which locals easily elevated family heritage to historical prominence was arguably ceding to another one. As part of a broader shift that I will consider in chapter 5, Carl Brasseaux's *In Search of Evangeline* changed the terms of local public history. The book led off with several sharp epistemological assertions, including a citation that "the printed document and the archival manuscript *are the source and the law*, and stand ever opposed to unverified tradition" (emphasis added).[24] Brasseaux's heavily footnoted argument proceeded to shred the case that Voorhies, Susan Anding, Andre Olivier, and their successors had accurately recounted historical events. Evangeline was thus an "excellent" example of how "legends are confused with historical fact by the general public . . . particularly . . . at the local level." Brasseaux clearly ranked these different kinds of historical speech, labeling such "folklore . . . [as] the 'handmaiden' of history." In this regime of knowledge and truth, academics, it seemed, would be the sole authorities. Yet Brasseaux also gave the last word to a folk musician whose lyrics mocked Evangeline, one of the many "egalitarian, blue-collar Cajuns" who were apathetic about the legend. Their "humor and even ridicule" of "anything placed on a pedestal," he implied, constituted another take on the past that should be heard.[25] To create the space to air it, the hegemony of a flawed history had to be challenged, or so one might conclude from such framing.

This perspective posits the historian as a civic referee, weighing historical truths and overseeing the entry of challenges and "minor" narratives into historical discourse. One can endorse such a view while still noting that, experientially, Brasseaux's intervention was lived as an intensely political matter, a contest *between* literates over the privilege of historical interpretation. Angela St. Armand certainly understood *In Search of Evangeline*'s impact in this way. A direct descendant of Voorhies's Acadian ancestor, St. Armand wanted to publish a response to it. She imagined a book in which she would reinterpret relevant sources and challenge Brasseaux's interpretation. But her initial attempts to interest a publisher were unsuccessful. In one of them, she felt that she was rebuffed because the prospect of "this little Acadian lady in St. Martinville" challenging an academic historian represented a bridge too far for the editor to cross. Importantly, a new regime of local historical knowledge entailed not simply a shift of speech, of narratives, but also of speakers, of those authorized to recount the past.

As St. Armand's response intimates, Brasseaux's inversion of the valence attributed to Evangeline promoters' behavior—instead of performing commendable deeds, he characterized them as profit-seekers and "fakelorists"—did not sit well with their descendants. Their indignant reactions revealed another dimension of historical remembering, another experiential anchor for it. Some felt personally targeted by the book; in these cases, remembering such a history was personal, part of how they fashioned their selves. For Jeannette Marcantel, Brasseaux's claim that Voorhies had "made it all up . . . maddened" her. Married to one of Voorhies's descendants, she resented that her children should "ever have to read the sentence saying that their great-great-grandfather fabricated a story and passed it off as truth . . . I mean, the man was a judge. His great-uncle had been governor of Louisiana. . . . This society wasn't into fabrication." Accustomed to transforming their ancestors' notable accomplishments into local history without challenge, *Brasseaux's characterizations "insulted" them,*

Marsha Greenhaw, descendant of another family linked to Evangeline history, claimed. These women's reactions suggest that remembering their historical precursors served as a means of self-fashioning, for both themselves and their posterity. Even as their ancestors' achievements had become public history, these St. Martinvillers recalled this past as an intensely subjective matter: Families had socialized it as part of their identities. Greenhaw's indignity at Brasseaux's book implied that her identification with her ancestor was such that his charge impugned her own reputation. In Marcantel's concern over how Brasseaux's claims would impact her children, transmitting a positive memory appeared as a means of shaping their subjectivity: They needed to learn of their descent from a prominent jurist (presumably to instill in them a large sense of their own potential) rather than suffer harm from the claim that he trafficked in falsehoods. For them, Evangeline history was historical memory in a strong, Halbwachsian sense: transmitted intergenerationally and experienced as profoundly self-formative.

Such reactions were limited; only a few people expressed them. Other St. Martinvillers thought less of Evangeline, if at all. Yet they were significant, since Evangeline history was not *merely* a fabricated legend. As these stances suggest, some prominent families embedded it in their mores, and through Evangeline sites, the town had anchored it in a certain public historical memory. Brasseaux's book undermined the legitimacy and raison d'être of both. One does not have to affirm these families' prerogative of turning familial lore into public history as they saw fit to appreciate that a new archival version of history had implications well beyond the printed page. Insofar as academics asserted that a respect for facts and truth should extend "to the local level," they called for subjectivity and praxis that differed from existing ones. They were entering a field of cultural practices, of modes of historical remembering, that their narratives disrupted. In sum, *In Search of Evangeline* amounted to a civic and cultural intervention as much as an intellectual one, in which academics challenged the long-standing predominance of regional elites in history-making. And these residents interpreted it precisely in these terms, as a loss inflicted by an adversary. *"There's something about the handed-down history that we're losing. It's beautiful," Greenhaw mused. By contrast, she asserted, historians' history was all about facts, "but facts can never cover everything," and their dry narratives were "dullsville" compared to the handed-down version.*

REMEMBERING COLLECTIVELY: INDIVIDUAL AND SOCIAL MEMORIES, HISTORICAL MEMORY

"This particular building was started in the 1830s." Launching a tour of downtown historic sites, Oscar Duplantis, a retired insurance salesman, narrated details about St. Martin of Tours Catholic Church to a group of visitors seated in its nave. As the town's oldest Catholic parish, the church was integral to its historic identity; founded in the 1750s, it anchored the open square in the oldest part of town, around which sites like the opera house were situated. For the most part, Duplantis framed his presentation as a historical one, narrating, in a documentary-like, third-person voice, tidbits about the church's past. He focused largely on distinctive features of its interior, like its baptismal font, which, legend had it, Louis XVI had gifted to the church. But as he continued, he wove details of his own life into the narration. At one point, pausing for effect, he gestured toward the font and told the group that his grandchild's recent baptism added another generation to a long line of Duplantises who received the sacrament at that spot.

With this shift to first-person speech and personal experience, Duplantis created an explicit intersection of individual memory and the collective past, recalling his own involvement in the parish's long-lived continuity and inserting it into his narrative. This articulation of the personal and the collective, of memory and history, produced an effect, as some visitors reacted with audible gasps. In connecting his own experience to the space and time of the church, Duplantis briefly embodied the history, the permanency of place and congregation, that he described. Not all Petit Paris history was as "open" to such personal identification as this. But this "bring[ing] of life history and [collective] story into mutual relevance" was a common practice among local guides, including those who, like Duplantis, had little "organic" link to much of Petit Paris history.[26] At the same time, Duplantis's endorsement of it was not total. Though he later led the tour group to the Petit Paris Museum, he told me that he was skeptical about its historical accuracy and declined to enter it with them.

For natives, the long-lived character of Petit Paris history operated as a substantial given: It represented, in socially and spatially dominant forms, what was significant about the historical past. Yet if, as I described, much of Petit Paris history featured a few affluent clans, how did it become memorable for individuals and groups who weren't "part of the family?" How does someone else's history—as Halbwachs noted, we initially encounter *any* time beyond our lifetimes as "other"—become "our own"? This moment in Duplantis's tour illustrates one instance of how this happened: He linked himself to Petit Paris by recollecting his own life in relation to a prominent object in a key site. At the same time, it suggests that for some, their articulation with Petit Paris history was partial, limited by other commitments, even a critical awareness. In subsequent chapters, I will evoke something of the breadth of memories as considered from this perspective; in the stratified context of St. Martinville, they were multiple, heterogeneous, and contested. Here, though, I focus on individuals who, while sharing similar social positions (especially middle-class and white racial status) with members of the town's "founding families," were not inducted into it through family memories (à la Marcantel and her children). Instead, they became connected to Petit Paris history by other routes. What did such people remember that linked them to that history? How did they come to claim it as their own?

Several things stand out in this regard. One dimension of this remembering was its embeddedness in social relationships. This means more than "people remembered history together" (though they did, of course). It signals as well that recalling the town's past composed but one aspect of relationships that were multifaceted, such that individuals mixed historical remembering with other interests and projects.

A clear sense of this mixing emerged in Adam Leger's reflections. "The history is just outstanding," he enthused. "There's just so many beautiful things." A retired school administrator, Leger rattled off a litany of places—"beautiful old plantation homes, old Victorian homes"—to substantiate his claim. Seated at his kitchen table, he then offered me a brochure about Oak and Pine Alley, which commemorated Durand's spiderweb wedding and which he placed at the top of his list of "beautiful histories." Most of the "beautiful things" Leger mentioned harkened back to that history and to the elites who built the structures, attended the operas, and married off their progeny with such panache.[27]

Given his enthusiasm, it was not surprising when he added that local officials often called on him to accompany VIP visitors. He offered a similarly positive and definitive explanation of this: "You know why? I was proud of my town. . . . I loved St. Martinville." His endorsement of Petit Paris seemed to be inspired by a deep sense of belonging and civic pride. Leger spent much of our long interview describing the substance of this pride in St. Martinville, thereby intimating how it was linked to his investment in its past. Reflecting on his life, he focused at length on its social dimensions, sketching out a particular trajectory. Raised in modest circumstances, Leger rose into the school system's upper echelons, and the relationships that accompanied this rise were important to him. He referred repeatedly to his interpersonal skills (e.g., "I get along with everyone") and went into detail about particular episodes in his career: managing and mentoring employees, organizing school board campaigns on behalf of allies, working to build relations with power brokers who facilitated his career, and leading projects with civic organizations.

In this telling, he anchored his identification with St. Martinville in a rich sociality, which offers context for grasping his attachment to Petit Paris history. Given the centrality of public history in the town's civic life and that of social capital in Leger's upwardly mobile trajectory, one glimpses here the significance of social relations in shaping historical memory. In an individual life centered on public-sector employment, local politics, and civic volunteerism, the sociality of these milieux apparently privileged the remembrance of Petit Paris as "our" history. Moreover, in linking his interest in the collective past to a sense of belonging—"I was proud of my town. I loved St. Martinville"—Leger was not unique. Many interviewees replied in this way, moving quickly from recalling past events to recalling contemporaries, shifting focus to the people whom they remembered and their shared interests. As such, moments of purely historical retrospection often seemed fleeting, interwoven as they were in recollections of other activities. Historical remembering could be evanescent, barely standing out from memories of social relations.

Austin Rodrigue's account of restoring a building he purchased offers further insight into this socially embedded character of historical remembering, which was co-constructed and sometimes tentative. A newcomer who relocated to rehab an old building and start a business in it, Rodrigue counted as one of many locals who approached the town's past through its historical structures. In addition to a remarkable ensemble of nineteenth-century architecture in the downtown core, older neighborhoods contained numerous residences of similar age. Locals with means, both natives and transplants, renovated them as homes and businesses. Like Leger, Rodrigue also brought an enthusiasm to his appreciation of historical buildings. The connection to historical structures was passionate, and he struggled to put his sense of it into words. "It just fascinates me," he began. "I get very excited when I see these old beams. . . . It's just the history of it. And knowing about those people [who built the structures], sometimes I almost feel like there's a connection there."

In recounting the renovation process in detail, Rodrigue punctuated his memories with the reported speech of his interlocutors, underscoring their significance. They brought a multiplicity of frames to his project, resulting in uneven negotiations through which his effort was enrolled into Petit Paris history. After scouring the region for the right building to renovate, Rodrigue settled on a structure not far from St. Martinville's downtown square. During his first visit with his sister to view it, he recalled, "When we drove up, the weeds were this high [*gestures to chest*]; the front porch was falling off, literally. And I said, 'I have *got to have* this building.' And my sister said—I'll never forget it—she said, 'I think you have lost your mind.'" Later, when touring the building with an inspector before purchasing it, the owner of a nearby property confronted him. "I was in there, and Mrs. Tremblay walked in, and she said, 'What the hell are you doing in this place?'" Rodrigue remembered, "I told her I was getting ready to buy it. They [Tremblay and other neighbors] were not happy." These comments present the diversity of perspectives—of individual and social remembering—vis-à-vis Rodrigue's effort to remember historically. With his passion for preservation, Rodrigue saw in the structure the potential for a satisfying encounter with history. Others, however, drawing tacitly on divergent schema, interpreted his act differently, according little or no historical significance to it. Rodrigue's sister saw the purchase as folly, presumably viewing it from the perspective of a failed investment. The irate neighbor felt suspicious or threatened, perhaps seeing Rodrigue as an unwelcome interloper. Both initially refused to join Rodrigue in his recollection of the past. And Rodrigue went far down the path of remembering as such: Once purchased, he researched the building's previous owners, gathered information on its original decor, accumulated early photographs of the structure, and the like. But at its start, he alone brought this frame to the purchase.

As his renovation proceeded, some neighbors shifted their opinions. Witnessing his effort to rehabilitate the structure, they responded: "But once they saw what I was doing with the building, [that I] cleaned up the property and landscaped around it, [they changed]. In fact, Mr. Gagnon [another neighbor] would come; I'd be working like a dog, all hours of the night. He said to me, 'You're the hardest working white man I've ever seen.' I said, 'Well, thank you.' So, you know, that was that." Here, a widely shared (though, as the racial qualifier suggests, differentially applied) notion about the value of work came into play. Bringing other schema to the fore, residents reevaluated their initial labels of "threat" or "folly," reframing Rodrigue's actions as an esteemed activity that conformed to their recollections of similar cases. Still, divergent social memories are evident here, insofar as no one shared Rodrigue's frame of renovation as recollecting the past.

Moreover, no one, including Rodrigue, associated his activity with historical narratives of Petit Paris. In Rodrigue's retelling, that first happened ascriptively, as others made the link: "I offered [the business] a lot to the town [i.e., municipal government, for receptions]. . . . When I first moved, there was a huge dinner party. The lieutenant governor [attended], there was, I don't know all these people [who were present]. And Deborah [a native] made the comment, she said, 'Well, Austin has brought a bit of Petit Paris back to St. Martinville [with his renovation].' I was so thrilled." One does not have to assume his recollections are flawless to presume that, for an outsider like him, some sort of induction, of locals narrating his renovated structure into Petit Paris history, needed to occur for it to qualify as such. The social dimensions of that process stand out in Rodrigue's account: At each step of the way, interpreting his effort as historical appears as a co-constructed activity. At the same time, as his project unfolded, there existed a certain trajectory, a movement from others' disagreement with or doubt about his acts to their joining him in remembering—as well as ongoing abstention.

As these accounts suggest, a profound investment in objects made up another prominent feature of this historical awareness. Like Duplantis gesturing toward the baptismal font, many used things to construct a meaningful link to the remote past. Objects could possess a well-recognized "past-ness," when, like the font, locals regularly affirmed their historical quality. Not all things had this taken-for-granted historical character, and by and large, those that did fell into relatively few categories. Rodrigue's restoration is a case in point. Initially an old structure falling apart, a potential ruin whose historical significance was fading, the easy recognition of its long-standing existence, along with prominent discourses valuing the preservation of historical structures,[28] made it a comparatively uncomplicated task to refurbish its historical meaning, to re-member it. Again, this underscores the importance of shared constructs that scaffolded subjective and social investments in history.

Laura Cormier's description of how genealogical research is a meaningful endeavor provides another illustration of this. While researching a family tree may seem straightforward in terms of how it enables memory and significance, it is loaded with culturally specific notions about how such an act connects individuals to "their" past. Cormier's synopsis of genealogy's importance encapsulated several of these ideas. A middle-aged teacher from a nearby town who assisted others in their research, she spoke from this experience when she claimed, "Genealogy . . . is a way of finding out, maybe for the first time, and in a very real sense, who you are. . . . Because until you see an ancestor's gravestone, or a picture, or a name on a census role, when you see any of those things, anything tangible, it makes the past suddenly become very real. You realize you're part of a larger continuum." Cormier's sentiment is complex, referencing several commonly held notions about genealogy as historical memory. For one, the dominance of the historiographic imaginary obscures the fact that while human being is thoroughly temporal, we do not possess an innate sense of time extending beyond our own lives—a stance Cormier evokes.[29] This sense is culturally elaborated, and her reflection opens a window onto its subjective dimensions. Quite possibly, she draws on an ingrained Euro-American notion that origin establishes identity, such that its discovery clarifies something fundamental about one's authentic self.[30] Echoing Rodrigue's sentiment about architectural beams, another inference has to do with the socially constructed power of the past's materiality—in this case, as it relates to family names. As Cormier put it, when "you see" a material trace of distant predecessors, "the past suddenly becomes very real": The material encounter engenders a capacity to re-member, as a sense of connection with one's ancestors and a temporal bridge ("continuum") between now and then replaces the gap between self and other, past and present.

Well-organized groups with focused interests recruited people like Cormier into their initiatives, channeling such passion into public projects. In this way, the heterogeneity of individual and social memories was routed in specific directions, privileging a certain collective historical memory. Though not a resident, Cormier met influential natives through her archival research in town. As they sought to launch a historical project, her skills made her attractive to them, and they enlisted her participation. Speaking about it afterward, she admitted she did not find the project entirely compelling. It emphasized the downtown's architectural history, which did not align with her own commitment to enabling access to genealogical resources. Yet she became a vital contributor to their project. During the 1990s and early 2000s, when St. Martinville buzzed with new initiatives, locals who promoted them recruited individuals from outside their circles to conceptualize, research, and manage them. Many of these recruits—not infrequently inspired by their own life-shaping contact with history—believed that enabling stronger historical memories was an important civic task. Cormier was convinced of the significance of "educating our children about who we really are" through history. She was philosophical about joining the architectural project; as she framed it, "Given the choice of basically . . . sitting on my hands and watching the situation develop or trying to have a positive impact," she had hoped that she could "nudge things along in the right direction" by participating. Those spearheading the renewal of local history-making leveraged such sentiments.

TURNING TO HISTORY AMID DECLINE: CHANGE, HERITAGE, AND THE PAST AS CIVIC FORCE

When the local garment factory, a Fruit of the Loom plant, welcomed with great fanfare in 1968, announced its closing in May 2001, residents recoiled. Many saw it coming, but that did not make it any less of an unwelcome blow. The factory had anchored economic activity in the area, and its slow contraction contributed to a decades-long economic slide, of which St. Martinvillers were acutely aware. Arguably, this event also signaled the demise of industrial recruitment as a major economic development strategy. Since mid-century, authorities promoted the notion that places like St. Martinville needed to make themselves attractive to industrial capital through measures that both enskilled the workforce and incentivized factory relocation (with low-interest loans, subsidized industrial parks, etc.). During the 1990s, however, observers acknowledged the obvious: With the expansive offshoring of manufacturing accelerating at the century's end, industrial recruitment's viability as an approach had cratered.

As an alternative, planners, politicians, civic boosters, and others increasingly proposed that local history could be developed, enabling "heritage tourism" to operate as a source of wealth creation. Of course, Louisiana, and New Orleans in particular, has long foregrounded its distinct history in attempts to make it a destination. Now proponents advocated a far-reaching expansion of these efforts throughout the state: increasing public investment in planning, coordination, and marketing; professionalizing exhibit design and curation; and creating multisite itineraries to entice visitors into longer stays and wider circuits. As mentioned in chapter 1, early history makers in St. Martinville had also sought to attract tourists to enhance business. This amounted to a sweeping intensification of that approach.

These two related trends—the economic decline of St. Martinville and the rise of heritage tourism as a response to it—help bring into view another meaning of history that bears on the ones already in play. Alongside the anxiety that factory's shuttering produced, many St. Martinvillers expressed a sense of inhabiting a town that had seen better days. In interviews, one of the few constellations of non–Petit Paris memories that emerged in any breadth concerned a series of past decisions by local leaders that, in hindsight, contributed to the town's current predicament. In these, residents referenced numerous events, including officials' choice during the nineteenth century to reject the Southern Pacific Railroad's passage through town; their refusal to host the region's first public university (today's University of Louisiana at Lafayette); and more recently, their ineffectiveness in competing with rival Breaux Bridge during the postwar years for the routing of US Interstate 10. Starting in the mid-twentieth century, demographic and economic growth in St. Martinville stalled as towns and cities around it boomed; retrospectively, these were remembered as unfortunate missteps contributing to that decline.

In this interpretation, there lies a "folk" theory of history as an account of change and continuity. Here, history's connotation is that of explanations for shifts over time, of how to mark boundaries that separate a collective "now" from a prior "then." To be sure, this everyday historical consciousness was not entirely separate from official discourses; those, too, mark turning points and divide time into eras, and they often stress the economic as a key driver of progress. One sharp difference, however, was that instead of advancing along a linear path into a future of greater prosperity (as dominant narratives predicted), St. Martinville was heading in reverse. In their comments, its residents sometimes expressed a lived sense of retrogression—of watching nearby cities and towns of Lafayette, New Iberia, and Breaux Bridge expand, grow wealthy, and create opportunities for residents while their town did not.[31] Another difference was that rather than being only a matter of knowledge or semantic memory, it possessed a visceral dimension, a shared experience of time's effects on their subjectivity.

Crucially, this remembered sense of the past (as a collective experience of temporal change) was mostly distinct from that of historical narratives. In accounts of the town's remote past, whether public (like Duplantis's tour) or informal (such as Leger's recollections), locals seldom mentioned this decline. For some residents, however, they did intersect. These proposed to make Petit Paris history the core of a heritage tourism strategy that would not only address the town's economic decline but also resolve a kind of malaise that accompanied it. According to them, a "reawakening" of the past (narratives of Petit Paris history) would animate the civic pride necessary to change time's downward-sloping direction (St. Martinville's socioeconomic stagnation) and overcome the accompanying doubt about the collective future. This intentional investment in the past composed another key dimension of the landscape of memory, emerging both in relation to and distinct from other conventions enabling historical remembrance.

This vision inspired a remarkable burst of history-making activity in St. Martinville. In the mayoral election of 1991, a group of heritage-minded citizens supported candidate Eric Martin and, with his victory, set to work executing their program. Their accomplishments during the next decade read like a master list from heritage tourism implementation guides. The town created a tourism commission composed of citizen appointees who advised officials on policy; established a downtown historic district and set about improving and popularizing it; inaugurated a Main Street Program and a Visitors' Center for tourists, hiring new permanent employees to staff them; embarked on several major historic projects (the opera house renovation, the Acadian Memorial site, and a museum devoted to African American history); and obtained an impressive amount of outside funding to create these. As a recipe for economic growth, the strategy had its detractors. Across the South, some experts considered tourism-centered development as an economic dead end, one that "offers only modest wages and few full-time jobs."[32] But by the turn of the millennium, state government went all-in on it, elevating the promotion of cultural tourism to featured status in Louisiana's economic master plan.[33] Many professionals agreed with the strategy. Scanning the bleak landscape of late-century rural Louisiana—where a long-standing decline in agriculture, a shrinking oil economy, and endemically high rates of poverty were hollowing out small towns—a consultant to one heritage project asserted, "[Heritage tourism] may in the long run be the only real economic hope this area has."[34]

Abiding local interests motivated this initiative. Some entrepreneurs kept close tabs on tour bus traffic, noticing when it began to dip in the late 1980s. Across the region, tourist officials knew that travelers had shifted their itineraries, replacing a stop in St. Martinville with one in Lafayette. With the program outlined previously, they consciously sought to address this. Yet robust consensus on this strategy eluded its proponents. Support among merchants whose businesses did not benefit from tourists (e.g., pharmacies) was soft; advocates had to stay on the offensive. During the fall of 2000, when the town was constructing three new sites and hiring new personnel to staff them, several town council members, some of whom were skeptical all along, began to balk at the budgetary implications. To push back against them, Mayor Martin convened a meeting, inviting about two dozen of his allies to the town hall, during which they endorsed the policy before critical council members. Looking at tens of thousands of dollars in outlays compared to the (in their eyes) meager tax revenue returns, they sounded an alarm: This was unsustainable. Later that fall, the mayor would analyze the latest sales tax figures to bolster his counterargument; during this meeting, however, no one forwarded anything so specific to refute the councilmembers' skepticism. A bed-and-breakfast owner's declaration typified one kind of intervention. She concluded the proceedings by asking, *"What other town of this size has this kind of tourism with this kind of tax structure? We have to make this work!"* With such support, the mayor's budget survived intact, for the moment.

Yet many of those who spoke did not engage with the economic rationale for investing in history. Instead, they made arguments more civic and psychological in character. *They underscored the benefits of history for themselves and those like them (never mind the tourists), like the satisfaction that came from living in a town in touch with its illustrious past and the increased self-esteem that flowed from being connected to one's ancestors.* In one sense, they attempted to limit the predominance of budgetary considerations on matters they viewed as pertaining to quality of life. But they were also engaging in another debate involving a distinct set of social concerns and how history could be deployed to address them. While these psychosocial desiderata may sound diffuse, they were at the center of an emergent formation concerning what history was *for*. Moreover, it, too, developed from a novel problematization of social dynamics, one as well defined as that proposing heritage as an economic strategy and as consequential in materializing the town's investments in it.

For instance, claims about history's capacity to stoke residents' pride were common. At another town council meeting that fall, *Mayor Martin asserted that the heritage tourism projects he promoted "produce a change of attitude among people in town."* During a heated council meeting two years earlier, he made a similar case. This unfolded as another occasion when opponents threatened to block one of his proposals, in this instance a new hire for a heritage project. At one critical juncture in the debate, he insisted, "There's a strong lack of interest . . . in our area as far as researching history. I want this gentleman to make [residents] excited and interested in actually going out and researching. And there's so much history there, and it's so much, there's a lot of good." He later explained, "My ultimate goal as mayor is to get people to stay here and to live here." From his perspective, this aim intersected straightforwardly with promoting the civic effects of local history. With the economic stagnation, the town's population was in steady decline; with such comments, the mayor sought to counter the pessimism he sensed among those who stayed and prevent more departures. In facing this challenge, he considered St. Martinville's history as an invaluable antidote to such hopelessness. Like others, he was committed to leveraging the town's past as part of economic development, but he also envisioned it as having profound effects on residents' subjectivity, on their feelings about and commitment to the town. Referencing the impact that historical awareness could have on St. Martinvillers, he contended, "We have so much to be proud of here."

Such a conceptualization of the benefits of contact with history permeated a heritage-focused "vision plan" written in the late 1990s. Confident assertions about history's civic effects punctuated this planning document. Developing particular downtown buildings into historic sites, for example, would "serve as a reminder of the determination many ancestors [had] in keeping St. Martinville alive and progressing."[35] The authors—including civil servants, small business people, and civic boosters—claimed that the plan focused on enhancing residents' quality of life, specifying how specific improvements (e.g., removing utility lines) would "re-establish the nostalgia [*sic*] of the Petit Paris Era."[36] Echoing the mayor's concern about the town's existential crisis, they posited that historic preservation would inspire individuals and create social cohesion, reminding residents of their predecessors' tenacity and offering them a "common dream" about which they could all "care."[37]

The enthusiasm for historical remembering illustrated throughout this chapter provided the basis for such a project. But the mayor's stance—that enhancing citizens' awareness of their past formed a critical *civic dimension of his duties*—signals a qualitatively distinct notion of its collective purpose and effects. This perspective aligned with how administrators, planners, consultants, and public officials increasingly theorized this nexus in late-century cultural policy. An earlier example is found in the sustained effort to maintain the architectural integrity of the French Quarter, in which preservation advocates in New Orleans limited the amount and kinds of renovation property owners could undertake on buildings there. They argued that apart from antiquarian or economic rationales, such efforts should "primarily . . . be thought of as having a flesh-and-blood social purpose, to enrich and give meaning to the daily life of the people of a community."[38] In such arguments, practitioners posited distinct benefits that contact with historical buildings, practices, and narratives would enable and that public projects should foster.[39] A discrete dimension of governance emerges here: History could operate as a means of *enhancing civic commitment and morale*. In the vision plan, this premise is explicit: Remembering their predecessors' laudable qualities would stimulate citizens' sociality and incite them to strive, for instance, by imitating their "ancestors' determination." Alongside and distinct from the economic rationale for them, this civic vision of history animated the commitment that sustained heritage efforts.

This project's reach was nonetheless circumscribed, as an abortive attempt to expand the downtown historic district illustrates. With dozens of buildings dating from the nineteenth century, many considered the town's center an exceptional ensemble, extensive enough, some thought, to serve as the basis for a living history initiative similar to Colonial Williamsburg. To begin realizing this potential, authorities doubled the district's size in 1996 to include neighborhoods ringing the downtown core. The Main Street Program manager claimed that the rationale was also to "help homeowners understand the history behind their homes." "You need to realize you're not just living in a subdivision," he later elaborated, "you're living in a place where the creators of St. Martinville once resided."[40] But within a year, the town council rescinded its endorsement of the expansion, as controversies eroded support for it.[41] Ultimately, the Historical District Commission's prerogative to approve renovation and new construction within the zone proved to be a divisive issue. As residents grasped the implications of this power to administer the past, they viewed it as an unacceptable infringement on their property rights. As a councilman put it, "You're going to start telling me how to put bricks around my house or what color to paint it? If you pay for it, you should be able to paint it the color you want."[42]

This illuminates how aligning the civic goals of historic preservation with everyday behaviors presented genuine challenges, even in a place where many appreciated its historic charm. As the councilman's comment suggests, historical awareness was relatively thin. When homeowners looked at their residences, they saw the privilege of making aesthetic choices and economic investments, not historic structures needing preservation. For these residents, other articulations of time held sway, ones that ostensibly privileged the homeowner's lifetime *alone*. Temporally, the satisfaction that a person might find in inhabiting the dwelling and the profit they might generate by maintaining it mattered more. When I attended a Historic District Commission meeting in 2001, the specter of these disputes lingered over their deliberations. Several businesses had installed vending machines on Main Street sidewalks, but commissioners dared only to "request" they be removed. Others contested their vision of the past, underscoring how history-making was both necessary (if it was to be widely shared) *and* tenuous.

CONCLUSION

This chapter engages with two enduring questions in anthropological studies of memory and history. First, what is the cultural status of historical remembrance? Is it a universally shared capacity, something like verb tenses in human languages—that is, present, available, and active in every individual? Or is it more contingent, more dependent on social and political circumstances for its emergence, elaboration, and significance? Taking Michel-Rolph Trouillot's *Silencing the Past* as an exemplary text, one would answer that yes, concerns with history and with rules governing its debatability are operative across cultures in both the Global North and South.[43] People everywhere are called to and do recollect remote pasts important within their political and cultural traditions. Similarly, Roy Rosenzweig and David Thelen seem to assume that everyday engagements with mementos of grandparents' lives or narratives of past family events comprise practices and idioms that constitute historical awareness as such.[44] From these perspectives, the remembering of distant pasts presents as a kind of ubiquitous, organic activity that all humans pursue.

This ethnography of the landscape of historical remembrance in St. Martinville suggests instead that it is more complex, motivated, and contingent than these views indicate. It was culturally complex in that it involved the stitching together of traces of remote pasts from documents, objects, and buildings; individual memories of lived experience; and personal and collective investments in future-oriented initiatives. Deeply embedded conventions particular to the area enabled it, and activities like the opera house dedication and the vision plan's implementation buttressed it. In terms of its motivations, a broad thrust emerged: Remembering the distant past of le Petit Paris was *for* pursuing specific kinds of social order. In remembering, people upheld models of conduct and achievement as inspirations and made attempts to transmit cherished codes of behavior and identity across generations in the name of the collective good. As such, historical remembering operated as an arena in which locals—in this case, largely white and middle class—affirmed particular models of agency, social relevance, and governance.

And far from being omnipresent, many did not engage in it. Austin Rodrigue found the apathy toward history that many of his neighbors displayed especially frustrating. After completing the renovation of the structure he acquired, he approached the owners of an adjacent old building about purchasing it for a second renovation. But they rebuffed him. "'Oh, it's junk.' They think it's junk," he explained. "Look, they thought I was crazy!" Locals like Rodrigue were quite conscious of an extensive "outside" to the historically aware field they tried to sustain. There were clear failures of historical remembrance, when others declined to join them.

From this perspective, historical remembrance exhibited a paradoxical, Janus-faced quality. It existed *both* as a social fact *and* as a project to be achieved.[45] It was a fact insofar as St. Martinville obviously possessed a distinct past, an unfolding in time and space that distinguished it from other places, traces of which locals cultivated in practices of active recollection. Yet as a dimension of awareness and desire oriented toward the future, these St. Martinvillers also treated it as undeveloped potential, a capacity in need of nurturance, whose cultivation required interventions. Residents' memories of their history were not given, secure, or inherently motivating. Thus, locals undertook initiatives—from the opera house renovation to the vision plan—to address this. They assumed that residents should be guided into a meaningful understanding of how the town's past impacted them: to be governed through historical memories for their own betterment.

The second issue to which this material speaks is that of memory's inferior epistemological status, especially the contention that the affective, self-interested thrust of remembering is at cross-purposes with a properly historical sense of time. According to this view, the embeddedness of remembrance in the reproduction of self and group identities renders it deeply suspect; conversely, a sound, robust historical awareness is based on the dispassionate reconstruction of time out of mind. History is (or *should be*) distinct from the motivated influences of remembering. This engenders a pervasive tendency to cast history as epistemologically distinct, as knowledge *alone*, and label all else as flawed oral memories and sugarcoated amateurism.[46]

For longer than I care to admit, my stance on this issue tracked the common historiographical one: Historical remembrance of le Petit Paris did not seem *authentically* historical, because it did not approach the past with the proper dispassion. There seemed to be few moments of retrospectively weighing the truth value of evidence or even lingering over extended accounts of past events. Instead, people constantly discussed their interests and aims, the purposes they remembered remote pasts *for*—instilling residents with optimism, enabling social uplift, expanding the local economy, transmitting values across generations, and more.

However, reflecting on this embedded, civically motivated cultural politics of St. Martinvillers' historical remembrance gave me a new lens through which to consider historians' contribution to the current status quo. In sifting through their project proposals, bureaucratic correspondence, and book prefaces, I noticed that historians' efforts sought not only intellectual goals of spreading knowledge and combating ignorance but also and simultaneously *social* ones—not unlike these St. Martinvillers. Anticipating an argument I develop in chapter 5, historian Glenn Conrad, who consulted on the effort to replace the false, Evangeline-based Acadian history with an accurate one, cast Cajuns' historical awareness as a serious problem. Not only had their "grandmas" told them "myths" that "clouded" their grasp of history, he claimed, but these false tales also put a chip on their shoulder, rendering them contentious and sowing social strife in the region.[47] Only a proper history—one possible, he implied, through the intervention of experts—would resolve this challenge. From this perspective, historians' rational retrospection no longer seemed decoupled from motivated civic and political goals. Following Michel Foucault's formulation, knowledge began to appear in its profound linkages to the exercise of power, and such efforts came to resemble discourses of historical remembrance in St. Martinville.

In St. Martinville, historical remembrance seemed a form of work "on" the present, of attempts to shape "emergent social and psychological realities."[48] Often, both the landscape of memory in which it was situated and the social projects in which it was interwoven affirmed particular visions of order, civility, and social significance. In important ways, the discourse of public history proper does not fundamentally differ from this. "History" and "memory" were much less distinct from each other than suggested by the academic models I carried into the field. When historical remembering is approached in this way, "as a social fact in lives of people. . . . , the difference between history and memory is [not] as sharp as it has been made out to be."[49]

Chapter Three

Forgetting Big Things in a Cursed Town

> The act of forgetting, I would even say, historical error, is an essential factor in the creation of a nation. . . . The essence of a nation is that all individuals have many things in common, and also that they have forgotten many things.
>
> Ernest Renan, "What Is a Nation?"

"Oh, they got a lot of things in there," Sterling Antoine mused. "Seems like I seen or heard about a lot of the big things too." Standing in front of the town hall, Antoine reacted to my declared interest in the local past. In stark contrast to how many whites addressed the topic, Antoine detailed a litany of events—some autobiographical, others collective and historical—in what he later referred to as a "dark, miserable past." Among the "big things" he remembered were executions of Black men during Jim Crow, the everyday aggressions and slights that he and his family endured, the whitecapping (stealing of land through fraudulent manipulation of legal documents) he claimed had been common, his own participation in struggles to integrate local schools and government, and plantation owners' customary practice of raping enslaved women. In this, Antoine, a retired mechanic, was not unusual: Many Black residents willingly specified how frustrating life in St. Martinville was and had been for them.

In doing so, they often made something of a historical argument, linking, as Antoine did, memories of their own lives with those of times past and asserting that, together, these formed a continuum during which too little had changed. Like others, Antoine went further, claiming St. Martinville was cursed. A Black man executed during Jim Crow, the story went, proclaimed his innocence and cursed the town before he died. For people like Antoine, the town's economic woes and much more provided evidence supporting their interpretation that whites' discrimination against Blacks operated as an ongoing scourge. That malediction, sometimes referred to as Johnson's curse, currently blocked the prosperity of everyone in St. Martinville.[1]

Antoine's remembrances mark one end of a spectrum of social memory among the town's residents and constitute something of the obverse of le Petit Paris. One might say that these memories were what whites had to forget in order to recall the town as a beacon of cultural refinement. Indeed, drawing on both oral sources and the archival record, a narrative could be composed that, in the spirit of Antoine's "dark, miserable past" of "big things," outlined many of the key events, trends, and forces characterizing the state's interracial relations over the past two centuries. Among these were the rise of a sugar cane plantation system lethal for the enslaved;[2] the antebellum fluorescence of a class of *gens de couleur libres*, or free people of color, who, through privileges of education and property ownership, acted as a social buffer between the enslaved and whites;[3] the brutal suppression of insurrections during the Civil War[4] and the campaign for "Redemption" by the Knights of the White Camelia and the White League, whose most fervent leaders along the Teche hailed from St. Martinville;[5] Jim Crow, whose onerous reign comprised "legal lynchings" (the executions Antoine referenced) as well as the most underfunded "separate but equal" school system in the state;[6] and a lengthy, uneasy transition into the postsegregation era, with white resistance that required court challenges and sit-ins and led to contentious electoral politics, including a pitched town council redistricting struggle during the 1990s and 2000s and a school desegregation case that lasted over fifty years.[7]

Moreover, many Black St. Martinvillers remembered, at times emotionally, a catalog of abuses and slights from their everyday lives: From ongoing practices of segregation (two racially defined Catholic churches stood six blocks apart); to collusive efforts more difficult to discern (e.g., when public agencies seemed to privilege white job candidates or businesses over Black ones); to unforgettable affronts born of intimacy, as when one woman recalled how the family of a white matron whom she nursed for years failed to attend her own mother's funeral. Blacks referenced all of this (in bits and pieces); whites mentioned it less frequently, if at all. *Summing up his version of such a litany, one middle-aged man sighed in exasperation, "It's hard being Black here."*

Blacks were aware of whites' propensity to marginalize them, and some actively decried it. During a town council meeting several weeks after the Duchamp Opera House dedication, the last agenda item involved the approval of airfare purchase for a municipal employee's trip to Senegal's Gorée Island, the town's newest international sister city. *When some white participants balked—upon hearing the trip's focus described, one councilman replied, "This sounds like a Red Cross mission. It's got nothing to do with us"—the mayor withdrew the request to avoid its defeat. Yet before he did so, Jimmy Charles, a Black council member, interrupted, declaring, "I want to say something before I die . . . so that everyone will know how I feel." Comparing their enthusiastic endorsement of the town's sister-city activities in France, Belgium, and Canada to their refusal to support this Senegalese relationship, he accused his counterparts of hypocrisy, his voice rising as he did so ("But when those folks came from France, y'all were parading all over with them! . . . That was city money, and y'all never said anything!"). Shouting as he left his seat for the exit, Charles acknowledged none of his colleagues' protestations. Instead, he chastised them as he exited: "Y'all should be ashamed! . . . It makes a difference [in St. Martinville] when it's Black and white!"*

This episode illustrates the dynamics of an active forgetting as it pertains to both cultural and historical remembrance. One could characterize the white councilman's stance as an act of mere racial bias: He seemed to want to privilege the town's white sister-city activities over those linked to its new African one. But as Charles pointed out, he justified his position through the convenient omission of his previous support for those other sister-city relationships. Forgetting as a socially constructed practice includes the effects of everyday silences and motivated selectivity like this, because they can produce a shared experience of marginalizing others, of not seeing, including, or remembering them as part of a collective "we" (as the councilman asserted, "This [trip] has nothing to do with *us*").[8] Moreover, the exchange illuminates how a minor act such as voting against the purchase of airfare might contribute to a kind of historical forgetting. Some white St. Martinvillers did indeed enjoy meeting with guests from Canada and Europe, which reinforced their sense of reproducing cultural values that dated back centuries. Opposing such an experience for African Americans would prevent them from cultivating a similar historical sense as well as maintaining a narrative about the town's history as a story solely about immigrants from Europe. As Ernest Renan intimated, forgetting is produced in just such ways, operating as a political force that holds a group together in its commitment to a certain amnesia.

Along these lines, I ask, What did St. Martinvillers forget in order to remember their town as le Petit Paris d'Amérique and the Birthplace of

Acadiana? Without suggesting that, for white residents like those featured in the previous chapter, it exhausts the breadth of socially constructed oblivion, interracial relations formed one significant local dimension of this forgetting. The case for this begins with demography: Both currently and during an extended moment in the past, Blacks constituted the majority of St. Martinville's residents, yet neither Little Paris nor Acadiana included them in their constructions of collective history. In pursuit of an answer, I disaggregate history (research-based narratives), cultural memory (like the public history in historic sites), and social and individual remembering (recollections uttered in everyday settings), approaching them as distinct fields of discourse about the past that interacted dynamically with each other. With respect to both whites' and Blacks' recollections of the Black past, I contend that the forgetting decried by Charles emerged as a result of various practices and effects of power. In short, whites succeeded in muffling the circulation of both critical historical accounts and memories like Antoine's. They were not monolithic in this regard, yet many saw Blacks as fundamentally different, judging them as inferior and recalling behaviors they criticized as wrong, depraved, even dangerous. At the same time, I underscore how moral and civic registers of discourse and practice shaped interracial remembrance and history-making. When local leaders decided to establish an African American museum—one of Louisiana's first permanent exhibits devoted to Black history—morally inflected conventions of public history and citizen formation fashioned an interracial consensus over how to recount such a past. The resulting limits fostered an active forgetting of the most fraught dimensions of the town's interracial history.

"EVERYTHING THAT WE'VE WORKED SO HARD FOR WILL SUFFER": THE MORALIZED CHRONOTOPE OF WHITES' INTERRACIAL MEMORIES

African Americans were not absent from whites' memories. To the contrary, whites' recollections of fellow Black residents could be extensive and intense. But instead of recalling the past's "bad things," many whites' interracial remembering unfolded in a different register. Those recollections often involved affirmations of radical difference, moral threat, and the prospect of troubling change. The slights and injustices that Blacks recalled went unacknowledged or were dismissed, as recent instances of Black inferiority stuck in their minds.

To be sure, a thorough outline of the interracial status quo included many counterpoints and contrary trends. By all accounts, Blacks successfully fought to dismantle numerous dimensions of de jure segregation during the late twentieth century. The public high school (though not the elementary schools) and a private primary school were integrated, as were electoral politics and the civil service; the spatial division between a white north side and Black south side was breached (though not eliminated); social groups, including some of the town's civic organizations, were racially integrated in their membership. Despite informal efforts to discourage interracial socializing, some bars and restaurants welcomed integrated clienteles, a few especially so. Many residents spoke at length of positive interracial associations that marked their lives. Some white St. Martinvillers joined Blacks in contesting the decade-long council redistricting dispute and the malfeasance that marred elections in 2002.[9]

At times, whites even reflected on how these changes rearticulated their views of Black people. One remarkable instance of this involved Debra Guillot, a barmaid at the Cool Spot, a working-class watering hole. It figured as the most integrated social scene I encountered; Black and white patrons consistently mingled there, and *Guillot spoke proudly of her effort to enable this scene. In an initial exchange that grew frank with unusual speed, Guillot reflected on her views of race, noting that while she herself could never date a Black man, she would not object if her daughter did. Then she admitted that a recent robbery had challenged her assumption about Black criminality. Recalling a recent burglary at the Cool Spot just after closing, she acknowledged, "I always thought it would be a Black man. But don't you know, when it happened, it was a white guy—a customer—that did it."* In such reflections, one can discern the effects of sociospatial shifts on whites' experience of African Americans as individuals. Not only had many younger patrons at the Cool Spot attended high school together, but they also worked together at Martin Mills, the local garment factory.[10] As Jim Crow rules receded and whites interacted with Blacks more regularly, sedimented discourses about Black delinquency and fears of social contamination faced counterevidence that undermined them.

Yet across many interviews, white St. Martinvillers sometimes struggled to make sense of these novel interactions. At times, their interpretations of African Americans' conduct were multistranded and contradictory. The recollections of George Trahan, a retired businessman and civic leader, offer one striking example of this. As the head of a prominent civic group, Trahan presided over its racial integration and groomed a younger Black man as a potential successor. Ultimately, the protégé chose not to seek the post of president, a decision Trahan regretted. Several times during the interview, Trahan recalled the man, praising his qualities and wondering what might have been had he become the organization's leader. At the same time, however, he categorically dismissed African American participation in electoral politics. "The Blacks are *idiots*, excuse the expression. Most of them," Trahan insisted, remembering instances in which, from his perspective, many of them were too easily swayed in their voting preferences.

Apart from the complexity of Trahan's views, moral judgment stood out as prominent in these recollections. Embedded in his memory of Blacks' conduct as voters was a sharp, negative valence. He recalled about them not merely a racial difference but also a morally charged one: a capacity (their reason) that was unquestionably benighted.[11] Yet his ambivalence raises a question about the persistence of racial bias in postsegregation social life. How did whites sustain prejudiced racializing in the face of challenges (like Charles's) and evidence to the contrary (like Trahan's experience with his protégé)? What steered their memories away from what their Black coresidents recalled and toward those loaded with such negative—and moralized—assessments?

Some (often older) white St. Martinvillers went further than others in remembering this conduct and making these judgments. In condemning the misdeeds of their Black neighbors, they offered sweeping characterizations of their moral bankruptcy. At the outset of our interview, Eugene Naquin declared himself vexed by the "decadence of society in general," which, when he became specific, translated into his Black neighbors' tendencies to play loud music, wear baggy trousers, litter the roadsides, and walk in the middle of the street. A retired contractor, Naquin recounted how he engaged residents on these issues, but his efforts had met with checkered success. This left him dissatisfied and ruminating about its causes. "[Their behavior] kind of gives you the impression that they're mad at the world, and all they want is a handout," he speculated, continuing, "They don't want to contribute to the welfare of the neighborhood, or the town, or their family. [They are focused on] just getting what they can out of the government." Many St. Martinvillers similarly concluded that social life had changed for the worse during their lives. Like Naquin, some explained this decadence by pointing to the deplorable ways in which Blacks conducted themselves.

Naquin's moral assessment was partly civic in character: He implied that individuals should "contribute" to collective well-being by engaging in activities beneficial to society. Interweaving personal memories with these criteria of civic and moral propriety, he and others posited a broad spectrum of behaviors susceptible to their judgment. As he recalled experiences with his Black neighbors, Naquin stipulated that it was "not prejudice" that motivated him; "granted," he allowed, "they don't have the standard of living that we do. But I feel like that's not my fault." He then broke into an autobiographical summary, in which these claims became explicit:

> I was born and raised in a dwelling that didn't have double walls. And raised in the country. Worked hard, didn't have much money. I should say didn't hardly have *any* money. My daddy couldn't afford to pay me for working . . . , but I knew that I had to help him. He was in a bind, trying to provide for ten kids. . . . He was a carpenter, often unemployed. . . . And I knew that I couldn't go to college, so I decided to join the army. Went to war, came back, had the GI Bill, made up my mind that I was going to take advantage of it. He couldn't afford to send me, [but] I went to college, got a degree. Worked hard for forty-somewhat years and made something of myself.

He concluded, "Now, all of this, this is still open to everybody if they want, instead of dragging the streets, in hip huggers and language that you'd never entice anybody to hire you [with]. And [they] don't want to change!"

Rather than referencing mediated discourses about problematic Black behavior (e.g., from the widespread trope about welfare queens—though perhaps these also shaped his views), Naquin grounds his characterizations in concrete experiences.[12] Not least among these is his own life trajectory, which he deploys as evidence for his claim about their immorality. In it, he fleshes out what an upright existence means to him: It is ambitious, educated, decorous, and possessing of personal qualities like fortitude and a penchant for hard work. In comparative perspective, his achievement against great odds demonstrates Blacks' flawed character: While they could have acted similarly (the path is "still open to everybody"), they fail to do so. Many whites moralized race in this way. Racial distinctions were simultaneously differences between virtuous and blameworthy behaviors, between right choices and wrong ones, between good people and bad ones.[13]

Beyond this, Naquin's account also intimates how whites' articulation of themselves as social beings in time could be interwoven with their moral distancing from Blacks. The moral and racial categories implicit in his memories intersected in complex and contradictory ways. On the one hand, by positing that Blacks were equally positioned to take advantage of the opportunities he created for himself, Naquin situates them on the same ethico-temporal plane. He stresses a time of shared presence and equivalent prospects with his Black neighbors, though it is arguably fictional.[14] Then, remembering his own virtue, he asserts that they failed to surmount the "same" challenges he overcame. Thus, he grounds his sense of moral differences between Blacks and whites in a skewed remembrance of a shared interracial past. On the other hand, his assertion of moral differences enables a profound sense of his distinction from Blacks, as if each race lived in a separate time and space. His narrative's overarching gist is that they were encroaching into a zone of respectable social life that he and other whites occupy.

Through her recollections, Mary Angelle, a retired teacher, also conveyed this twisted interweaving of moralized agency, race, and spacetime. While she began by characterizing St. Martinville as a "wonderful place" filled with cherished memories stretching back to her childhood, she grew pessimistic about it as her attention shifted to the present. Like Naquin, she linked her sense of the town's decline to her perception of Blacks' effect on social mores. She, too, interacted regularly with Blacks; she recalled the efforts she made as a teacher to shift their behaviors. But she had a "hard time . . . trying to get them to get an education and start a new history" beyond the one bequeathed to them by their parents. "Having babies, you know," she sighed. "You can't prevent that if it keeps repeating itself over and over and over again."

Her convictions about the intractability of Black dysfunction led Angelle to make the most categorical assertion of racial difference that I heard, which in turn grounded her anxieties about an apocalyptic future. Reflecting on those recollected experiences with Black students, she claimed, "A lot of them don't think the way we do. They don't act the way we do. They don't speak at all the way we do. Let's face it, they're just a different breed altogether!" Imbued with this absolute sense of racial difference, she expected a takeover of the spacetime she occupied, as Blacks' inferior ways threatened to overwhelm it. The cycle of teenage pregnancy Angelle described not only led to a dependency on welfare, she asserted, but also contributed to a troubling predicament for whites. "They have grown and they're prolific, and they've taken over the town," she claimed. Angelle feared that the Black political ascendance she saw on the horizon would translate not only into lost political power but also into a dramatic regression. "I just pity the day that the Blacks take over this town," she worried, "because I think tourism is going to go downhill. . . . *Everything* that we've worked so hard for [will suffer]."[15] The separation she draws between races—spatiotemporal and moral—is profound. White achievements and well-being will collapse, Angelle dreads, the more Blacks enter her world as empowered peers.

This emplotment of social difference and moral value also inflected whites' memories of Blacks in space. The racial divide before and after Jim Crow involved a complex spatial politics, whereby contact between Blacks and whites could be close and extended in some contexts (e.g., as when Black maids raised white children), while whites proscribed proximity in other relationships (e.g., adjacent residences). Within these various norms, whites infused their subjectivity with dispositions concerning the control of space. Simply put, a crucial dimension of whiteness resided in the ability to enforce boundaries between themselves and Blacks and to compel deference from them.

In recollections of their Black neighbors, many whites foregrounded elements of this sense of space and difference. As a de facto ban on Black property ownership in certain neighborhoods dissolved, the novel prospect of heightened proximity disconcerted them. A civil servant, Zachary Dugas, known for his efforts to bridge the racial divide, mentioned that "there's a lot of ill feeling" between whites and Blacks in St. Martinville, which he claimed "doesn't help [social relations] at all." When I asked what contributed to this, he recalled that "a lot of the Blacks are able to get low-interest loans, and they're buying houses as soon as they come up in the white part of the community." Explaining how this exacerbated racial tensions, he continued, "So they're taking over, and that puts the white people ill at ease. I mean, don't get me wrong. I don't blame them. You naturally want to do the best thing for you and your kids. But it's causing that ill feeling again."

In these recollections, Dugas's language is suggestive. Across the semantic range evoked by the two verbs he uses for their actions—"buying" and "taking over"—one hears again a framing of Black behavior as morally problematic, alongside a privileging of white prerogatives.[16] The bodily dimension of his construction is also significant: As Blacks purchase homes, whites feel ill at ease, with this discomfort presented as *the* civic problem in need of a remedy. His formulation implies that, in relation to whites' need for a comfortable distance, African Americans bear responsibility for respecting that sensibility. To be sure, in his ambivalence, Dugas recognized the validity of these competing stances, which many whites did. Yet the stress ("I don't blame them, *but* . . .") remained on Blacks' indiscretion and the ill will it fostered.[17]

The subject positioning consistent across these exchanges—of whites as defenders of a moral and civic order—had implications for how these St. Martinvillers remembered their Black coresidents. If they did not share Blacks' memories of their common past, it was partly because they retained an abiding cultural schema, a chronotope, for interpreting Black difference in negative terms. With some exceptions, they were not their peers. Such an assessment possessed visceral salience, as they linked it to their commitments to proper behavior. As a result, events that animated Blacks' memories of interracial relations found little purchase in whites' imaginaries. Jennifer Cole suggests that remembering is a moral dimension of behavior, since what people remember is shaped by "their personal dreams of who they think they are, what they want the world to be like, and their attempts to make life come out that way."[18] Given their commitment to upholding a moral-qua-racial order, Blacks' flaws and transgressions often stuck in whites' memories. And this remembering had an orientation toward the future: They invoked it to thwart the anticipated chaos that, in their view, Blacks' sociopolitical ascendance threatened to trigger.

FORCES OF OBLIVION

The sentiments and memories these whites shared in the intimacy of their homes differed in degree but not in kind from those that whites expressed publicly. A similar schema inflected remembering linked to social and political matters in which the positions they took had historical dimensions to them. In these instances, whites often dismissed Blacks as immature and downplayed racial discrimination in both the recent and more distant pasts. As they linked these narratives to public acts they performed or resisted, they actively contributed to the oblivion that many Blacks decried, buttressing whites' predominance in the process.

This selective remembering was perhaps most evident in the town council redistricting dispute, which reached its climax during the early 2000s. While the threshold of Black participation in elected office had long been crossed, many whites worked to avoid traversing another one: that of Black "control" of town government (i.e., by winning the mayor's office *and* a majority of town council seats). Throughout the decade-long effort to redraw council districts following the 1990 census, white politicians battled to limit Black electoral strength, especially in remapping a critical third or "swing" district (of the five-seat council) that would determine the racial composition of the council's majority. As the federal Department of Justice tried to mediate a settlement, they vetoed its proposals, challenging Blacks' assertions about the status quo.[19] When the parties reached a negotiated agreement in 2002, extensive misconduct marred the ensuing election, as the winning white candidate and her allies pursued an organized scheme to register ineligible white voters to cast ballots. Eight people (including the candidate) pled guilty to vote fraud charges in the election's aftermath.[20]

During this episode, white principals articulated a skewed take on the recent past. They insisted that they acted in good faith, proposing plans that were "in anybody's mind fair."[21] Arguing on behalf of the white council members and mayor, the town's attorney affirmed the acceptability of white bloc voting, suggesting that Black voters simply needed to attain the same degree of political cohesion.[22] Meanwhile, Department of Justice officials and Black officeholders contended that their efforts were discriminatory and sought to minimize Black political representation: The town's recurring proposals underrepresented Blacks in the swing district by 9 to 10 percent, vote fraud convictions tainted previous elections, and whites' had threatened retaliatory legal action against Black politicians.[23] The clique's aim of maintaining political dominance clearly shaped these narratives. Surveying the aftermath of the redistricting standoff and the flawed election, Mary Frances Berry cast it as a matter of "a small, tight-knit group of white politicians [who] suppressed the city's Black majority."[24] But as accounts of the recent past, they also worked to abet a certain oblivion. Part dubious assertion that racial discrimination had been superseded and part exculpatory denial of a history of disempowering Black voters, they attempted to erase the fractious reality of postsegregation electoral politics.

While a few people spearheaded this public stance in the redistricting dispute, it intersected with widely circulating views about Blacks' fatuity as political actors. In editorials in the *Teche News*, newspaper editor Henri Bienvenu targeted councilman Jimmy Charles in this regard, characterizing him as petty and juvenile. When Charles protested that commemorative plaques on public projects did not accurately reflect his status as mayor pro tem when they were approved, Bienvenu singled him out for creating "a tempest in a teapot," suggesting that the councilman irresponsibly took offense because he egotistically sought more credit than he deserved.[25] At times, whites endorsed this claim about Black immaturity in descriptive terms, as if it were a rule of social development. *They just needed to "get organized," Leonard Marceaux replied matter-of-factly to my query about the redistricting dispute. Eschewing the notion that the town's position disadvantaged Blacks, he noted how, in the 1970s, Cajuns coalesced politically to elect white ethnic politicians like Edwin Edwards. Echoing the town attorney's position, he claimed that Blacks were "behind," not as far along in their progress, and should accelerate their pursuit of a similar strategy. When they did, Marceaux surmised, they would achieve the power they sought.* Marceaux evokes a well-known modernist conceit: that different social groups are situated along a historical axis such that *racial* differences can be interpreted as *temporal* ones—for example, underdeveloped political skills placed Blacks "earlier in time" relative to whites.[26] While less anxious than Angelle's fear of the collapse of racial separation, such views similarly convey a tendency toward allochronism: They placed Blacks in a separate time from themselves, disallowing that they shared the present and its political predicaments with them.

While such statements could be diffuse in their effects, another effort, explicitly genealogical and historical in character, amounted to an unambiguous attempt to suppress the interracial past. Initially, the African American Museum project (to which I return shortly) included a proposal to digitize sacramental records of free people of color and slaves, aiming to incorporate them into the exhibit. Its Black proponents were excited about this prospect, both because many of them were interested in genealogical research and as a matter of equity. The Acadian Memorial featured such a genealogical database; more generally, such records for whites had circulated publicly for decades. Even libraries in the region's smallest towns contained copies of a thirty-volume compilation of Catholic sacramental registries, which gathered the birth, baptism, marriage, and death records for generations of white Louisianans in this majority Catholic region. However, this series did not systematically include records for people of color. For the compilation's author as for the museum project, accessing these registries required the consent of the region's oldest, historically white parishes; their clerics commonly balked at such requests. Citing administrative difficulties, the pastor of St. Martin of Tours Church did so as well, and museum proponents could not create the database.[27]

Participants in the museum initiative agreed, however, that other motives were in play. For varied reasons, whites desired to silence this past. Because these records would document interracial family connections dating to the colonial and antebellum eras, "the core issue is miscegenation," acknowledged one white contributor. "The pastors [at St. Martin of Tours and similar parishes]— . . . I assume they're catering to objections from old-line families—are afraid that skeletons still exist in the closet." In St. Martinville, these ties were acknowledged: readily by Blacks, more tentatively among whites. If the latter were aware of these distant relations, they might voluntarily mention them after several conversations, as Elizabeth Prudhomme did. *But Prudhomme, a working-class retiree, quickly added that she didn't talk openly about it, because "no good can come of it."* Recognizing Black relatives remained potentially stigmatizing across the social spectrum. Just as Virginia Domínguez noted among white Creole New Orleanians, white St. Martinvillers were concerned with the cultural politics of blood "contaminated" by contact with Blacks through miscegenation, through contemporary relationships but also those that were centuries old.[28]

One of the project's Black proponents also asserted an economic rationale for squelching this history. "I think the underlying bottom line is a lot of people of African descent would be able to claim property," he claimed. "*That's* what everybody's *afraid of*." Even if such cases were rare—whereby the descendants of mixed (i.e., planter and slave or manumitted free person of color) liaisons sued whites to redistribute assets as a matter of shared paternity—they were not completely unknown. Notions about the prevalence of these relationships differed across the color line; Blacks believed that many of the patronyms they shared with whites resulted from common ancestors, a view whites contested.[29] If well-to-do whites had the most to fear from the records' dissemination, even the less affluent like Prudhomme acknowledged their genealogies carefully, muffling this aspect of the interracial past such that it hovered over the present as a shared secret. Under a regime of historical truth governed by recourse to archival records, this concealment mattered. These records were not just fodder for public history initiatives; they also operated as a cornerstone of the social order and its distribution of privileges and resources.

In the case of the curse—one of the few historical events about which I heard widely circulating narratives and memories—interpretations differed across racial lines. This divergence was meaningful, signaling a consequential divide in views about the effect of the racist past on the present. Like Antoine, many knew of what they called Johnson's curse, in which a Black executee cursed the town before he died, claiming cryptically that as long as

St. Martinville kept the same name, it would never prosper. In the references to the curse I encountered both orally and in print, no consensus existed as to who uttered it or what offense the condemned had committed. Some locals offered no details; those who did often cited one of two infamous cases of violent Jim Crow–era crimes. Each of them—one in the early 1890s, the other during World War II—led to the execution of Black men.[30] Both now appear to have been "legal lynchings" of innocent men for crimes committed by others.[31] In the moment, the executions were great spectacles, covered by the local press and attended by large crowds.

Among whites, accounts of these stories sometimes reinforced notions of Black criminality and the need for security against them.[32] Most with whom I brought up the curse dismissed it, considering it superstitious. Insofar as they weighed in on this troubled history, many downplayed its notorious dimensions. Instead, they offered some version of the Tannenbaum thesis, affirming the relative benevolence of slavery under the French and Spanish. In his comparative study of enslavement across the Americas, historian Frank Tannenbaum suggested that humane influences of Catholic tradition and Latin culture produced master-slave relationships that were gentler than those elsewhere in the New World.[33] Some went further, claiming that these forces possessed a long-lived impact such that the more recent history of race relations in Louisiana was not as fraught as that elsewhere in the South.[34] Thus, they posited a historical continuum of (relatively) enlightened interracial understanding stretching into the present.

Some declared such positive interpretations of the interracial past publicly before mixed audiences. "There's so much history there, and it's so much, there's a lot of good. It's not all bad," Mayor Eric Martin asserted during a town council meeting. "First thing you think of is that it's all slavery, and depression and suppression, and it's not."[35] Martin sought to foreground the history of local free people of color and considered it something about which "we could really toot our horn." In this regard, he implicitly referenced one aspect of the antebellum social order that Tannenbaum thesis supporters stressed: the existence of an intermediary social status in the three-tiered antebellum racial hierarchy, that of free people of color who, in practice, were largely mixed-race descendants of master-slave relationships, manumitted and allowed to own property and become educated (though not to vote or own weapons).

To be sure, there were outliers; some whites recognized racial discrimination, recalling dark pasts resembling those remembered by their Black neighbors. A fortysomething civil servant bearing the name of a prominent white family, *Andrew Carmouche did research for a documentary film project on one of the infamous executions, in part because he believed in the victim's innocence and wanted to "exonerate him."*[36] *But he also acknowledged that there was perhaps some truth to the notion that St. Martinville was cursed. The evidence for this, he believed, pertained to something that "keeps people from being successful here," which he discerned by comparing his own moderate success with the more ample accomplishments of those in his age cohort who moved away. "Well, it has a lot to do with the slave days, and the plantations here," he admitted anxiously.* Carmouche's diagnosis aligned with the temporal dynamic that Blacks like Antoine identified. They each posited that the past was not past: History's racist excesses had ongoing effects.

Blacks like Antoine interpreted the curse's meaning in precisely this way. They held that the many unpunished injustices—of which executions were the nadir—had unleashed an ongoing blight on the town. And rather than recalling it as a past event without contemporary ramifications, they repeated it to convey pressing concerns about discrimination in the present. Those past injustices inflected contemporary social relations, they claimed, and the curse hinted that rectifying them required some sort of reckoning, a transformative shift. As his more educated peers did (see the next section), Antoine thought that the racist past constituted an active, nefarious force and needed to be addressed as such. *After convincing his church's pastor to support it, he approached leaders of the town's largest white congregation with the idea of an interracial prayer service, during which "everybody would just take responsibility for all the bad things that happened."* Intriguingly, religious modes of self-formation inspired Antoine's idea for a public ceremony; he envisioned transforming civic discourse with positive effects from a religious ceremony.

But the proposal failed: White church leaders declined, he explained, because "it was that word—responsibility—they didn't like that." Despite its lack of success, this proposal comprised a striking juncture of historical and moral modes of memory and reflection, which was typical rather than unique. Blacks like Antoine could imagine ways of reshaping subjectivity through an ethically charged engagement with the past such that racial relations would improve. As we will see, Blacks and whites who supported the African American Museum similarly conceived of their effort as a moral intervention that would address racial issues. The particular configuration of these that Antoine sought to enable, however—a frank remembrance of the past's "bad things" and a contrite embrace of responsibility for their ongoing effects—proved unacceptable to his interlocutors.

WHITE PREROGATIVES AND CITIZEN FORMATION AS PASTORAL CARE: THE THERAPEUTIC FORGETTING OF BLACK HISTORY

The effort to represent African American history in a permanent exhibit space—one of the first of its kind in the state—constituted a significant moment in the unfolding of local history and memory. It should be clear, though, that prior to its opening in 2001, no singular account of the Black past shared by all St. Martinvillers, no narrative that could readily be enshrined in a public setting, circulated. From this perspective, the site's historical narrative required work, history-*making*, distinct from archival accounts and everyday memories even as it drew on or bracketed them.

While Black participants played a crucial role in this making, whites' involvement turned out to be equally if not more consequential. Late in his first term in office, Mayor Martin proposed to his Black allies that the town seek funding to construct the site, which would feature the colonial- and early American–era history of the region's African American population. The proposal's focus dovetailed with criteria of the new Atchafalaya Trace Commission; in seeking to diversify the region's public history beyond its concentration on white elites and Cajuns, the associated Atchafalaya Basin Project funded the site with an inaugural grant. Some of the mayor's white allies disagreed with this move, viewing it as a white politician pandering to voters in a majority-Black town, as one interviewee put it. Others considered it courageous though politically risky, given the possibility that its content might satisfy neither Blacks nor whites. In keeping with his comment about slavery not being "all bad," Martin insisted that the site focus solely on African American "triumphs and successes" and reviewed the exhibit's drafts.[37]

In itself, such a move enacted a bifurcated practice of history-making. As it happened, the staff and board at the Acadian Memorial were busy adding a historical exhibit to its commemorative space at the same moment. But its elaboration unfolded largely "in house." At a key juncture, a member of the memorial's board took on the task of finalizing its text panels, sidelining the exhibit consultants hired by the town. For the African American Museum, the opposite occurred: A biracial steering committee of residents and municipal employees oversaw the elaboration of its text panels, with multiple drafts circulating between them, the same consultants working on the memorial (an all-white team), and the mayor. Some of these white participants intervened decisively. One fraught moment in deliberations occurred when they vetoed the proposal that shackles be displayed in the museum, arguing that "in this area, most of the slaves were not treated as bad as some would like to make it look," as one of them put it. "The only negative part is slaves coming from Africa," he continued. "But after they got to this part of the country, it was pretty much more positive, in how the free people of color had owned property. They bought a lot of their relatives and managed to get them out of slavery." Ultimately, the site's narrative focused tightly on free people of color, allowing it to avoid the darker aspects of enslavement and construe the Black past as a bootstrapping story of upward mobility (about which more shortly).

As one local politico cynically explained, more pragmatic reasons also existed to skew the representation of slavery. *In the midst of a meeting of the Acadian Memorial board, Myrtle Comeaux explained that Blacks currently think, "'You owe me,' because they feel like you enslaved their ancestors. And two weeks later, it doubles; they feel like you owe them that much more." She expected that with the opening of the African American Museum, however, that leverage would be undermined. It would debunk "the myth" that "it was all slavery" and show "the real story": "Their ancestors were slaveholders too."* Comeaux refers here to the fact that some free people of color became slave owners, an aspect of local history that the exhibit mentioned. To her mind, such a narrative would muddy the waters for Blacks' political claims, and as an elected official and member of the steering committee, she played a role in shaping it. In the racially homogeneous setting of the memorial board meeting, Comeaux referenced what was, as the stories of Charles and Antoine suggest, a common occurrence: As part of staking claims on resources and participation in decision-making, Blacks challenged whites' obfuscation surrounding racial domination and its legacy. Suggesting that people of color also engaged in slavery's brutality would undermine that complaint, Comeaux believed, and thereby buttress the project of maintaining white rule.

At the same time, these stances alone are insufficient to explain why the public narrative of local Black history took the form that it did. Modes of interracial consensus also sustained it. As they collaborated to elaborate the site, many of the steering committee members, curators, historians, and consultants articulated a distinct set of behavioral preoccupations that guided them. Together, these formed a set of morally inflected conventions concerning public history and citizen formation that shaped interracial agreement over how to recount such a history.

For their part, African American participants articulated their own reasons for avoiding a detailed story of enslavement. Some believed that "there's nothing positive about slavery," as Ferdinand Moreau put it; because it had so degraded Blacks' humanity, remembering it offered no fodder, they thought, for building strong selves or collective purpose. After reading research during the exhibit design process, Arlene Darby said, "I got so fed up with the subject . . . [because] I know there was more to my culture than slavery." Members of the steering committee, Moreau and Darby each defended their decisions about the exhibit's content in these subjectifying terms. While it was an unchallenged assumption among many Blacks that whites had brutalized the enslaved, they also assumed that slaves had thereby been reduced to a destitute existence, deprived of the autonomy, creativity, and dignity that people sought to realize in their own lives.[38]

Such a stance was grounded in existing Black History Month celebrations sponsored by local churches; several steering committee members were involved in these, and they sought to transpose its ethos into the museum. In describing reasons for their participation in them, organizers articulated a particular rationale that acknowledged Blacks' need to overcome white racism yet to pursue this in an indirect and ennobling way. Summarizing a set of "feeling rules" that her parents conveyed to her,[39] Denise Howard, a social worker who led one such event, specified them succinctly: "You don't sit there and feel sorry for yourself. You make things happen in your life. You don't wait for somebody else or some system to make it happen for you . . . and you don't look upon those situations in a negative kind of way. You look at them as strengthening your character." To do otherwise—to offer excuses for one's situation like "'the [white] man stopped me'" or to "just complain" instead of seeking to "understand"—was, she claimed, to engage unproductively with memories of injustice.[40] Inflected by this vision of how remembrance and moral agency properly intersected, those Black History Month ceremonies possessed a forward-looking, inspirational purpose. They focused on everyday ethics (e.g., setting positive future goals) or reflected on contemporary moral challenges (e.g., the lack of hope that deterred some from striving). Intriguingly, references to collective local struggles past or present were largely absent, apart from vague references made in passing (e.g., *"We've come a long way in St. Martinville"*). In this vernacular practice, reflecting on history possessed a moral, subject-forming thrust; it employed the unjust past tacitly as fodder for reshaping Blacks' desire and motivation.

Many participants in the museum project shared this psychosocial lens on relations among the self, the past, and the shaping of future behavior. As educators convinced that new information could inflect action in positive ways or as civil servants and entrepreneurs working in milieus stressing self-esteem and emotional labor as key to effective service and profitable commerce, they jointly held assumptions about conduct, subjectivity, and the effects of specific interventions on them. They argued that this historic site should be judged by its potential to enable civil conduct among local visitors, avoiding the intensification of negative feelings among African Americans. "It's easy to make someone angry. It's easy to make someone hate. . . . It's very hard to make someone love, and hard to make someone happy. [But] that was the idea [guiding choices about the exhibit]," insisted Moreau. Approaching the exhibit as an intervention meant to foster cognitive and emotional impacts on individuals, they took seriously the potential of texts and images to produce subjective effects and suspected that an exhibit presenting a detailed account of slavery's injustices would stoke Black anger and hatred. This vision for the site—that of inflecting Black subjectivity positively and contributing to improved interracial relations—translated into an explicit strategy of avoiding those emotions.

The intentional pairing of the Black history exhibit with the Museum of the Acadian Memorial reflected an interracial consensus on this approach to using historic sites as tools for shaping conduct. Housed in the same building, the foyer leading to the entrances for each exhibit featured parallel maps of the Atlantic, one for the respective African and Acadian diasporas. The site's two curators shared the inspiration to stress similarities in the historical experiences of the two groups, both of whom had been scattered against their will across the New World. In a successful submission to a statewide competition after both sites opened, they made these aspirations explicit. The exhibits, they wrote, would "set in motion a healing process against the racial and cultural prejudices stunting our economic development and overall well-being." Indeed, they claimed that this dynamic had already begun, as members of the biracial steering committee "learned about each other's cultures and overcame fears," engendering "an increased awareness of a common ground for forging stronger relationships between races."[41] They considered this stress on enabling positive self-fashioning and civic amelioration as crucial. More than participating in knowledge's diffusion, they saw their history-making as an effort to form selves, in the mode of therapists.

Along these lines, Black participants voiced another concern about the exhibit's impact on locals' subjectivity. It pertained to their fear of whites' reaction, specifically the backlash that might result from their encounter with representations of enslavement's depravity. This suggests again that racial hierarchy shaped the exhibit. "We could have possibly put a little more emphasis on the slavery issue," Darby surmised, "but you never know how that's going to be accepted right now." When I probed further, she explained that narrating slavery's injustice would have resulted in "a lot of anger, a lot of confusion," which she opposed. As Darby and her steering committee colleagues finalized the exhibit, they met on two occasions with museum practitioners directing African American programming at other sites, and their queries to these guests signaled this anxiety. *"It's not the [museum's] purpose to make people feel guilty," Suzanne Papillon explained to one of them, but these emotions "inevitably" emerged. Recalling her experience of teaching the television series* Roots *in the classroom—which involved "putting out the fire" of students' emotions—Papillon asked for recommendations to "prime our visitors . . . to help them not feel guilty."* Even whites articulated this fear. Some were "not ready" for a critical history, as one manager put it; if the narrative tried to "do it all at one time, . . . we would overwhelm and lose the buildup of understanding and acceptance." She offered this opinion after viewing the exhibit with a racially mixed group of residents, all of whom were critical of its omissions. But even in arguing for a sharper narrative that included an apology, a Black minister conceded that "it is difficult for [whites] to deal with African slavery."

In terms of specifying why such scenarios should be avoided, Black steering committee members may have been circumspect with me, as they did not detail the roots of their apprehensions. But others did not hesitate to name the source of their fears. Standing in the parking lot of the Cool Spot at dusk, construction worker Dallas Dickey pressed me about my research. When I responded that while the town had numerous historical sites, some locals didn't seem to like its history, *he replied gravely, "It's just a bad place. It's a nasty, rotten, bad place." After attributing this rottenness to whites' racism, Dickey fixed me with his gaze and intoned, "Whatever you do, you better be careful. They don't fucking mess around here. Man, you'll disappear, and they'll never know what happened to you."* Alone with me in the gathering darkness, a memory of white violence came readily to Dickey. That this legacy operated in the present and that people (including white outsiders like me) should take it into account comprised part of an everyday savoir faire that he articulated without pause. This fearsome specter of retribution suggests that a certain memory of past violence shaped Blacks' sense of agency and initiative. In any case, fears of whites' potential reactions guided Blacks' calculations in representing the past, translating into a clear politico-moral aim. Preoccupied with designing an exhibit that would shape Black subjectivity, they also felt a pressing need to manage that of whites.

That perspective offered a distinct vantage point for judging the museum, which many locals adopted. The steering committee's Black members expressed satisfaction with the outcome; when the site opened, journalists featured their claim that it did not "sugarcoat" historical reality.[42] That the exhibit even mentioned slavery—something of a first in Louisiana—was perhaps the savory flavor they referenced with such an assertion. A white consultant to the project shared this optimistic assessment, claiming that it had a "huge" positive impact. By merely acknowledging enslavement as historical fact, the site amounted to a watershed, she asserted, which would allow more critical narratives to emerge down the line. But since the exhibit de-emphasized slavery's brutality, any criticism would mark an advance. In the way that it summarized the Black Code (highlighting that slaves could work for wages and purchase their freedom) and described slave concubinage (stressing the genuine affection that developed between masters and enslaved mistresses), it implied that enslavement had humane dimensions. As promised, it centered African American triumphs and successes, which translated into the property owning, educational achievement, and public service of free people of color.

Others rejected this as partial and flawed. In a focus group that toured the exhibit the week it opened, a Black participant protested that "something is missing" from the exhibit's narrative. When I asked for specifics, she shouted, "The whip!" For her, the site's failure to evoke slavery's violence compromised it. As a white participant in another focus group put it, the exhibit risked reinforcing the sense that "slavery wasn't that bad" and that Blacks exaggerated its depravity. And though I invited Antoine to tour the museum and share his impressions, he refused. He had seen enough half-measures. Referencing the truncated narratives of Black History Month, he held that Black educators had "traded away" the chance to teach a critical history of race for ungraded assignments that "nobody's gonna even remember." Antoine had his own notions about what should be in such an exhibit, which were also focused on history's moral, subject-forming potential. He explained that he insisted on showing his own children a piece of scrip he possessed, which came from a plantation where he worked as a youth; he was certain it could teach a better lesson than the authorized narratives he rejected.[43] Seeing the scrip, he maintained, would allow his children to "do better in life" by "know[ing] who they are and where [they] come from."

CONCLUSION

This chapter problematizes any notion of a neat concordance among history, memory, and remembering when it comes to the past of white-Black relations in St. Martinville. Instead, they were in conflict with each other. Compared to other parts of south Louisiana, a certain paucity of published *history* on slavery and Jim Crow in the Teche region existed at the turn of the millennium. Nonetheless, enough archival research circulated to suggest the broad contours of slavery's brutality as well as the malicious severity of Reconstruction and Jim Crow.[44] Meanwhile, in terms of *memory*, which I might gloss here as recollections abetted by literature and other mediated forms like historic sites, a comforting narrative echoing the Tannenbaum thesis governed public discourse. In panels on "Slavery in Africa" and "The Louisiana Experience" of slavery, the museum recognized only Africans and slaves as subjects with agency—for example, "African rulers" were opportunistic merchants who "realized" the economic potential for selling slaves and "seized" captives from other tribes. In Louisiana, however, it offered no parallel politicization of slavery. Plantation owners, slave traders, white politicians in antebellum and confederate Louisiana: All were absent from its account. Finally, in everyday *remembering*—in what people recalled about remote and more recent pasts, considered in all the centrifugal heterogeneity presented earlier, from Naquin's insistence on the comparative validity of his mid-century bootstrapping to Antoine's invocation of Johnson's curse—something else held sway. Recollections that were contentious and adversarial competed against each other, reflecting the fractious reality of the interracial status quo. Rather than smooth alignment, the relationships across these distinct yet interwoven fields of discourse about the past were characterized by a gear-grinding tension.

From this perspective, the curse can be seen as a provocative countermemory. In it, some Blacks conveyed a lived sense that the oppressive past and troubled present were aligned in a continuum; by repeating it, they sought to break through opposition to their claims for justice. During the late 1990s and 2000s, Black residents organized and contested the status quo in high-profile ways: in the legal challenges surrounding the council redistricting dispute and its aftermath, in a series of protests on sentencing in the judiciary system, on the school board's skewed promotion practices, and in the renewed effort to address racial segregation in public schools.[45] In the wake of a failed attempt to correct issues with Blacks' advancement in the school system, Sally Thompson, a woman who participated in protests, recalled another incident that resembled the executions evoked by the curse. Reflecting on her frustration over whites' inability to acknowledge racism, a memory came to her:

> Sometime, I look at that bayou [Teche] and I wonder, how many dead people . . . is down there. How many dead Black people? . . . A lot of people jumps up and says, around here, "There's no racism—well, other than by years, years, years ago." There was this man, his last name was Caesar. He used to work on cars. . . . The [white] man came, and [this] man called him [Caesar] to ask him to go with him to fix on a tractor he got. . . . The next day, somebody found [Caesar] floating on that bayou by the levee with his penis cut in his mouth. Exactly, they found his body. . . . It happened about in the seventies. . . . And, you know, a lot of people know who did it, but people never face no time. . . . But, you know, when you talk to them about discrimination or about racism, they want to say it doesn't exist. It never exists [for them], but it exists!

As with Antoine and Dickey, something about the specter of past murders and executions—of how they related to their current experiences of negation, social if not existential—made such a memory salient to Thompson. Fully aware that many whites did not recognize their claims, they remembered moments of unpunished violence to push back against that lack of justice and recognition, in remembrance shaped by a politics keyed to the present.

Alongside efforts such as white leaders' stance in the council redistricting dispute and the corresponding narrative they forwarded with it, the African

American Museum presented as an attempt to pacify such counter memories as well as to forestall the wider diffusion of existing historical accounts. A dynamic relationship was very much in play. As Comeaux openly stated, some whites explicitly wanted to check those Black memories and the demands for redress that accompanied them. The historical account in the resulting exhibit was partly the result of their successful efforts to achieve this. In this sense, these collective forms of memory simultaneously sought to foster a certain oblivion about the past they referenced, evoking Johannes Fabian's claim that "memory requires memory work carried out as remembering and forgetting."[46] Though cracks in this formation have emerged more recently, this has been typical of postsegregation remembrance in Louisiana: The historical oppression of Blacks could not readily be represented in the state's public historical sphere.[47] As we will see, this contrasted sharply with new narratives about the Acadian past.

Still, while certainly potent influences, neither post-civil-rights-era white supremacist politics nor whites' denials of coevalness with their Black neighbors fully explained this mix of remembrance and forgetting. Operating as an animating force, strong commitments to using history to heal wounds and form a decorous social order also limited the discursive options for history-making. As mentioned, an interracial consensus emerged about this. Supporters of the Acadian Memorial considered that their site fulfilled a similar function: By offering an accurate, positive account of Acadian history, it would shift Cajuns' negative self-image and increase their self-esteem (a topic to which I return in subsequent chapters). Accordingly, it seemed that a melodramatic ethos shaped public history in St. Martinville.[48] Virtuous heroes and inspiring role models could be represented and remembered. But to recall enslavement, Jim Crow, and their legacies, in any of the strife and violence that either memories of the curse or the historical record suggested, risked inciting turmoil in the present. Many St. Martinvillers believed that it would involve telling a darker story about the past, coping with difficult emotions like anger and guilt, and posing challenges to the social order. Yet this bracketing of the past's unresolved conflicts is arguably typical. Multivocal, critical public histories that engage such complexities are rare. "At base, public histories are moral narratives," asserts Geoffrey White, comprising a genre whose proponents have successfully "[resisted] efforts . . . to present history as unfinished business."[49]

Chapter Four

Where Cajuns Fit In, God Knows

Remembering White Ethnicity—or Not

It is said that the good Lord protects morons, stray dogs, and babies, but where [Cajuns] fit in—God knows.

John Bergeron, *Bayou Cajuns*

If . . . our life narration and our sense of self are inextricably linked to our sense of the good, the chronotope of memory must be a moral space.

Michael Lambek, "Past Imperfect"

In the introduction, Julia Cormier articulated an intriguing mix of autobiographical remembrance and historical narrative. Recalling a modest rural childhood, she essentially recollected the former, interpreting it through the positive light that the Acadian Memorial's representations offered her. Consider now the trajectory of a contemporary. A fortysomething entrepreneur who identified as Cajun, Sophie Pitre repeated a question she once fielded from an older acquaintance: "'How can you be proud of being Cajun?' Because that was such a dirty word. *Nobody* aspired to be Cajun fifty years ago." This query—with its premise that Cajun ethnicity was irredeemably corrupted—prompted Pitre to reflect on her own family's behavior, in which she recognized a silent echo. Hailing from a town near St. Martinville, her parents and grandparents had gone to great lengths to shed any association with Cajun traits. They anglicized the family name (to Pete) and abandoned the use of French to the point that they declined to speak the language with her, even after, following her English-only upbringing, she became fluent in it as an adult. Most strikingly for Pitre, her father systematically avoided staying in Baton Rouge when his work as a salesman brought him there. Over the years, he and other family members divulged few details, but Pitre knew enough to grasp that as a young man living there, residents of the capital had callously derided him as Cajun. It was likely memories of this "shitty treatment," she concluded, that motivated her family's distancing from markers of white ethnicity. Moreover, their silence about these everyday tactics of social positioning—Pitre assembled her interpretation from bits and pieces of behavior and discourse—amounted to an effort at oblivion.

Scholars have commented on the lack of fine-grained analyses of how people make social constructions of history and memory meaningful for themselves—or indeed, whether they do so at all. To be sure, the voluminous research on social and cultural memory produced since the 1990s has compellingly explored commemorative landscapes and practices.[1] These studies illuminate the genealogies of historic and monumental sites, suggesting how, in the material forms and commemorative practices associated with them, memory is channeled in particular directions. But in this scholarship, there also exists "a broad tendency to forget that people, in addition to archives and monuments, are essential to the process of remembering as well as the content of what gets remembered."[2] Such work sustains the particular stresses of Maurice Halbwachs and his mentor Emile Durkheim, emphases that undertheorize the heterogeneity of social groups and ignore the importance of individual memories. Simply put, the problem is that from this perspective, collective remembering can seem static and stable. Meanwhile, "the points where one is likely to see tension and change are precisely the junctures between socially constructed memory and individual experience."[3] Cormier's spirited recollections, Pitre's father's definitive forgetting of his Cajun youth, and Pitre's own "return" to those practices by, for example, reclaiming the family's French patronym: The dynamism of such shifts and their divergent junctures with formations of historical and social memory are missing from this body of work.

Having considered this challenge with respect to historical memories in chapter 2, I approach it from the angle of autobiographical memories in this one. These are linked, yet the shape and character of their interconnections are precisely what another Halbwachsian tendency obscures. In emphasizing the primacy of social processes in collective remembering—the ways that spatial representations and commemorative acts serve to moor recollecting and influence its shape and feeling—Halbwachs often tied memory to politics. From his perspective, current group interests, especially political ones, offer the clearest explanations for why particular events are selected for remembering. While studies of the influence of social differentiation on remembering are not uncommon, they often renew this recourse to political dynamics as the primary influence on mnemonic processes.[4]

Without denying its significance, I make one specific conceptual shift to complement this stress on the political. A compelling case can be made that, in trying to link individual remembering to social dynamics, a political lens can be exaggerated. Instead, many scholars have laid the groundwork for approaching memory as an activity deeply inflected by moral praxis.[5] As I outlined in the introduction, the prompt is to grasp the visceral footings that ethical commitments and worldviews carve out for remembrance.

Along these lines, anthropologist Maurice Bloch makes a related point that links such ordinary ethics to historical remembering. In a suggestive article, Bloch claims that in certain contexts, autobiographical and historical memory are not *generically* distinct. That is, in terms of *how* we remember, evidence points to ways in which processes of recalling an episode of lived experience can resemble those used for semantic memories (recall of learned narratives and facts, including historical ones) and vice versa. As he shows, this resemblance emerges especially in the context of stories of a distant past that are "highly relevant to the identity and moral life" of a given group.[6] Simplifying his argument, when historical narratives matter for one's life, when they become practically integrated into one's life story, they are remembered "not in linguistic narrative forms but in terms of imaginations of 'what it was like.'"[7]

Later, I will use this insight to explore historical remembrance in the Acadian Memorial, showing how Cormier and other visitors found the site's narrative compelling in relation to memories of their own lives. But before attempting that analysis, Bloch's claim begs these first-order questions: In a place like St. Martinville, how do individuals remember their own lives? What kind of moral commitments and judgments do they evoke and imply? Do these vary relative to orders of social difference? More specifically, what autobiographical memories and corresponding moral positions do self-identified Cajuns have? Do these differ from memories of those who, like Pitre's father, could identify as Cajun but did not?

With these questions in mind, my focus in this chapter is on recollections among individuals who, by conventional criteria (e.g., Acadian ancestry, French-speaking or descended from francophones, rural/working-class family backgrounds), *could* easily identify as Cajun (or Acadian). Alongside questions of identity, I pay close attention to the moral positioning of interviewees "in and around" their recollections. That is, I consider both the moral valence of autobiographical events (or episodic memories)—how individuals cast themselves as moral actors in their memories—and elements of context that bore on their interpretations of those recollections. Not infrequently, for instance, interviewees remembered past events in their lives as part of making claims about their current situation. (Thus, in practice, these were often deeply intertwined.)[8]

I encountered a range of memories and positionings, and the following foregrounds this heterogeneity. Significantly, only one of the three groups I describe identified as Cajun and associated memories with that label.[9] Comparatively, their moral positioning in autobiographical memories was distinctive, creating an intriguing narrative arc across the recollections and claims articulated in the interview. In sum, most self-identified Cajuns remembered experiences when others judged them negatively and/or socially marginalized them. This lack of respect and challenge to their dignity endured into the present and was integral to how they identified as white ethnics.

For two other cohorts, I also sketch out the prominent aspects of memory and positioning in their responses, but as "potential" Cajuns who did not identify as such. What stands out, I argue, are the distinctive articulations of memory and moral evaluation that accompany each cohort's identitarian stance. On the one hand, the differences suggest the impact of processes of social differentiation and identity formation beyond white ethnicity, including race, class, and gender. On the other hand, they also hint at the individual agency that contributes to a mnemonic dynamism. One sees how, in limited yet substantive ways, individuals affirm, refuse, sidestep, and bemoan the lack of affiliation with others, with corresponding effects on their work of remembrance and social positioning.

COHORT 1: INDIGNITY, BLOCKAGE, AND MEMORIES OF A RACIALIZED CAJUN-NESS

When I announced my focus as understanding what living in St. Martinville was like, Genevieve Barriot, a middle-aged housewife, quickly interjected, "It's not a pretty picture." Sitting at her kitchen table, she went on to explain the difference between herself and those whom she held responsible for this state of affairs:

> But there are a certain group of people, and—I don't like to say that—aside from the French Acadian people . . . and I guess it has to go back to the first French people who came here. . . . They pretty much look down on you. . . . Like us, looking back and thinking, we weren't a materialistic people, you know. I don't know how to explain this to you. So we didn't worry about how we dressed, what we looked like, and all this, you know. Just so we were clean and wore clean clothes, that's all we cared about. . . . And I have to say, it's like the people in town, you see? The town people seemed like some stiff-necked people, you know, that won't bend and, you know, just won't look at you, don't want to know you.

In describing the "town people's" "stiff-necked" ways, it became clear that Barriot was recalling moments from her elementary school days. It was her fellow students who would not return her gaze, communicating to her that her simple clothes were inappropriate. As chapter 1 described, differences in hygiene, dress, and comportment often composed the crux of how other whites distinguished themselves from Cajuns. Like many, Barriot first became subject to this boundary-making at school. Crucially, she defines the social difference in play here in ethnic terms, as "the French" and the "French Acadian" (with whom she identifies), which is then overlaid with a distinction between "town" and (implied) "country." She used this memory to elaborate her claim that living in St. Martinville was not a "pretty picture," making it a reproach of their conduct. Recalling the literal lack of respect, the way that town people "just won't look at you" (i.e., her), Barriot positioned herself as a person who deserved the intersubjective care that the French did not give (or *will* not give? Significantly, she toggled back and forth between past and present tenses in her remarks).

One similarity that led me to classify Barriot's response together with those of others involves family's centrality in their memories. While I began asking what it was like to "live in St. Martinville," members of this cohort often went away from the town and back in time, as Barriot did here, to the countryside and family life during childhood and adolescence and even to memories of their parents' or grandparents' lives. Many St. Martinvillers had trajectories like Barriot's, in which they left one of numerous surrounding hamlets, where they farmed in tight, family-based units, and moved into town. These largely positive memories operated as one thread of historical awareness; through remembering stories of grandparents, many affirmed something specific about a time beyond memory.

But in the context of St. Martinville, they also recalled family as a social fact with a complicated valence. More significantly, another key correspondence in the remembrances of self-identified Cajuns like Barriot pertained to the distressful character of such recollections. In a lasting way, such moments challenged the self morally. This emerged in the kinds of self-validations that preceded or followed their recollection, justifications affirming a dignity that, from their perspective, their interlocutors denied them in these encounters. Rejecting the opposite interpretation implied by these events, they asserted their own fundamental goodness. Before the remarks I just cited, Barriot juxtaposed the interpersonal relations she experienced with "the French" to those that she practiced with her family: "Well, here's my roots. Here's all my family. And we are a close family. I stay in touch with all my sisters and brothers. We eat suppers together every once in a while; we do things together all the time. You know, sometimes, we have disagreements, but we get back together again. . . . And, for the most part, most of the people are friendly people [like us]. But there are a certain group of people . . ." Heard together, these two statements express clear moral judgments. Barriot uses the way she and her siblings treat each other—being "close family," "do[ing] things together," "hav[ing] disagreements" but "get[ting] back together again"—as a standard for proper social relations. She employs the moral category "friendly" to characterize their conduct, implying that behaviors of the French were the opposite. Importantly, across both statements, she situates most of her narrative in the present tense, shifting to recollect ("looking back and thinking") the vexing moments that resonate into the present. It seems the denial of respect was ongoing—as was the need to negate it.

All these individuals recalled moments when they felt socially challenged or marginalized. These memories were prominent, recollected recurrently or at length. Some made them emblematic of their experience, suggesting they were formative and/or summarized the gist of social life in St. Martinville. Many of these memories dated from early in life, to episodes during school or young adulthood. In this way, they evoke what Sherry Ortner calls "memory tattoos," or the searingly painful recollections that high school often burns into Americans' memories.[10] Invariably, these were indeed difficult moments of embarrassment, rejection, or isolation, which, in recalling them, interviewees cast as a lack of respect from others.

In analyzing her interlocutors' memories of secondary education, Ortner suggests that high school generates memory tattoos because it operates as a system that "forces" identities onto individuals, placing them into categories "based on seemingly natural . . . and randomly distributed characteristics (e.g., beauty, 'personality,' athletic prowess)."[11] Individuals adopt but also struggle with and unwillingly endure labels that sometimes constrain and shame them. Ortner goes on to say that, while ostensibly natural, these identities are inflected by class. "Class baggage," she claims—"family income, family quality . . . , and family cultural capital"—are in play as factors that shape both social categories and individuals' capacities and behaviors. These recollections offer clear parallels with Ortner's analysis. The categories French/Cajun and town/country appeared as givens; the adequacy, provenance, and motivation for their use largely went unquestioned. Similarly, class-based disparities in income and cultural capital loomed large in these memories. Like many others, Ortner's claim about how class recedes into the background of such narratives is that its influence on sociality is both suppressed and misrecognized; more accurate characterizations of social circumstance and identity would acknowledge its formative force.

However, a subtle aspect of the cultural logic of ethnicity, prominent in these narratives, suggests why it, not class, predominates. In these recollections, adversarial others deprecated the self as flawed and inferior, asserting that the flaws were intergenerational, deeply ingrained, and Cajun. While class-based identities are certainly laden with moral judgments that generate profound subjective effects, there is arguably an existential "stickiness" to the quasi-racial logic in play here.[12] The antagonists in these remembered episodes asserted an *inherited* defect in the rememberer's self. Early in an interview, Nora Chiasson, a teacher, recalled a moment when, after disciplining a student in her class, the child's parent challenged her authority. In a statement to another parent that was repeated to Chiasson, the rebuked student's mother said of her, "Well, who does she think she is? After all, you know where she grew up."[13] The implication was that the ethnic self does not escape the effects of its marginal social provenance: Cajuns are somehow *genealogically* inferior.

Andrea Sabatier's recollections contained the most elaborate version of this. In an unusually sustained version of such a narrative, Sabatier outlined a multigenerational litany of indignities—from discrimination and insults endured by grandparents and parents to her own experiences, stretching from her childhood through the present. Among these, she remembered that an acquaintance recently dismissed her Acadian ancestry by characterizing it as "'that riffraff they took from the prisons in France and brought to Louisiana.' I said, 'Oh, no, that's not so. That was John Law who emptied the prisons to bring some of those French names into Louisiana.' He made me furious! The Acadians did not come from the jails! But these attitudes." Intriguingly, Sabatier interprets her interlocutor to have impugned her by implying that after more than two centuries, her ancestors' misconduct indicated something negative about *her*. Not surprisingly, individuals countered such characterizations as false, defending themselves in the present from these recollected challenges. At the same time, the positive connotations associated with families and the belief that behaviors *are* passed down within them (Barriot and Chiasson were explicit on this) made the accusations plausible enough, giving them a sharp, subjective "bite." Consequently, white ethnicity gained a discursive foothold not only in social relations but also in the body. The label carried a charged indictment that carnally, congenitally, *permanently*, Cajuns are flawed social beings. And it was precisely this charge that evoked emotion; as Sabatier did, these interviewees articulated such memories to feelings of indignation, anger, regret, or shame. This had considerable implications for constructing a historical awareness of the distant Acadian past, as we will see.

In addition to this racialized impeachment of Cajuns as people, these memories conjured another trial that tied these individuals together. In them, they remembered a certain marginality, a lack of acceptance or an explicit challenge *in the present*. This was true even for those who, by middle-class standards, had achieved "success" and merited respect. Individuals in this group spanned a range of the class spectrum; some of them had middle-class occupations, while others were hourly wage earners or homemakers in working-class households. Yet in situating themselves in the town, they often spoke of seeking opportunities—to circulate, participate in activities, or access resources—that were denied them or beyond their reach. They felt they were capable of if not entitled to such privileges and sought them but did not reach them as easily as expected, if at all. In sum, they spoke of personal horizons that, while seemingly open, were contested, of social barriers to pursuing greater agency.

In the context of local dynamics of class and status, these individuals were situated outside of some of the more resource-rich and exclusive social networks. Conventionally, a common route of upward mobility required establishing a relationship with someone in these circles. As one interviewee explained it, "For businesses, for work, if we needed something, we'd go to one of the big families, and they could get you whatever you wanted." Some recalled unsuccessful attempts to pursue such a relationship or to overcome active resistance from powerful members of these groups. Jeannette Richard, the proprietor of a small business, remembered how, in purchasing the building where she operated, she and her partner sought a loan from a bank in a distant city, not daring to approach a local one. Intimating that as a Cajun from the countryside, others perceived her as an unwelcome, even undeserving rival, she claimed, "People are nice here, but there's competition. If the word would've got out that we were trying to buy this, we would've never got the option [for the purchase]."

Based on her experience, she believed that if given the chance, one of the town's prominent families would leverage its privilege and purchase the property ahead of her. So in addition to going elsewhere for credit, she completed the loan application and drove it to the out-of-town bank rather than mailing the forms and allowing more time for word of her effort to leak out. Richard made her business prosperous, but the experience was not smooth and seamless. The more we talked, the more she pointed to evidence supporting her claim that prominent locals resented her success. Though a native of the area who effectively pursued her interests, Richard recalled her experience in St. Martinville as a "country girl" whose presence others contested—as an outsider.

To be clear, in their memories, many of these locals stressed their winning efforts to overcome obstacles, like Richard's plucky plan to outwit would-be competitors. At the same time, they often articulated continuity between early memories of disrespect and more recent ones, a permanence that enabled an enduring sense of self as different and challenged by others. This continuity may have worked to ground a recollected sense of a Cajun self. As these interview excerpts intimate, many were not remembering a past that was "complete" or "finished." Rather, they acted on those memories in the present. In Richard's account, she projected her remembered experience as a Cajun from the countryside into anticipation of how she would fare in the real estate market. From there, she planned her tactics accordingly. Thus, as opposed to being inert or forgotten, they used such recollections to narrate social relations and guide action. Memories not only are retrospective but also operate as a basis for action and prospection; recollected experience shapes praxis.[14]

Significantly, most of these interviewees were women. Like Richard, several of them entered previously all-male domains and encountered challenges to their status as legitimate actors. While women's participation in the workforce spiked in Louisiana during the 1960s and '70s, some spheres (e.g., electoral politics) in small towns remained firmly male-dominated through the turn of the millennium.[15] Given this, it may be that these women's statuses—their very dignity—were often contested, leading them to feel less secure during experiences that resembled their earlier recollections. Along these lines, it bears emphasizing that as a marginalized and minor social category, *Cajun* has often been feminized.[16] Consequently, it may well be easier for women to articulate the linkages of memory, identity, and moral positioning outlined here. In my fieldwork, only men who might have identified as Cajun explicitly rejected it, *as when a farmer told me he didn't want to be seen as a Cajun or Cajun American but rather "just plain American."*

COHORT 2: UPWARD MOBILITY, ACHIEVEMENT, WHITENESS

Sitting at his dining room table, Sam Benoit spent most of our exchange recounting cheerful memories of his life. He had reason to be satisfied. From humble beginnings—which he quickly passed over—he spent much of our time together recounting highlights of his social trajectory. Following a GI Bill–funded college degree, Benoit moved into law enforcement, climbing into the hierarchy of the sheriff's department. With obvious pride, he recalled the pleasure he took in serving the public and managing employees, peppering his account with memories of episodes in a career that would soon end with his retirement. Throughout that time, he also participated in prominent civic organizations, taking up leadership positions in several of them. By the end of the interview, he was sharing mementos, recollecting with satisfaction the successful events he coordinated. Before I left, he insisted on showing me the well-landscaped yard surrounding his century-old house on Bayou Teche. "Look at this," Benoit said, gesturing at flowering azaleas stretching toward the bank. "Why would you want to live anywhere else?"

Like the individuals profiled earlier, those I group together with Benoit had similar backgrounds: They bore Acadian patronyms, with parents who were francophones and farmed or performed other types of manual labor. Though less likely to recount memory tattoos, they did have some to share. As mentioned in chapter 2, a Bienvenu, one of the town's "elites," denied Benoit credit as a young man. As a result, he never again set foot in their department store.

Yet overall, these interviewees remembered lives permeated by improvement relative to their modest origins. As the previous summary suggests, their focus was personal, highlighting their own achievements. In their remembrances, they recalled experiences of acceptance and respect in contrast to the indignities stressed by Cajuns. "I feel I was very fortunate, coming here," claimed Gerald Authement, who migrated from the countryside to town and rose in the civil service, "because my father was middle class, and not [of] the old families in St. Martinville." But since he "worked hard," they "appreciated and rewarded" him with senior appointments in municipal government. Such appreciation formed a recurrent theme in Authement's reflections; about his experience in general, he claimed, "One thing I like about St. Martinville is that I was given the chance to prove myself."

Not unlike members of the previous cohort, Authement acknowledged that class-based differences created difficulties for people like themselves. But because his life had been substantively different—he successfully overcame the challenges his class position presented—he situated himself otherwise vis-à-vis that order. Individuals in this group reflected explicitly on such remembered moments of inclusion, as when Benoit recalled the groundbreaking character of his own trajectory. Formerly, "a Benoit would never have been allowed to join the PTO [Parent-Teacher Organization] Executive Council," he claimed, "but I was. I became a member of the Kiwanis Club [which was similarly exclusive]. I became its vice president. . . . Why? Because I was accepted all the way down the line." By this, he meant that his accession to these posts showed how prominent families acknowledged him as a peer—including members of the Bienvenu family, the store owners who refused him credit. As such, these memories were suffused with a positive tint of respect. In them, powerful interlocutors "accepted" the self's competence and goodness and "rewarded" it with access to opportunities and resources.

To be sure, a certain variety of attitudes existed among these individuals. Many of these individuals either participated in or had strong opinions about local political issues. Not unlike residents in the previous cohort, they recalled disagreements in which they were involved or challenges they faced. Several lived in neighborhoods just outside of the town's corporate limits, which the municipal government had recently targeted for annexation into St. Martinville. These residents opposed that project, some vigorously. Yet while they criticized this status quo forcefully, they did not connect it to remembered moments of marginalization in their own lives. Instead, they focused on the annexation proposal itself, repeating their claims about its drawbacks or belittling its proponents for *their* personal flaws. Perhaps their success enabled this: They had defeated the annexation push. As one of them, Brian Boudreaux, explained, the local powers-that-be tended to hold "secret meetings" and make decisions in which "everything's under cover," which led him to relocate outside the corporate limits. According to Boudreaux, the annexation provided another example of this, so defeating it preserved the privilege he secured by moving beyond the town's corporate limits. In recalling such episodes, Boudreaux and others emphasized that through alliances and other means, they had successfully countered elites' attempts to influence their lives, a contrast with how Cajuns foregrounded ongoing blockages from the same groups.

This points to another key dimension of their recollections that stands out in comparison: their stress on agency, of which Benoit's interview marks the most enthusiastic example. Yet whether, like Benoit and Authement, they had built alliances with local elites or, like Boudreaux and others, had defied them, they all emphasized that they had successfully acted in their interests. In St. Martinville, they had exercised agency throughout their lives, which unfolded in unimpeded upward trajectories. This contrasts sharply with those of the previous group. While they situated themselves "outside," centering remembered moments of marginalization, these locals put themselves "inside." Except for one issue (to which I return later), they seemed content with the status quo, remembering lives in which their success was either unchallenged or successfully defended.

In such memories of agentive potency—of achievement and earned respect through social mobility—the antagonism that characterized any memory tattoos (like that of Benoit) had ostensibly been overcome. Those negative experiences had not become a "structuring force in their everyday lives" but had instead morphed into "a past [that] had simply passed," memories that had little salience in their present.[17] As a consequence, these mnemonic emphases served as grounds for a distinct construction of identity, morality, and order. While these could have enabled a range of identitarian stances, these individuals largely articulated a self-presentation that displaced ethnicity.

The significance of class and status politics in their lives suggests one reason for this. As the foregoing makes clear, these loomed large in their trajectories. This cohort was composed of men who shared similar paths, participating in the region's extended postwar expansion that propelled individuals out of agriculture and wage labor and into technical, managerial, and professional livelihoods.[18] As their remarks intimate, relationships of alliance with prominent families also fostered upward mobility. Marriage into well-to-do clans served as one form of this, but a more prevalent path involved sponsorship of one's career. Several interviewees described their members offering them "breaks" at critical moments in their professional lives, as they were recruited into a type of patron-client relationship. Among these was Adam Leger, the upwardly mobile resident mentioned in chapter 2 who served as the go-to tour guide for VIP visitors. Given the centrality of these relationships in their lives, it is unsurprising that their recollections foregrounded them as much as they did.

Relative to the first cohort, which included several upwardly mobile women, gender also intersected this configuration in life-defining ways. In practice, these pathways privileged men; as we saw with Richard, the advantages associated with them were precisely what women sought, at times without success. In addition to broader cultural dynamics that skewed women's participation in certain occupations, other social practices distorted the distribution of opportunities along gender lines. The local chapter of the Rotary Club, for instance, which brought together professionals, managers, and entrepreneurs and had the highest public profile of all civic groups, was exclusively male in its membership.[19] Yet neither gender nor class per se figured prominently in their narratives. One reason for this may be that the most critical dimension of their socioeconomic trajectories—relationships with elite families, which they did acknowledge—took their place, so to speak.

Along these lines, one might expect that ethnicity would be prominent here. Some work suggests that middle-class Louisianans of Acadian descent such as these are more likely to self-identify as Cajun.[20] But these interviews suggest a need to qualify that finding, as none of these middle-class interviewees affirmed a Cajun identity. They did not use Cajun as a label to classify themselves or others, nor to describe any of their memories, even though recollections like Benoit's failed attempt to obtain credit from the Bienvenus were precisely the kind of moments members of the first group named as such. A certain disconnect between their remembered lives and a Cajun subject position offers one possible way to grasp this. Since *Cajun* signified "working class" and "country" (and, for some non-Cajuns, "crass")—and since many others experienced it as entailing marginalization and social blockage—these agentive, upwardly mobile narratives were incompatible with it. White ethnicity's social implications aligned with neither the "substance" of their lives nor the ways they remembered it. While they could identify as Cajun—and others like them have—they did not.

At the same time, this mismatch only partially accounts for why they might have eschewed the label and what they affirmed instead. Building on the preceding analysis, I am suggesting that these individuals actively pursued other ways of remembering and constructing their identities. In addition to an eschewal of ethnicity—both Cajun and French—this formation involved a certain articulation of whiteness.

As previously underscored, ethnic categories in south Louisiana have conventionally operated in a hierarchical manner, with Creole marking a superior rank above Cajun and other "hyphenated" labels within the broader classification of whiteness.[21] An Anglo-American slot implicitly tops this ranking, though it often signifies in an unmarked fashion. For the upwardly mobile—Pitre's father, for example—it was possible to attempt reclassification, shedding markers of ethnic belonging (e.g., by anglicizing a French patronym) in pursuit of this higher rank of white identity. By now, the rationale for this should be clear: Cajun and other white ethnic labels were experienced as limits on agency and opportunity. Practically, then, an opening toward redefinition existed, away from a circumscribed minor form of whiteness and toward a more desirable major one.

There were two ways in which these interviewees pursued such a reclassification in memory and discourse. The first involves how they narrated their lives, which ostensibly tracked the cultural schema of the individualized, unmarked white self. One prominent template for autobiographical remembering focuses tightly on the individual, often excluding the effects, positive or negative, of social relationships, commitments, or allegiances. Beginning from a situation in which the self's social station or customary behaviors operate as obstacles needing to be overcome, they succeed through their own effort to lift these burdens and achieve success.[22] In some Cajun autobiographies, that initial obstacle is ethnicized; the shame and limits imposed on individuals *as Cajuns* set them at a disadvantage, which they subsequently surmount.[23] Yet it would be a small step to de-emphasize or eliminate the ethnic dimension of these obstacles altogether, making them nondescript and generic—and, in doing so, to "de-ethnicize" the self. Several of these men made such a move. Its most condensed version came in Eugene Naquin's recollection, which I featured in chapter 3:

> I was born and raised in a dwelling that didn't have double walls. And raised in the country. Worked hard, didn't have much money. I should say didn't hardly have *any* money. My daddy couldn't afford to pay me for working . . . , but I knew that I had to help him. He was in a bind, trying to provide for ten kids. . . . He was a carpenter, often unemployed. . . . And I knew that I couldn't go to college, so I decided to join the army. Went to war, came back, had the GI Bill, made up my mind that I was going to take advantage of it. He couldn't afford to send me, [but] I went to college, got a degree. Worked hard for forty-somewhat years and made something of myself.

Where others labeled these limiting circumstances as Cajun, Naquin chose not to. As such, these memories of overcoming impediments and achieving success sketched out a trajectory that was ethnically unmarked—and, at least implicitly, normatively white.

To be sure, some variation emerged in these interviews. I mentioned how some of these interviewees acknowledged the assistance of others in furthering their careers. Overall, however, the mnemonic gist of responses like those of Benoit evinced an elaborate version of the arc outlined earlier: A strong emphasis on the self, whose actions were recounted in active, indicative language, with others who appeared intermittently or as weak characters. An enthusiastic raconteur, Benoit spent much of the exchange describing his professional career, stressing his personal commitments (e.g., being a "hard worker," having a knack for "organizing" projects) and skills ("I can talk to anybody") that contributed to his success. In this vein, these interviewees concentrated on their adult lives, with only fleeting references to their childhoods, parents, or rural backgrounds. This differs substantially from the Cajuns I described; these individuals recounted their own lives with a tight focus on their successful adulthoods. Even as Naquin recalled his childhood circumstances somewhat extensively (in detail unusual for this cohort), his conclusion tracks the schema closely: "[I] worked hard [to overcome obstacles] . . . and made something of myself." Again, these narratives contained strong moral evaluations of the self. Such memories were not merely described but rather deployed to affirm their good, proper behavior.

While in American public discourse generally, this schema of rising above hurdles toward acceptance and achievement may not be racialized as such, it was in this context. As we saw in chapter 3, many white locals remembered their Black coresidents selectively, in comparisons that set out racial distinctions in morally charged terms. Though not ubiquitous, such memories were common here and compose a second way in which most members of this group opted for white identities. Recall that, immediately following the succinct life summary quoted previously, Naquin insisted, "Now, all of this, this is still open to everybody if they want, instead of dragging the streets, in hip huggers and language that you'd never entice anybody to hire you [with]. And [Blacks] don't want to change!" These individuals mentioned African Americans frequently in their narratives, drawing sharp boundaries between themselves and their Black neighbors. At times, they made the ethically and racially charged distinction between "my proper, individual striving" and "their offensive, collective torpor" explicit, as Naquin did in this case.

Among these St. Martinvillers, there were meaningful variations in the intensity of these views. Yet they voiced many of the interracial fears I analyzed in chapter 3—of unfair encroachment into previously all-white neighborhoods, of the "havoc" created by school integration, and of the projected chaos that would ensue in the wake of an anticipated takeover. The gist of these whites' complaints—especially about Blacks' "intrusion" into homogeneous neighborhoods and the contested realm of electoral politics—points to their own somewhat tenuous social positions. As upwardly mobile individuals who, during their lifetime, gained access to unprecedented opportunities and resources, these men's gains were directly challenged by African Americans' sociopolitical advances. For some of them, these concerns came together in their move outside the municipal limits and opposition to annexation. As one interviewee openly admitted, he and many of his neighbors had moved outside of the town's boundary to sidestep the emergent Black majority within it. Another bragged that as a civil servant, he had rebuffed the demands of "big Black bosses" to hire their cronies in his division, a privilege they assumed came with their election to office. Yet whites conventionally held this prerogative—a key dimension of political power—which he proudly recalled having retained. Such concerns followed the well-traced configuration of whiteness illustrated in the previous chapter, whereby the status quo required defense from Black threats, menaces cast as intolerable challenges to order and white privilege.

COHORT 3: CLASS, BACK TALK, AND "MY KIND OF PEOPLE"

Walking into the windowless darkness of The Lafitte, it took a moment to spot Sam Bergeron. A retired jack-of-all-trades, Bergeron sat at the intersection of considerable traffic during happy hours at this local bar; with about a dozen people already present on a Friday afternoon, this one promised to be more animated than usual. I settled in next to him as Jim Gautreaux, a painter in his late forties to whom Bergeron had previously introduced me, entered. Seeing us, Gautreaux called over, "Hey, we gotta talk! I'm coming!" During our initial encounter two weeks prior, I explained my research focus to Gautreaux; today, having reflected on that first meeting, he now returned to it. After we exchanged greetings, he offered, "Now, I could tell you some things about the history around here, but it wouldn't make the people in control look too good." I signaled that I wanted to hear more, so he continued. "You see, when I was young, I used to run around with the other boys. And one day my father pulled me aside, and he told me, 'Son, if something happens and y'all end up in jail, their fathers can make a phone call, and they'll be out of there in no time. I can't make phone calls like that.'"

Hoping that Gautreaux might comment further, I reacted with a surprised "Is that so?" But instead, he shifted focus, gestured toward the middle of the barroom, and declared a preference for "my kind of people." In turn, he pointed to the individuals he knew, offering short biographies of each. Seated just down from us was Leo DeJean, one of Gautreaux's high school classmates, who, when his tenth-grade teacher asked what he wanted to do with his life, had, in Gautreaux's recollection, answered, "I'm gonna make four million dollars as a housing contractor." Gautreaux imitated DeJean's gravelly voice and thick accent, suggesting skills and cultural capital that were unlikely to achieve such an ambitious goal. But the project was unfolding as planned; Gautreaux estimated that "he's probably a quarter of the way right now." There was also a young man sitting a few stools away in the other direction, whose brother Gautreaux had known as "a guy who liked to run around." He remembered that man, Alex Ardoin, once telling him, "'You know, the most beautiful woman I ever had, the best lay in my whole life, when I woke up the next morning, she was gone, and had wrote on the mirror, 'Welcome to the wonderful world of AIDS.' The guy's been dead five years now," Gautreaux said. He continued in this vein until he completed his tour of the bar's patrons, outlining lives whose trajectories he alternately cast as droll, ironic, or melancholic.

This final cohort consists of working-class St. Martinvillers whose modes of remembrance and moral positioning were distinct from the other two.

In Gautreaux's juxtaposition of "my kind of people" with those "in control" lies the most profound difference between their discourse and that of other cohorts. In their memories, they foregrounded a St. Martinville riddled by hierarchical asymmetry, in which they found themselves at the margins. Their self-positioning signified sharp boundaries between themselves and their local "others," as Gautreaux did first by remembering his father's counsel—which both warned him and indicted the social order—then contrasting that with warm memories of "my people." This intense sociality, buttressed by recollections that celebrated it, coexisted with memories of being located firmly "outside" of privilege and opportunity.

In a way, such remembrances resembled those of the first cohort, which identified as Cajuns. This group expressed a similar sense of having lived in a "bad situation"—in a town whose social order unfairly disadvantaged them, inhabited by others who derided them. But they diverged in how they remembered their response to this marginal status. While the first cohort was composed of "outsiders" who "wanted in," seeking social mobility and integration into more exclusive social circles, these individuals were outsiders who "stayed out." Recognizing the obstacles they encountered as insurmountable—or as markers of a flawed status quo they rejected—they foregrounded recollected moments of transgressing norms they did not respect. *Over coffee in her kitchen, Joanna Dugas reflected on things I should know when she suddenly recalled a recent brouhaha over the Catholic cemetery. The Catholic parish's proposal that parishioners begin to pay "perpetual dues" for its maintenance had so incensed Dugas, a retired secretary, that she "wrote a letter to the pope." She described what she put in it—a laundry list of clerical excesses in dealing with the graveyard—but said she got no response. So she composed a second missive, this time to the local pastor: "I wrote 'Dear Henry.' I didn't put anything else. So one day, he called. I had company that day, but I answered the phone. 'I was very disturbed by your letter,' he said. 'I have a title, but you didn't address me with it.' I told him, 'Listen, I was taught by my mother that I don't call anyone father except the Lord Jesus Christ!' [I told him that] I looked at him, and I didn't see God. Oh, he didn't like that."*

Recollections of such "back talk" to others comprised a meaningful difference in this group's positioning vis-à-vis conventional mores. In their detail and attention to reported speech, these were performative transgressions, rendering contradictions and lies visible while literally "playing them out."[24] Critiquing the local priest was something of a pastime among Catholics in small-town south Louisiana, but Dugas pushed it into the realm of provocation. For her, the priest's insistence on decorum (rather than arguing his case on the merits) precisely defined what was so offensive about the social order in this "*petit crapule de village*" (shitty little town). As with Gautreaux, Dugas had no respect for it, made no effort to become part of it, because, as a pretentious sham, it deserved neither. She also used it to position herself confidently in the world, affirming the righteousness of her actions compared to those of her morally challenged antagonists. *When the priest justified the parish's position (claiming it was "following the law" as they did in New Orleans), she recalled that she had already confirmed this wasn't the case. So she challenged him. "You want to make a bet? I got the number [of the Archdiocese of New Orleans] right here for you to call," Dugas taunted. "This thing about it being the law was a bunch of crap," she insisted, a deception meriting the scorn she heaped on it.*

By common measures, these were individuals whom one might expect to identify as Cajun. In addition to meeting the usual demographic criteria, their cultural practices align with those recognized in scholarship. Dugas's memory of her feisty back talk tracks the subversive antielitism that some find characteristic of Cajuns' everyday humor, while their blue-collar class positions constitute the "socioeconomic center of Cajun life" that others deem fundamental to their identity formation.[25] Yet in conversations, these locals never used the label to describe themselves, another way they differed from the first group. In one sense, this was not unexpected. As researchers had found a generation before, residents whom they assumed would identify as Cajun used no such classification, instead using terms such as "people like us" as labels for themselves.[26] As the foregoing showed, identifying as Cajun in St. Martinville proved difficult for those who did so. They felt derided, so it took effort to claim such a subject position. These St. Martinvillers foregrounded a distinct response to that challenge, marking a significant regional variation in boundary-making and remembrance that is arguably overlooked.

Instead, more than the other cohorts, these locals engaged in a certain kind of status or class consciousness. Two of its features bear emphasis. The first is already in evidence: They often recalled moments of status inequality, challenging the implied inferiority of their position by situating themselves as morally superior to social others. As with Dugas's retort to the priest's insistence that she employ his title, they often focused on privileges related to social rank. To be sure, Dugas sought to resist the church's proposal to extract rent for cemetery maintenance, a matter of economic resources. But in her recollected narrative, she foregrounded the dispute's interpersonal dimension, with a corresponding stress on personal attributes (her own and the priest's). This tendency to personalize the social sometimes gave their analyses of collective matters a moralizing character. They remembered such confrontations as conflicts between bad actors and good ones, defined in terms of the moral valence of individuals' character traits.

At the same time, they also recalled problems with access to material resources. Such memories were legion: stories of whitecapping going back generations, of fallout from the displacement of fisher families from the Atchafalaya Basin, and of ongoing efforts to limit access to subsistence fishing there.[27] These memories flowed into conversation with remarkable ease. *On one damp evening in late fall, I greeted Sam Bergeron by asking how the fishing was going. He supplemented his Social Security check by selling what he caught in the basin, and his response—"Not good"—presently spiraled out into memories of people stealing fish off his lines and trouble with game wardens. Soon, Bergeron introduced me to Ben Daigle, a fortysomething seated next to us, and the two of them continued in the same vein. Daigle complained bitterly about how unfair hunting laws were to people like himself, in a rant drawn from experience. "What if I just want to go out and kill enough food to eat? If you only take enough food for a meal, they shouldn't be able to do anything." Only when you clearly possess too much to consume at one meal should you be penalized, he argued.* Within ten minutes, greetings gave way to complaints inflected by past experience, grievances that never seemed far from people's minds. Though they shifted only occasionally into considerations of class relations as such, their memories and commentaries on them condemned the unfairness of how their lives had become more difficult as, in a variety of ways, their access to productive resources shrunk.

Finally, a distinct rapport with the past held sway among these individuals. While other cohorts evinced an openness to public history, a desire and capacity to participate in it, these individuals did not. In this way, they were again situated and situated themselves "outside" the normative sociality that sustains conventional histories. At times, however, they nonetheless engaged in an intensely meaningful relationship with remembered pasts, distinct from and somewhat opposed to historical discourse.

On a Friday after Christmas, with lights still strung high on the walls, the barmaid offered Bergeron and me drinks that we hadn't requested, purchased by someone she called Arthur. Sam turned and gestured: Wearing blue work overalls and a baseball cap, Arthur LeBlanc, a large man in his fifties, stood off the bar behind us. He and Bergeron knew each other, so we left our seats to greet him. As Bergeron did when presenting me to others, he told LeBlanc that I was studying to be a professor and writing a book. "He's interested in history," Bergeron explained, as if this vague explication was enough to justify my presence in the bar. This made me uncomfortable, since "professor," "book," and "history" seemed like a high bar for launching a conversation at The Lafitte. I wanted to translate them into something closer to home, so when Bergeron finished, I said, "Yeah, I'm interested in the history of St. Martinville." Luckily, LeBlanc was game, responding, "Well, that's gonna have to be an awfully big book."

The two of them then began a batch of stories about "the old days" in the basin, where both grew up and continued to spend time. Bergeron began with a story about how once, years ago, the fishermen along one stretch of the basin got together to pull straws and charged the person pulling the short straw with the task of scaring off a much-hated game warden. Begun in this way, this account announced itself as a bravado tale of macho exploits that I often heard at The Lafitte. But in Bergeron's telling, the plan backfired, and the protagonist had to be rescued from the law by the rest of the group. Changing the subject slightly, LeBlanc recalled how fishing used to be so much better: "You could catch crabs that measured two feet from claw to claw. Ask Sam." Bergeron responded in kind: "Now, you not gonna believe me, but one time, I ran fourteen crawfish traps and got fifteen sacks of crawfish. I'm not kidding. That's how good it used to be." A common theme in talk about the basin, this "used to be" quality of life referred, among other things, to the deleterious effect that its gradual infilling with sediment from the Atchafalaya River was having on fishing and trapping. Shaking their heads, they traded stories about particular places in the swamp that, though formerly under water, were now silted up. From there, Bergeron asked about LeBlanc's elderly father, who he claimed was a one-of-a-kind swamp dweller in his day. "They don't make no more like that," Bergeron said approvingly. They both agreed that if I wanted some "good stuff for my book," I would do well to seek him out and speak with him.

As noted in chapter 2, everyday historical awareness in St. Martinville, even among those who cultivated an interest in public history proper, seemed partial and intermittent: Individuals tethered it tightly to their current interests. That quality also manifested in this mundane encounter, as Bergeron and LeBlanc skillfully interwove autobiographical memories into a social exchange, occasionally reaching toward time beyond memory (e.g., in referencing LeBlanc's father's long career in the basin). Yet rather than developing a sustained focus on the past, they tacked heavily back and forth between remembering and their present concerns (e.g., in the underlying refrain that things were not what they used to be or when Bergeron shifted the stream of their recollections to ask about LeBlanc's father's health).

Two further aspects of this feature bear stressing here. First, Bergeron's and LeBlanc's shared recollections implied a sociality with moral underpinnings, ostensibly affirming mutual recognition and solidarity. The turn-taking they each facilitated; the way Bergeron inquired about LeBlanc's father; and at the level of active context, the enactment of the unspoken rule of reciprocal buying of rounds that framed the encounter: These practices oriented their remembering, anchoring its purpose. Secondly, their memories seemed to possess a nostalgic bent, a recurrent contrast between a meager, run-down *now* and a more bountiful, desirable *then*. But among this cohort, telling a story about the "old days" often made a claim on the present rather than expressing a desire for a lost past. Whether latent, in Gautreaux's implied critique of social hierarchy, or more explicit, when Ben Daigle denounced the priority of bag limits restricting the number of animals hunters could kill over subsistence, they drew memories hard into the present, deploying them for staking moral claims that it *should be different than it is*. Labeling it "nostalgia" does not fully illuminate such remembering. As Johannes Fabian writes about the mnemonics of Zairian popular painting, memories of important aspects of social life "are not just remembered nostalgically; they are invoked as the foundations on which present life and consciousness grow, or should grow."[28] For these individuals, everyday remembrance did not primarily ponder distant moments separate from the here and now, which is integral to conventional historical discourse. Instead, this cohort grounded the past in the present, using the former to nurse expectations about a better time to come.

CONCLUSION

All these individuals shared similar family backgrounds and even formative experiences. In theory, these might have served as a shared core of memory and identity, yet they did not. Social trajectories differed considerably, and the differences seem determinative in shaping distinct formations of memory. Clearly, social class is important in this regard. But it was not the only order of difference that mattered. Instead, experientially, the fulcrum of memory varied, as gender, ethnicity, and race were also in the mix. Of equal importance, each groups' memories possessed distinctive moral codings. Variably situated in a stratified social landscape, these individuals' recollections conveyed discrete moral positions, in which they articulated a sense of belonging or exclusion vis-à-vis others. In turn, these can now be seen in their alignment with the regime of social memory and public history, forming an intriguing constellation in what I referred to earlier as the local memoryscape.

Consider first the "Cajuns." For those St. Martinvillers who identified as such, their autobiographical memories involved repeated moments when others judged them negatively and/or relegated them to the sidelines of social activity. Even the upwardly mobile among them described their agency as being unfairly blocked. Significantly, most of these individuals were women. Like Jeannette Richard, many of them entered domains that were previously all male and encountered challenges to their status as legitimate actors. Significantly, their interlocutors ethnicized the "blockage" to fuller belonging and expression of agency with a hint of racial logic: The Cajun identity ascribed to them was grounded in their genealogy, their membership in a (putatively) tainted lineage through which they inherited an organically flawed identity. Crucially, the existential "bite" of this racialized insult filled the space of memory and discourse. In interviews, their effort to dispute this character defamation featured quite prominently (arguably displacing the role that, e.g., class might have played). And it posed an active dilemma for them, not one that had been overcome by decades of "Cajun pride."

The comparison of this formation with those of the second and third cohorts is striking. The second group, mostly middle-class men, recalled many moments of upwardly mobile improvement and respect, through which they seemed to secure a sense of dignity that eluded many in the previous cohort. Compared to Cajuns, who mostly remembered themselves as marginalized "outsiders," these individuals spoke of themselves as "insiders"—recognized as peers by high-status others and capable of successfully accessing resources and decision-making power. Moreover, in remembering moments pertaining to housing, work, and local politics, these St. Martinvillers asserted that distance and distinction from Blacks mattered to them. As such, they defined themselves as white, both adamantly vis-à-vis African Americans and in how they narrated their personal trajectories as matters of autonomy and self-realization. Socially and experientially, these individuals charted a distinct route of memory and positionality toward a more normative whiteness and away from ethnicity.

Like "Cajuns," those whom I situate in the third group also voiced a sense of their exclusion in St. Martinville. Similar to that first cohort, they adamantly affirmed their dignity in the face of challenges to it, often creating, through recollection and practice, an inclusive "place to stand" with similarly situated others.[29] But rather than seeking to overcome the barriers that marginalized them (by maintaining existing "rules of the game," as the Cajuns ostensibly did), they often mocked them in aggressive back talk. These individuals voiced the sharpest criticisms of (some aspects of) the status quo that I heard; in this regard, their discourse centered class relations and political economy more than the other groups. Yet character, behavior, and other person-centered moral concerns were arguably more central to them. Reversing others' explicit critiques of them over improper conduct and lack of couth, they skewered the recollected behavioral foibles of their interlocutors, congealing social conflicts into matters of "good versus bad" people. And while they might have identified as Cajuns—and so many narratives define the ethnic group in terms of such working-class individuals—they, too, eschewed the label, marking yet another path into identity and memory.

One can map this heterogeneity onto stable formations of public history and cultural memory. On the one hand, the animated bonhomie of this third group's sociality shares something in common with the depictions of Cajun joie de vivre that, during the past several decades, became ubiquitous in the popular press and media campaigns. On the other hand, the details of their sometimes hardscrabble lives—not to mention the brashness of their challenge to norms of civility, taste, and (at times) legality—have contributed to white elites' discomfort and motivated the latter to marginalize the former's presence in public discourse. Simply put, the lifeways of this third group may be (partially) good for *culture* (in its commodified form) but not for *history*. Their sharp opposition to the status quo was neither the stuff of historical discourse nor fodder for tropes of the American Dream. Moreover, Petit Paris's "theme"—roughly, "sophisticated people did remarkable things here"—did not align with their own remembered experiences, to say the least. Thus, public culture offered few symbolic resources through which they might reproduce and congeal their remembered experiences. And they recognized this. During one of my first visits to The Lafitte, *a patron responded to my stated interest in local history by asking, "Which one: the real history or the fake stuff* [e.g., Petit Paris history]?"

Meanwhile, the autobiographical memories of the second group clearly existed in a centripetal relationship to common patterns of public discourse and history. These men remembered their lives in ways that track the schema of the American Dream, with their stress on overcoming obstacles, individualistic striving, and social success, narrowly defined. Some members of this group also took an active interest in Petit Paris history, the only of these three to do so. In addition to Adam Leger's enthusiastic tour guiding, others participated in the elaboration of some key sites. As I outlined in chapter 2, it appeared that the sociality of these men's careers involved investing in local historical culture. In addition to this social shaping, the particular emphases of, for example, the opera house dedication—its focus on individuals, on notable (white, male, and middle-class) achievement, and on certain kinds of service to the public—sketched out strong parallels with these men's lives.

Viewed from the perspective of the memoryscape concept, one can arguably see, in these articulations, the constructive, morally validating effects of this formation on their remembering. As Carol Greenhouse suggests, dominant "time narratives" are ultimately about agency and its social distribution: They name what counts as important actions and circumscribe who can legitimately perform them.[30] In light of the temporal trajectories that the American Dream and Petit Paris authorize, it is not surprising that these men remembered selves in ways aligned with those schema.

Finally, the Cajuns in the first group share much in common with the working-class members of the third one. Given the narrative gist of their memories—that of good individuals who, throughout their lives, encountered an undeserved lack of respect and opportunities—these individuals were largely blasé about Petit Paris history, including the Evangeline sites. Recall also that the entire Petit Paris complex was tightly associated with "the French" and several elite families. To claim that history, one seemingly had to shed one's ties to Cajun ethnicity, as the second cohort did. These individuals, meanwhile, identified as Cajun, affirming themselves and their family heritage in the face of denigration. At the same time, one might say that many of their recollections included a melodramatic element of the American Dream. In their upright, upwardly mobile striving, they were innocent targets of mistreatment. And their efforts, crowned with some success, deserved to be rewarded with more of it. In this regard, the link between these individuals and the Acadian Memorial was striking. Opened several years before I began fieldwork, they were already familiar with this new site; they had visited or become connected to it in some way, finding it compelling. As Andrea Sabatier put it, "When I personally found out the history of my ancestors, then a lightbulb went off," igniting a reappraisal of her self-image. It also motivated an extended commitment to the venue, whose historical account engaged her own memories of being a Cajun in St. Martinville.

In this regard, the Acadian Memorial added something to the memoryscape. It engaged locals who identified as Cajuns in ways that Evangeline history in particular, and the narratives of Petit Paris more broadly, did not. How it represented that past in terms of agency and progress and why residents like Sabatier were enamored of it will be the subject of chapters 6 and 7. First, though, the very existence of a new Acadian site in St. Martinville begs a question. As we have seen, apart from Evangeline history, which traded heavily on the national reputation of Longfellow's poem, the history of Acadians in Louisiana created a problem for society, not a contribution to its advance. How did that change? What shifts created the conditions for a new history site, one that could garner widespread support and engage the recollected experiences of self-identified Cajuns? I turn now to these questions.

Chapter Five

Making the Happy Minority

Cajuns, History, and Projects of Governance since the 1960s

> There is "something altogether different" behind things: not a timeless and essential secret, but the secret that they have no essence or that their essence was fabricated in a piecemeal fashion from alien forms.
>
> Michel Foucault, "Nietzsche, Genealogy, History"

Devon Melançon left a message, inviting me to join him at the yet-to-be-completed Museum of the Acadian Memorial. As a memorial board member leading the effort to write the museum's text panels, Melançon was finalizing their composition and wanted to check their mock-ups on the exhibit space's walls. Could I give him a hand to tape them up and verify measurements? Prior to this, he asked me for feedback on a draft narrative, so in joining him that day, I was keen to know what he made of it and better understand why he and his colleagues wanted to recount this particular history. The site's leadership had determined that without an explicit narrative framing the representations in the memorial's commemorative space (opened five years earlier), visitors (not least many locals) could not fully appreciate what they were seeing. So the exhibit would add necessary context: a brief history of Acadians/Cajuns from late medieval France to the present.

In a building that once housed St. Martinville's fire engine, we hung sheets of easel paper on freshly Sheetrocked walls. As we worked, I inquired about the process for composing the exhibit's narrative. Who participated in composing the text panels? Had there been debate about how to craft the narrative? Melançon's responses made it clear that while he reached out to others for contributions, he largely proceeded solo. Funded by a grant from the Louisiana Endowment for the Humanities, historian Carl Brasseaux, from the nearby University of Louisiana at Lafayette, provided the memorial with a database of entries from primary sources, essentially a collection of research notes. Working from them and his own research, Melançon did the rest.

When we arrived at a panel entitled "Pride," I noted that Melançon had rewritten its first paragraph to read that "the civil rights movement inspired Cajuns to counter abuses and prejudices during the 1960s." As evidence for this, he cited the creation of the Council for the Development of French in Louisiana (CODOFIL). Under the inaugural leadership of a former congressman, James Domengeaux, the state agency promoted Louisiana's French language and culture. Such an affirmation could be seen as the crux of new historical narratives about Cajuns that began circulating in the 1970s. This new public history foregrounded accounts of the discrimination they endured since arriving in Louisiana, centering a political and cultural "renaissance"—a self-directed ascent into recognition, civic agency, and full citizenship.

Yet I questioned this characterization, noting that when it came to CODOFIL's signature initiative, Domengeaux adamantly defended the teaching of standard French and not local vernaculars, even in the face of fervent grassroots opposition.[1] *Wasn't this an elitist project aligned with the class oppression that preceded it? A veteran of years in the classroom, he calmly replied, "Given that I don't have a lot of space, I don't want to speak just about conflict. And even if Domengeaux was elitist, he was a Cajun. And if he did elitist things, it was because of everything that he endured before [pointing to a paragraph describing the mid-century English-only policy in public schools]. He wouldn't have acted like that if he hadn't experienced oppression like everyone else." I accepted this without comment, and we moved on to finish the work.*

But I immediately thought this exchange was significant. In field notes, I wrote that Melançon's response could help clinch the argument I sought to prove. To my mind, class conflict in Louisiana was as clear as day, and one question my research attempted to answer was, Why wasn't it more open in discourse and identity formation? In so many words, Melançon replied, because ethnicity is more fundamental; it trumps class, or it should. I interpreted this as a kind of ideological obfuscation that provided an answer to my question. Class struggle among whites could be more open, but a discourse of Cajun ethnicity camouflaged it. I recall feeling satisfaction, the pleasure of theory's vindication.

Ultimately, however, I decided I was wrong as to why this exchange is critical for this study. I still believe that there is nothing foundational about a given identitarian idiom and that class discourse could (and perhaps should) become more prominent in Louisiana.[2] Yet I understand Melançon's reply differently now. Though seemingly toiling alone on those text panels, he did not share this sentiment about the Cajun past as a personal opinion but rather inscribed it in public space, with the sanction of the memorial's staff and board, the town's mayor and council, nongovernmental organizations, the state legislature, and many others at his back. Moreover, Melançon was shaping the elaboration of the eighth of nine Acadian historic initiatives to emerge in Louisiana since 1974. Committed to conducting a rigorous materialist analysis of the historical representation of Cajuns, I realized I was oblivious to an expanding material apparatus that stared me in the face. Instead of an ethereal "superstructure," historical discourse in this situation was quite concrete. And many others had preceded Melançon, in efforts that stretched back to the 1960s; spanned institutions from St. Martinville to Washington, DC; and resulted in a network of venues similarly centered on enabling historical awareness and ethnic identity. After much reflection on this emerging complex, I pivoted to engage his response on its merits.

In what follows, I approach this from the perspective of power and politics, broadly construed. I engage with several views about this, starting with Melançon's. In his text panel on Domengeaux and CODOFIL, he described an effort to address a power imbalance, "to counter abuses and prejudices," evoking the politics of status and hierarchy. A related version centers electoral politics: Edwin Edwards, the state's flamboyant (later convicted) Cajun governor, takes Domengeaux's place as the movement's leader, and his electoral campaigns (especially that of 1971) are its locus of agency. This comprised a central thread in a new narrative about Cajuns and their place in the body politic. Far from the apathetic, benighted citizens they were portrayed to be, Cajuns had organized to affirm their civic right to cultural expression and elect one of their own as the state's chief executive. They did this despite having ample justification for resenting their decades-long marginalization—which is where the narrative became historical—acting instead to effect change. In contrast with so many "aggrieved minorities," Cajuns became a "powerful" ethnic group, buoyed by an irrepressible joie de vivre and offering a model for social integration in fractious times. In the public discourse of that era, they were said to comprise a "happy minority."

As an explanation of this history's emergence and link to relations of power, such accounts get one significant feature of this right: A desire to shed their second-class status motivated many Louisianans' investment in this narrative.

As shown in chapter 1, efforts to reform Cajuns, accompanied by historical narratives about their degeneracy, were pervasive; many were eager to negate that discourse. But these "self-directed" efforts were not the only dimension of power that mattered in the happy minority's rise, nor the sole initiative that sparked the complex's unfolding. Considering the many ways that history has long been central to civic politics, other relationships and developments, other struggles of social transformation, must enter the analysis to explain how this happened.

Across the chapter, I describe five distinct yet overlapping social *projects*, visions and programs for governing and transforming society, and how the history of Cajuns as the happy minority emerged from their trajectories and intersections. Each of them is *political* insofar as they involve a conception of existing relations of power and of how its efforts would modify them. Following Michel Foucault's method of analyzing power's "microphysics," I highlight two dimensions of these projects insofar as they promoted the history of Cajuns as the happy minority.[3] The first concentrates on Cajuns and their history *not* as stable objects but on discerning the *conditions of their constitution*. Far from maintaining a continuity, becoming model white ethnics whose history needed to be grounded in truth involved a dramatic shift. This emergence drew on existing practices of knowledge and power to create a novelty, a domain in which "good" Cajuns and a "positive" account of their past could stand out and counter the negative histories that predominated before. The other dimension comprises locating those implicated in each project as actors in antagonistic landscapes, pursuing *strategies and tactics* to achieve their goals. From this perspective, the seemingly apolitical character of historical narratives, their amorphous "view from nowhere," congeals into a depiction of situated agents who actively sought this new history, for particular reasons and against adversarial forces. An appreciation of such micropolitics is arguably the most serious gap in conventional accounts of public history's power.

PURSUING CAJUN POWER I: THE HAPPY MINORITY AS WHITE ETHNIC BACKLASH

As an explanation of how narratives about Cajuns' past changed, the argument that Cajuns themselves brought it about predominates in the region. Authoring the first robust version of it, geographer Cécyle Trépanier underscored the role played by the electoral successes of Edwin Edwards, a self-described Cajun whose avowedly ethnic gubernatorial campaign in 1971 legitimized the label.[4] This analysis certainly has merit. Edwards took notes on how his predecessor John McKeithen reversed his electoral fortunes in south Louisiana by running a regionalized campaign there in 1967. Edwards's success then created something of a template that others have tried to replicate. Candidates with French ancestry who hail from south Louisiana often appeal to Cajuns in various ways, from campaign stops at St. Martinville's Acadian historic sites to policy proposals designed to address their interests.[5] This is one dimension of what some referred to as "Cajun power": electoral victories that translated into a white ethnic political project.[6]

As a public entity mandated to preserve Louisiana's French heritage through teaching French in public schools, CODOFIL's founding often appears as the project's signal accomplishment. As Melançon framed it, it is also cast as a matter of Cajun politicians combating their second-class status. But *pace* the claim that Blacks' activism inspired Cajuns, the organization seems to have emerged as an electoral tactic in the wake of the Voting Rights Act (VRA)—one meant to *counter* Black political mobilization. Before its creation, CODOFIL gestated for years inside Governor McKeithen's office, as the volatile politics of Black civil rights preoccupied him and other white politicians. During the 1960s, ascendant segregationists defeated the racially moderate Long machine, the dynastic political bloc led first by Huey Long and then by his brother Earl, and those forces joined the rest of the South in "vigorously opposing school integration and viciously attacking the NAACP."[7] White voters veered rightward; Alabama Governor George Wallace won all but five of the state's sixty-four parishes in the 1968 presidential election. In these moments when race became the main issue, white majorities consistently "opposed change."[8]

In this context, Cajun power possessed a clear interracial dimension. Seeking to animate white voting blocs, senior politicos apparently conceived of CODOFIL as an effort to stress the European heritage of Louisiana's white residents. In a series of letters during the 1967 gubernatorial campaign, Raymond Rodgers, a Canadian political scientist who served as McKeithen's aide-de-camp and the éminence grise behind CODOFIL,[9] specified the strategy's logic. Writing surreptitiously to both candidates before the runoff election, Rodgers urged the incumbent McKeithen that "*now* is the hour" to "get election mileage" from a "states' rights and pro-Acadiana" platform of concluding a cultural exchange agreement with the provincial government of Quebec.[10] To McKeithen's challenger John Rarick, Rodgers also wrote and suggested running on two "States' Rights and Education" programs: the Quebec initiative for south Louisiana and "an educational exchange program with South Africa" for the north.[11] In another confidential missive to politicians in the state's federal delegation, Rodgers explained that similar efforts in Alabama inspired him to advance this proposal; while working there in 1965, he learned that officials under Wallace reached out to Southern Rhodesia and South Africa to create exchanges and "promote friendly relationships, et cetera."[12] Communicating at a crucial moment with these politicians, Rodgers rendered explicit the initiative's potential electoral value for reinforcing white Louisianans' identification as whites in a proposal targeting the racially fraught domain of public education. McKeithen carried south Louisiana in a landslide (he had lost there in 1963); the following year, he supported the legislation establishing CODOFIL and headlined a gala in St. Martinville to celebrate its passage.[13] While it became an organ of cultural policy, officials launched the agency partly as a tactical experiment for bolstering the white vote in post-VRA elections.

A corresponding shift in public discourse emerged, a change in speech about Cajuns' civic belonging embedded in a new historical narrative. Cajuns and their past began to signify differently through a positive contrast with Blacks. As Aihwa Ong summarizes, "Racial categories are fundamentally about degrees of undeserving or deserving citizenship."[14] In the country's "moral order," free, white working men "embody republican citizenship," with Blacks' servitude and lassitude operating as their despised, excluded opposite. In between, there exists "a black–white continuum of status and dignity," Ong claims, "and the relative positioning of a (sub)ethnic group determines its perceived moral claim to certain areas of privilege and advantage." In the *New York Times*, journalist Roy Reed's account of Edwards's first gubernatorial victory presents the lineaments of such a repositioning along this continuum. Given their long relegation to second-class status, it would have been understandable if Cajuns were resentful, but instead of joining the ranks of "aggrieved minorities" they sustained their inimitable joie de vivre.[15] In Reed's telling, this "choice" explained Edwards's success: Rather than indulging in a politics of grievance, Cajuns mobilized to elect him.

The historical dimension of this shift in Cajuns' racial classification soon became more explicit. Because of their positive qualities—contrasted sharply with Blacks' negative ones—Cajuns deserved the reevaluation of the lowly status they were receiving. In the mid-1970s, Revon Reed, a journalist from the small town of Mamou, asserted defiantly,

> In these times, *when the distressed cry of minority groups is heard in every section of the nation*, it is appropriate . . . to concentrate on the way of life that we Cajuns have learned, following a distraught, persecuted, and often at times degraded life. Today, the Cajun culture that was born as a result of this exodus [i.e., the Great Deportation] *offers to America a cultural alternative to suburbia and to the big-city ghettoes*, because Cajun culture offers a lust for life [joie de vivre], full of vigor . . . that refuses to die. . . . Cajun philosophy tells us that it is better to live than to exist; better to sing, dance, and laugh than to swear, weep, and complain; and certainly better to love, maintain a peaceful demeanor, and have faith in one's neighbor than to spread hate, war, and fear.[16]

In contrast to the malicious distress emanating from Black neighborhoods, Reed insists that Cajuns had distilled their historical trauma into a life-affirming praxis that merited the country's respect. Prior to this moment, Cajun elites avoided featuring the Grand Dérangement in their histories. During commemorative events in 1955, they deliberately eschewed using "expulsion" to describe their ancestors' exit from Nova Scotia, referring to it instead as their "migration" to Louisiana.[17] Subsequently, however, advocates centered it as Reed does here, intensifying the comparison with Blacks and using it to heighten the civic significance of Cajuns' conviviality. This change suggests how transformative civil rights discourse was for Cajuns as white ethnics; in replacing liberalism's conventional focus on individual rights as a core political value, they embraced this "contagious idiom of group identity and group rights" and deployed it against Blacks, with collective suffering from the Grand Dérangement and its aftermath operating as an equivalent to the racism endured by African Americans.[18]

Since then, this trope often frames their representation in public discourse. Spokespersons increasingly foregrounded their moral standing as victims: in a high-profile legislative effort to render Cajuns eligible for affirmative action programs, because they "have suffered cultural discrimination and repressed [*sic*] in the exercise of language"; in disputes with Blacks over Cajuns' growing predominance in regional public culture, with advocates casting them as casualties of "reverse racism" and "political correctness"; and in public history proper, where the deportation increasingly became *the* day zero in the group's past, epitomized by a successful campaign to extract a public apology from the British crown for the colonial deportation.[19] In the wake of Hurricanes Katrina and Rita during the 2000s, both natives and outsiders renewed the interracial comparison that subtends this figure. A New Orleans journalist asserted that while Katrina's Black victims in New Orleans were stuck in "paralysis," Cajuns responded to Rita by doing "what their forebears had done for centuries before them: survive, adapt, and thrive in hostile environments."[20] In this context, Cajuns' moral qualities—fortitude, autonomy, solidarity—were expressly opposed to African Americans' laziness, dependency, and dysfunction in a zero-sum game with civic implications. Others claimed that these divergent responses to the hurricanes offered a lesson for government: They valued Cajuns' self-sufficient ethic, informed by their history of surviving deportation, as appropriate while discrediting Blacks' vulnerability as the product of their excessive reliance on the welfare state.[21]

Compared to the regressive narrative that formerly prevailed, such a history represented a dramatic discursive shift. While this project did not generate the most public forms of the new history, it catalyzed this narrative. Used to buttress Cajuns' claims for greater inclusion and "full" whiteness, the history linked to Cajun power simultaneously positioned them over and against Blacks, subtending the maintenance of whites' predominance. As such, the history of Cajuns as the happy minority developed as a sort of postsegregation racecraft.[22] Employed in efforts to reposition them in the body politic, Cajuns' past suffering often worked to obscure anti-Black racism and explain racial hierarchy by blaming Blacks' alleged deficiencies.

PURSUING CAJUN POWER II: UPWARDLY MOBILE BOOTSTRAPPING AND THE SOCIAL POLITICS OF DECORUM

Cajun power also comprised an ambitious vision of sociopolitical transformation. The project's proponents imagined remaking society by recasting the region's past, using it to build a future that included Cajuns' formerly disparaged differences. In a speech on the House floor in Washington, Congressman F. Edward Hébert cataloged the first half-dozen years of such efforts: Cajuns' vernacular now served as a resource serving the country's "dire need of language development . . . [for] national defense"; learning it would become part of "career education," given how multinational corporations' need for multilingual employees "is increasing in leaps and bounds"; the region's "unique cultural heritage" would transform it into "a tremendously . . . stimulating place to live and work"; and more.[23] In retrospect, this reads as a grandiose forecast. But its underlying logic—that the Cajun past had become relevant for meeting *contemporary* challenges—is integral to history's salience in the public sphere. As Carol Greenhouse contends, history as a discourse of social time is "wedded to the time-space formulas of states, nations, and citizenship."[24] Referring not only to the past but also to the present and future, historical narratives help explain the status quo as well as the nation's becoming, what citizens and the state should aspire to accomplish. Since Cajuns and their past had been irrelevant to its progress, the case had to be made that they were now germane to its future. The region's francophone and francophile elites waged just such a campaign; rearticulating the Cajun past often unfolded in this future-oriented way.

In terms of their small-*p* politics, however, these efforts foundered. As Hébert's vision intimates, building a bilingual society in Louisiana formed its nominal goal. But the means and motivations to do so escaped its leaders, for several reasons. In what was arguably a fundamental prerequisite, they never gained access to and control of the media necessary to create a francophone public sphere. Though they were aware of its importance from the start, mass media remained subject to market forces; without substantial subsidy, neither government officials nor entrepreneurs could crack the challenge of simultaneously creating and attracting audiences.[25] Secondly, in the consequential field of public education, where state agents did have the means to enact change, they succeeded in alienating the public for an extended moment. When he lauded French instruction in public schools, Hébert singled out CODOFIL's first chairman, Domengeaux, who was charged with overseeing that effort. By the end of the 1970s, however, Domengeaux and the agency were embroiled in controversy over which language schools taught. He adamantly defended his preference for standard French and insistently excoriated Cajun French as the equivalent of "redneck English" before the public backlash to this stance forced him to "Louisianify" the curriculum by teaching local vernaculars.[26] By the 1980s, many of the state's most francophone parishes dropped French instruction, and CODOFIL gained a popular reputation as elitist.[27] Consequently, these efforts did not prevent the long retreat of French from the public sphere. In its politics, the project's ambitious vision required a mass effort of motivation, of inducing citizens to join in; instead, the agency's initial policies disaffected many.

Another explanation for Cajun power's limits as a political project involves its elected sponsors' circumscribed concept of it. Some did not share Congressman Hébert's expansive concept; their efforts to promote Cajun agency and history were more muted. In a 1973 League of Women Voters' forum on revising the state's constitution, "the French" were accorded a position on the dais (which would be unthinkable now). Yet John Breaux, then a congressman representing the state's Seventh District and speaking on their behalf, immediately downplayed the need for distinct civil rights based on cultural or linguistic difference. "The subject for this panel discussion ['What does my particular group hope for from a new constitution?'] is almost undemocratic," he intoned. Reporting on a survey his office conducted among residents of French descent, Breaux claimed, "The message came through unmistakably that [they] want to be treated as any other group, and not set apart."[28] At this key moment, Breaux, Edwards, and their cohort of Cajun lawmakers rejected making Cajuns' inclusion a matter of law and policy.

Moreover, not all who identified as Cajun believed that history and heritage furnished a path to the power they sought. When, in the late 1970s, cable network CNN produced a celebratory profile of Louisiana's many folk cultures and their histories, Governor Edwards became furious. After the feature's screening at the Governor's Mansion in Baton Rouge, Edwards approached the person he thought responsible and demanded, "Why did you do that? . . . You made a film about Louisiana, and you didn't show all the bridges and roads we've built. You didn't show the hospitals and the schools we've built. You didn't show one thing that had to do with our progress as a state, out of all this. All you showed was all *that*." As this civil servant explained, Edwards shared a widely held view that Cajun culture and history were so retrograde that they "would embarrass people." Like Breaux, Edwards thought in conventional political terms about what Cajun power should be used for. While committed to expanding opportunities through infrastructure and social services, he was ambivalent about furthering white ethnic agency per se. Later, other politicians did play a decisive role in some Cajun public history projects at critical junctures. Yet as CODOFIL's early antivernacular stance intimates, Cajun political leaders modulated reforms that would have boosted the civic inclusion of Cajun difference as such.[29]

One could also cast Cajun power less as a movement driven by electoral politics (though that was part of it) and more as a social one, though not in the conventional sense of that term. In statements from those buoyed by the state's postwar economic boom, one sentiment that comes through in spades was that of being fed up with their inferior status.[30] Edwards himself surmised that for his white ethnic supporters, the significance of his victory lay in how they appreciated that "he [Edwards] has proved that a Cajun is as good as anybody else."[31] Upset when his superiors complained about "cheap crooked coonasses" (on this term as a synonym for "Cajun," more shortly), an oil company engineer objected to the slur and was fired; he successfully sued for discrimination, asserting that he sought "to protect what they consider inferior second-class citizens."[32] All these were interventions in everyday dynamics of power, focused on claims for respect as well as on access to previously unobtainable opportunities. Thus, along the lines that Edwards and Breaux made explicit, Cajun power can also be seen as a social movement in the sense of a "campaign for material success, social respect, and . . . 'whiteness.'"[33] For them, the goal was Cajuns' inclusion as acceptable participants in white spheres of politics, business, and civil society.

Part of this "bootstrapping" project—and noting its raced, middle-class, and upwardly mobile location is crucial—involved rearticulating Cajun identity in historical terms. Chapter 1 clarified why this would be so: As part of insisting on their reform, authorities had identified Cajuns' historicity, their relationship to time, as malign. A pent-up desire to reject that discourse and rearticulate a positive identity *in historical terms* bursts from pages written at that moment. "How many people can grow up experiencing a cultural legacy of three nations flowing through their consciousness?" asked Myron Tassin, referring to centuries of Acadian history stretching back to France. "We can," he replied, "and it's exhilarating! . . . *Vive la difference!*"[34] In *Lâche pas la patate*, Revon Reed cast the Cajun past as "a history of cultural struggle, of relentless though never desperate combat, by an ethnic group to preserve its identity in the larger context of American society."[35] Such statements are suffused with an adamant affirmation of dignity, whose inspiration is best seen against the backdrop of decades of historical negation. Some experienced that dismissal viscerally; their rejoinders were correspondingly impassioned.

As a bootstrapping social movement, however, the project remained class specific, limited by tensions in a fractious social landscape. Significantly, the stigma linked to Cajuns' behavior did not disappear; in spats over the label "coonass," middle-class Cajuns rebuked its largely working-class users in an ongoing struggle keyed to a politics of respectability. As mentioned before, *coonass* circulates as an analog to "redneck" or "white trash," a contested, complex term that indexes "multiple axes of social relations"[36]—race, class, rurality, and francophone ancestry, among others—and operates as one of many name-calling traditions in Louisiana. CODOFIL's Domengeaux began an enduring practice of threatening litigation against those who used the term publicly, including natives who employed it among themselves as a term of endearment. Evoking a moral register of dignity and respect, his successors continue to condemn their use of it, insisting it "erode[s]" their "pride and morale" and "drag[s] the culture down" into disgrace.[37] Middle-class and affluent Acadians thus fortified the boundary between themselves and the region's working-class residents, retracing a border long drawn through concerns with the latter's ill-mannered conduct.

In this conflict, positions pro and con generated divergent politics of remembrance. By the 1990s, when many sites in the new Cajun historical complex had opened, working-class Cajuns were nonplussed by its narratives. To them, the distant Acadian past seemed like "an ethereal trace," something that was "supposed to be memorable, but was not."[38] Instead, the past that *coonass* evoked, both recent and more remote—folk traditions, family, and even the denigrated aspects of living close to the land and "com[ing] up the hard way"—merited remembrance.[39] The new public history, associated with professionals' enabling of the commodification of Cajun culture, did not.[40] Meanwhile, by this moment, some Cajun professionals reversed course from Edwards's earlier ambivalence about historical discourse. For those like attorney Warren Perrin, who founded a Cajun historic site in his hometown of Erath, *coonass*'s public use threatened to undermine its positive effects. A veteran anti-*coonass* campaigner, he contended the label's use endangered the "little victories" in "the war of pride" over the "shame we had been under so long."[41] For Perrin, achievements like CODOFIL's efforts merited commemoration, which *coonass* weakened by "show[ing] a total lack of respect for so many people [who] fought . . . to bring us up by the bootstraps."[42] Thus, with respect to opinions as to what merited remembrance, the tendencies were centrifugal. In practice, one of Cajun power's abiding thrusts has been this social politics of boundary maintenance and respectability.

GUIDING THE NATION WITH HISTORICAL KNOWLEDGE: LIVING IN THE TRUTH OF THE CAJUN PAST

Another dimension of the new Acadian history's emergence involves professional public historians becoming advocates for it. But the conjunction of their uses of history with those linked to these shifts in Cajuns' civil and social status did not unfold seamlessly. As noted, ethnic politicians like Governor Edwards did not prioritize elaborating a Cajun public history as part of their agenda. Appearing before a congressional subcommittee considering a national park in the state, Edwards said nothing about Cajun history's significance; his sole historical reference was to Indigenous peoples.[43] Yet when Congress later authorized that venue, Jean Lafitte National Historical Park, the legislation featured Cajuns. The park now contains a unit with three sites devoted to their history. How did this happen?

From one angle, this irony is unsurprising. Until the 1970s, state agencies like the Office of State Parks (OSP) did not systematically theorize how Louisiana's own history could be used as a tool for governing its citizens. By contrast, OSP administrators advanced nuanced rationales as to why residents needed access to nature and outdoor recreation and how these would improve their lives. In the 1940s, OSP officials contended that since citizens needed "to regain freedom . . . [and] escape from oppression and artificiality," in parks they could "[seek] and [find] a sane readjustment in Nature." By the 1960s, their argument was that, given declines in family cohesion and increases in juvenile delinquency, OSP's recreational programs provided "an outlet for excess energy" and fostered the sense of "fair play and competition . . . necessary to a well-rounded character."[44] These same reports articulated no parallel conceptualization of history's civic purpose, even though OSP was founded in part to manage the first state-run historic site, St. Martinville's Longfellow-Evangeline State Park.[45] Theorizing historical narratives' civic utility, operationalizing them in policy, materializing them in sites according to plans: In Louisiana, such a regime emerged fitfully and unevenly.

As it happened, the push to represent the Cajun past in historic sites arose as part of a considerable expansion in the state's deployment of history to govern citizens. However, this development arguably starts in Washington, where using the past to govern did have elaborate rationales. But federal authorities adopted Cajun history as their focus by accident, as the antidote to a proposal they judged too noxious for public consumption. In the late 1960s, a push to site a national park in Louisiana coalesced in New Orleans, centered on preserving a swath of marsh near the city. Though focused on its natural significance, the park's Louisiana proponents used the "colorful legend of [Jean] Lafitte the Pirate" loosely as a historical theme for their proposal.[46] National Park Service (NPS) officials determined the area did not meet criteria for inclusion as a natural site but counterproposed that the state's cultural history did qualify as nationally significant. Yet they also found the Lafitte idea repellant; the prospect of naming a park after a notorious pirate and slave trader offended them. In memos, staff dismissed "the Lafitte thing" as "pretty marginal," wondering "just what the hell to do about the proposal" and averring that they would "hate to see the Service have to base a park" on it.[47] Serving on a task force for NPS's Advisory Board, historian Joe Frantz spurned it, claiming that if the NPS honored Lafitte, "we must set aside parks for Bonnie and Clyde, Dillinger, and Billy the Kid."[48]

In a last-ditch effort to subvert the Lafitte theme, NPS administrators endorsed Frantz's halfhearted suggestion that Cajuns could serve as the core element for structuring the national park. Surprisingly, it stuck.[49] The site's enabling legislation kept Lafitte's name but stipulated that the park "portray the development of cultural diversity in the region" and specified inclusion of "Acadian towns and villages."[50] NPS insiders found its feasibility study for the park to be uncharacteristically "cursory" and criticized its analysis—which did not foreground Cajuns.[51] Apparently, Cajun history and culture were a hastily devised, anti-Lafitte placeholder, a "creative reaction" (NPS staff's term for their countermoves against proposals they disliked) by determined professionals in an antagonistic struggle.[52]

Jean Lafitte's launch evolved as part of an expansion of NPS historic sites, an intentional effort to enlarge national history beyond its conventional foci on elites and patriotic commemoration.[53] Social movements across the country—the civil rights movement, second-wave feminism, and other struggles—drove such change in many domains, including professional corners of the public historical sphere.[54] Still, one can ask a more fundamental question about this increase: Why did the public need so much more history? What values were fostered by imparting so much historical knowledge to citizens? A dominant faction of public historians at this moment eschewed thinking in terms of history's significance for citizens. They employed "public" as "a synonym for a generalized and somewhat passive 'audience'" and focused on research "products" rather than people and civic effects. Similarly, many academic historians mistrusted the rise of public history into a distinct subfield, worrying about its practitioners' objectivity and frowning on their involvement in policy matters.[55]

Yet these were not the only actors using history in the public sphere, and taking their stances as the best frame for answering such questions neglects a key thrust in history-making. Considering it more broadly, history had long been embedded in political discourse, public education, civic representations like memorials and monuments, and other vulgarizing efforts.[56] Along these lines, one might say that since the first half of the twentieth century, an influential group of practitioners advanced using history to foster a truth-speaking subject, a citizen who lives by the wisdom that history incites them to discover. Through their efforts, history operates as a pragmatic idiom of citizen-making.

An illustration of this minor tradition of public history lies in the consequential impact of Freeman Tilden, the sage of historical interpretation who widely influenced practice, not least at the NPS.[57] Tilden advocated an engaged approach to interpreting the past with and for the public. In an illustrative example of his method, Tilden wrote an essay for the NPS during the American Bicentennial entitled *Who Am I?* Describing the present as a moment of profound crises (e.g., a "tendency toward violence and abnormality"), he suggested that contact with history could help address them. Through vignettes in which he imagined visitors reflecting at specific historic sites, he posited how this might occur. Of visitors to Independence Hall, he asserted, "From history we learn who and what we are, as individuals and as a nation. Not only at Independence Hall, but in all the National Park System's historical preserves, *the thinking visitor is revealed to himself*. He asks himself the questions: 'What would *I* have done, under these circumstances? How would *I* have measured up to need and opportunity?' The . . . school children who come to see and reverently to touch The Bell go home with *that something* which the schoolroom and the book cannot impart."[58] For Tilden and his many disciples, this describes a fundamental aspiration for historic sites: to shape individuals' thoughts *and actions* such that they align with democratic principles of self-governance and problem-solving. The aim is to effect this through consent; in theory, the historic site does not indoctrinate. But it does seek to provoke profound subjective change: "The thoughtful visitor . . . places himself back in those days. . . . Would I have been happy in that simple life? . . . [Asking] questions like that. Finding one's self. Answering the question: 'Who am I?'"[59] Far from a passive subject, Tilden's imagined citizen-visitor is called to question and work on the self, discerning history's meaning and applying it to their life. In this way, practitioners proposed "[inflecting] . . . the subject towards its own truth" by "putting oneself in [historical] discourse."[60]

Tilden's vision of using history to govern citizens can readily be discerned in Louisiana contexts. In the prologue to a feasibility study for the Jean Lafitte Park, NPS staff invented an inner monologue for an imagined New Orleanian, conducting just such a truth-seeking inquiry. It begins, "Why aren't there any national parks here—here where all these people come?"[61] As the reflection unfolds, the resident considers various moments in the state's past, parsing out their meaning. The rumination culminates in the proposal that "we ought to have . . . something to . . . sort of make everything into a story for all the people to hear so they could know about it and take part in it."[62] By projecting the study's findings into the mouth of an imaginary local, the authors staged the Tildenesque practice—an individual questioning the historical record and discerning its importance—that they encouraged the public to emulate.[63] In summary form, the fictional monologue also encapsulated the protocols NPS staff themselves followed, evaluating the state's history against criteria for national significance and drawing conclusions about its lessons for the country.

At one of Jean Lafitte's Acadian Unit sites, a documentary film offers another example of this stress on subjective transformation through engagement with history's truths. *The Cajun Way: Echoes of Acadia* models such contemplation in the first person, as a male voice-over considers Cajun history from late medieval France to the present. During the thirty-seven-minute film, this voice of a contemporary Cajun alternates with a wispy feminine one, a personification of the colonial Acadian past itself ("I am Acadie. . . . Remember the paradise of hope and happiness"). Strikingly, the production performs a reckoning of the past's significance (e.g., identifying "dreams of liberty and liberation" as the motivation for Cajuns' immigration to the New World) as well as the Cajun subject's appropriation of its lessons (the male voice recites, "I know this story. I am Cadien. . . . Our traditions continue"). Throughout, the film illustrates a motivated subject discerning important historical truths, verities like the yearning for freedom consequential for self and nation. And it depicts history as personally empowering, inviting Cajun viewers to embrace a past presented as vital (the female voice whispers, "I am with you forever in your heart").[64]

Such uptake of Tilden's method implemented a pragmatics for using historical knowledge as a means of citizen formation. It bears emphasizing that this approach goes beyond the passive reception of facts. Instead, practitioners of this minor tradition sought to "[inculcate] . . . particular kinds of relations that the human being has with itself."[65] In this vision of how history could govern Cajuns and other citizens, their engagement with the past would consist of aligning their lives with the "greater truths" that it revealed.[66]

ELIMINATING CAJUNS' HISTORICAL IGNORANCE: PUBLIC HISTORY AND THE RISE OF EXPERT AUTHORITY

Yet another permutation of historical expertise inflected the emergence of the new Acadian history, a shift that overlapped with Tilden's vision yet targeted distinct social and political concerns. In Louisiana, the state's history increasingly became a matter for professionals, whose rise reconfigured discourse and its material anchors.

In the late 1950s, a reorientation of the academic history space began to unfold as professionals focused more intently on Louisiana history. Wresting control of the Louisiana Historical Association (LHA) from its Confederate-focused sponsors, a group of professionals reorganized it, calling for "more intensive study of state and local history" and "the development of groups interested in all aspects of Louisiana's cultural heritage."[67] Its initial thrust was inclusive and heterogeneous. In addition to items of the association's business, its early newsletters listed announcements from other historical organizations, including museums, genealogical societies, and plantation homes; mentioned historical anniversaries, public commemorations, and exhibit openings; and referenced recent newspaper articles and op-ed pieces about the state's past. When, after a lapse, the LHA relaunched the newsletter in 1975, its format changed considerably. Rubrics organized the news items, with the headings "Affairs of the Association" and "Colleges and Universities" containing the most entries. While "Miscellany" and "Allied Organizations" sections existed, they contained much less coverage of popular interests and more items related to those of experts. As LHA members' interest in Louisiana history grew, they reshaped the character of what they reported to themselves as news about it, with an emergent skew toward academic concerns.[68]

The relations of power involved in such a development can be grasped in the trajectory of another organization, the Attakapas Historical Association (AHA). To be sure, these were not exclusively hierarchical. Amateurs from several parish seats in the region (including St. Martinville) launched it, and the AHA grew into a large membership organization in which nonexperts and professionals collaborated. At its inauguration in 1966, members established thematic foci that crosscut these groups' interests, such as those centered on marking significant local historical sites and on collecting artifacts and memorabilia. At a molecular level, however, asymmetries soon emerged. At its first meeting, a credentialed historian "impress[ed] upon the members with [*sic*] the necessity of authenticating and recording their research," since it was only historical work "substantiated with factual sources" that constituted "valuable material."[69] In his first appearance before the group, Glenn Conrad, the new archivist at the University of Southwestern Louisiana (USL, now the University of Louisiana at Lafayette), claimed, "Most of Louisiana history as written today has been romanticized to such an extent it is not historically accurate," a situation that, he assured them, professionals like himself were laboring to rectify.[70] Later, Conrad convinced the organization to sponsor a grant for graduate students at USL, telling its board that the university was "*the center* for the study of Louisiana history" (emphasis added), with faculty members capable of training students in authoritative methods.[71]

This collaboration had clear effects on the association's trajectory. By the end of its first decade, its functioning shifted as the emphasis on expertise and its accompanying technologies transformed it. Academics assumed the association's officer positions, and its publications committee was integrated into the operations of USL's nascent Center for Louisiana Studies. Other changes were granular but no less impactful, reshaping norms over who could participate in historical speech.[72] "No untyped manuscripts will be accepted," decided the AHA Publications Committee members in 1976, and "only individuals with some experience in publishing should be qualified to serve on the Committee." Another new policy required authors to pay 30 percent of publication costs.[73] This privileging of expertise proceeded as matters of common sense and expediency, inflected by the exigencies of a public institution. Incrementally, however, such measures reconfigured historical discourse in the region. By the end of the 1970s, the AHA's lay membership atrophied, and the organization later went dormant. As history-making became a technical, highly literate practice, those with certain skills and resources claimed the role of its main practitioners and ultimate arbiters.

From another perspective, this project was far from apolitical, as it involved a conscious strategy of pushback against adversaries. And a material intervention—an archival collection—served as its point of leverage. Under Conrad's leadership, USL embarked on an ambitious project to gather all French and Spanish colonial records pertaining to Louisiana in its archives.[74]

Before that initiative materialized, however, Conrad was claiming it would "*reveal . . . the authentic* history of Louisiana" (emphasis added).[75] He highlighted the impact these documents would have on Acadian history, asserting they would correct widespread "myths and inaccuracies" whereby Cajuns were depicted as either "superstitious swamp-dweller[s] living in squalor" or "creature[s] of simple but solid virtue who . . . [inhabit] a timeless . . . land."[76] As culprits, Conrad identified journalists and scholars from outside the region, who were "haphazard" and "shallow" in their research.[77] He also blamed local elites like the St. Martinvillers who maintained Evangeline-based history, built as it was on commercial "publicity" and fabricated "mystique."[78] In such polemics, Conrad invoked the archives as a kind of center of calculation or interpretation.[79] With so many traces of the past gathered in a single space, he and others could combine them into novel, document-rich interpretations of Acadian history, making the archives an "obligatory passage point" for new narratives and for all who might claim to know history's truths.[80] As Conrad's prose indicated, the resulting modification in power dynamics involved not only epistemological but also ethical stakes. His knowledge was more authentic and sincere than theirs, "a sign . . . of authority [and] of a certain right to speak."[81]

A warrant subsequently emerged for disseminating this new history across the population and making it vital. In addition to the Longfellow-Evangeline site, circumscribed attempts to do so had occurred,[82] but now efforts intensified, like a state curriculum guide seeking to instill in students "a deep appreciation of the tremendous impact made by these remarkable [Acadian] people on [Louisiana] history."[83] The novel charge that citizens know the *Acadian* past piggybacked on that offered for national history, that historical ignorance threatened civic well-being, for example, by eroding public commitment to democracy itself. For his part, Conrad again justified it polemically. Writing in 1991, he expressed concern about a popular historical narrative, according to which wealthy Creole and American planters displaced Acadians from prime riverine real estate in antebellum Louisiana, leading to a second *dérangement* that remarginalized them.[84] His analysis of property deeds led him to conclude that the narrative was false, but Conrad went further. He offered a theory about why this deceptive history gained popularity and suggested that something be done about it:

> The picture projected by many writers of Acadian history between the 1950s and 1980s is . . . largely based upon what

> "grandma" related. . . . But popular oral tradition disregarded the complex factors contributing to the ruination of the agricultural economy and substituted instead simplistic reasons that . . . were constructed around words like "carpetbagger" and "greedy neighbors." . . . Unfortunately, . . . the vision of the writers did not sufficiently penetrate the fog of ethnic or racial pride to permit perception of the real causes for the long degradation of a people. Only through careful examination of the extensive documentation available and only after trained critical analysis can historians and other writers hope to produce what has so long been wanting in the literature of Louisiana, a social history of our state.[85]

Stoked by the "exclusive ethnic focus" of CODOFIL's programs, Conrad added, this problematic pride fostered a "tendency [among Cajuns] in local society to speak of 'them' and 'us,' rather than 'we.'" To spare the body politic from grandma's falsehoods and this disruptive conceit, "literate Louisiana" needed the authoritative skills—"careful examination" and "critical analysis"—that trained academics could provide. In this formulation, Conrad foregrounds relations of knowledge and power in public history: Cajun ignorance licensed the professional expertise needed to correct it. Like the federal actors described previously, he anchored this project in diagnoses of particular social problems, seeking to "act on the social" and reform regional dynamics of citizenship.[86]

Carl Brasseaux, the historian whose criticism of St. Martinville's Evangeline-based history discredited it (see chapter 2), articulated the situation differently but no less agonistically. In his characterization, the politics were more complex and the means of tackling the issue more technical. In a 1992 grant proposal for the Acadian Memorial, Brasseaux cast the problem the site sought to address as two centuries of "fanciful speculation" by "history buffs," producing histories with "absolutely no factual basis." While scholarship since the 1970s had corrected this, "the reluctance of Louisianians to acquire and read about new historical findings . . . , the continuing use of . . . inaccurate . . . textbooks, the strong popular devotion to . . . inaccurate historical traditions, and Louisiana's perennially low levels of literacy" undermined the circulation of that "accurate, factual account."[87] As Conrad did, Brasseaux situates the intervention in a troubled social landscape. Far from being amorphous, specific agents produce historical ignorance: unskilled amateurs, flawed textbooks, indolent readers. Yet he and his allies were also actors, strategizing about how to manifest a proper historical consciousness. Brasseaux wrote that the memorial would offer an engaging exhibit to attract the public's attention, conveying the new knowledge where books and classroom instruction had failed to do so.[88]

In the next two chapters, I will explore the memorial and the goals that others brought to its realization. But well before its creation, this long turn toward expertise altered the regional landscape of historical speech, laying the groundwork for such an intervention. Never before had authorities diagnosed ignorance of Acadian history as a challenge for the body politic, nor had academics proposed diffusing their research as a remedy for it. These historians cast their use of history as a complicated *political* act: It was interpellated by social problems, shaped by expert knowledge targeting adversaries, and aimed at civic transformation.

HEALING THE NATION THROUGH CAJUN COMMUNITY: THE HAPPY MINORITY AS WHITE ETHNIC IDEAL

As chapter 1 illustrated, liberal policy through the 1960s targeted the eradication of racial and ethnic differences, seeking to dissolve individuals' parochial commitments and move them into a uniform citizenship in which everyone pledged allegiance to the nation-state alone. In the public historical sphere, the melting-pot narrative served as its corollary, remaining prominent into the 1970s.[89] At this moment, however, a rupture occurred in which actors in federal institutions proposed new approaches to race and ethnicity, envisioning them as surfaces for possible interventions. This reconceptualization of the nation and its governance proved decisive for the emergence of the new public history of Cajuns.

A key development involved prominent voices analyzing sociopolitical problems in unique ways, using new conceptualizations of racial and ethnic communities and imagining unprecedented approaches for governing them. Alan Lomax, the ethnomusicologist who influenced cultural heritage policies, was one such voice.[90] Referencing recent unrest in testimony before the Senate in 1970, he asserted the political stakes were alarmingly high:

> If we don't solve the [tension in our national life], we're going to have breaking out everywhere now in America the kind of bitterness that the black community feels. [They are] an example

> of a community that has been not reflected, that has . . . been denied an avenue of expression. A black child sitting in a school now sees and feels how foreign his teacher is to him, because she's teaching him Western European culture and in a Western European style. Which says to him: "Those things of your parents are worthless." . . . Now, this is what we're saying to this whole great nation of national subcultures . . . through our system of education and communication.[91]

Such a characterization introduced a crucial shift in approaches to social governance, insofar as it defined ethnoracial groups as entities whose integrity needed to be respected rather than reformed. In positing that institutional practices violated their psychosocial needs, Lomax recast them as populations with internal dynamics the state should recognize and foster, not smother. Though implicit in his statement, the solution was manifest in the hearing's purpose (which Lomax supported): to fund folklife programming providing these groups with "avenues of expression."

Lomax's proposed remedy evokes Toby Miller and George Yúdice's claim that through organizations like the National Endowment for the Arts (NEA), which later received funding for such projects, the federal government "used subsidies for cultural activism to channel the expression of opposition."[92] Appointed to lead the cultural organizations that the NEA sponsored, Black activists, for instance, were drawn into responsibilities that undermined their ability to participate in protests and change efforts. As mentioned, some Louisiana politicians shared a version of this vision, seeking to deploy Cajun culture to inflect political participation such that it reinforced racial divisions. The claim that elites pursued a hegemonic project through cultural policy is compelling, as far as it goes. As this chapter illustrates, diffusing a history of Cajuns as the happy minority was, as an emancipatory project, circumscribed. It operated in polyvalent ways, used to divide and rank as much as to promote and empower.

Still, positing a rigid equation of cultural policy initiatives with reactionary political outcomes misses key dimensions of how these professionals conceptualized their efforts' civic politics. As Matthew Jacobson claims about the white ethnic revival generally, a "powerful current of antimodernism" drove it, which theorized that "mass production and consumption, mass media, commodification, bureaucratization, and suburbanization" operated as "bloodless, homogenizing forces" that were destroying the country.[93] In professional circles, such views peppered many of the era's public historical analyses and innovations, including those from practitioners on the center-left. "One of our great problems in this country is that we don't know who we are," opined George Hartzog, the National Park Service's director during the 1960s and '70s. He believed that the country's rising social mobility damaged individuals' sense of historical continuity, leading to their loss of "roots." "We are isolated in these concrete jungles," he complained, and "don't even know who our grandparents are." As one solution, Hartzog experimented with living history reenactments, whose purpose was "to make that program come alive for [young people] so that they felt that they were part of a continuum."[94] Hartzog and others sensed that existing techniques were ineffective, both due to their lackluster design and because they ignored the past that people most needed to know (e.g., that of their grandparents). They understood themselves to be countering anomie by initiating a pluralizing thrust in public history.

In the adjacent folk arts space, Lomax penned a plea for a presidential commission in which he sketched similar remedies for a bleak status quo. Focused on "the hard-hat and rural lower-middle-class folks" whom the "melting-pot policy" had "over-nationalized," Lomax insisted that they felt "inferior, anxious, cynical, and angry." In a country of disdainful elites who controlled mass media, they "lack[ed] the means and opportunities . . . to get a hearing [and] show what [they] have to offer" and so felt "cheated" out of their "birth-right" of free speech. Like Hartzog, Lomax yoked his diagnoses to a concrete plan for addressing the problem, outlining an agenda that ranged from media and educational initiatives tailored to these groups' needs to cultural-sensitivity training for mental health professionals. He claimed that, if pursued, such initiatives would "make our ethnicities . . . self-aware and self-proud, develop[ing] a self-consciously multi-directional national culture."[95]

From this perspective, the problems and methods these practitioners identified exceeded a focus on circumscribing the leisure that enabled protest. Instead, questioning postwar governance's assimilationist paradigm, they reconceptualized the nation's population and proposed interventions catering to its ethnoracial diversity. Nor did this constitute a wholesale break into neoliberalism; they maintained, for instance, a commitment to state intervention as opposed to its retrenchment. But their antimodernist sensibilities did lead them to imagine supporting ethnoracial groups with projects that would cure the ills modernism inflicted on them. Rather than reactionary or neoliberal, this is more accurately described as participating in experiments to govern through "third spaces."[96]

Others implemented this vision through initiatives that, like that of Tilden, sought to induce changes in citizens' subjectivity. Bess Lomax Hawes, Alan Lomax's sister and the inaugural director of the National Endowment for the Arts' Folklife Program, used the term "inreach" to describe one of the main strategies her fledging unit employed.[97] Following Immanuel Kant's influential claim that aesthetics are a distinct dimension of experience and judgment and thus a potential tool for enlightenment, bureaucrats and curators of public exhibition and performance have sought to define canons of important works of art as stimuli for refining the population's sense of the beautiful and the good. Applying this method to folk art, Hawes theorized that if a folk genre's finest artists performed in settings where audiences could appreciate their excellence, their art would have ennobling effects. Alongside curated interpretations of it, folk music would "reach in" to ethnoracial hearts and minds, offsetting their sense of inferiority and inciting them to believe that they, too, were capable of beauty and goodness. Thus, another innovation was that instead of aiming to homogenize citizens' subjectivity, such efforts enabled ethnoracial selves. In a profound break with the past, they were designed to induce racial and ethnic identification, encouraging citizens to inhabit their selfhood as ethnoracial subjects.

Practitioners like Hawes and NPS staff pursued this vision in Louisiana. Similar to how the former reconceptualized approaches to shaping subjectivity, the latter reimagined relationships between the state's ethnoracial groups, designing its interventions such that these might be deployed to renew national belonging. As they framed Jean Lafitte National Historical Park's interpretative thrust, NPS staff and contractors viewed south Louisiana as a distinct regional society with internal dynamics whose positive aspects needed to be incorporated into the park's representations.[98] In an ethnographic survey that helped set the park's interpretive parameters, a team of academics described this as a "tradition of ethnic co-existence and co-mingling," a striking "unity in diversity."[99] Where assimilationist policies had cast such situations as problems of unmelted holdouts in need of Americanization, the park's mandate instead called for supporting these relationships and representing the social concord they engendered.[100]

According to this vision, the park would deploy these beneficial and "naturally occurring" sociocultural dynamics by re-presenting them and their history to the public in exhibits and performances. In so many words, they proposed staging the region's harmonious social life, transforming it into a force that would teach locals and the rest of the nation a lesson in solidarity. And in the folklorists' analysis, Cajuns were the straw that stirred this drink. To clinch their "unity in diversity" argument, they offered an informant's story about a Cajun Santa Claus at a petroleum company's Christmas celebration. In his performance, Santa defined *Cajun* for his audience of nonnatives as "a mixture of all races, white, black, and red, and *only in Louisiana can you find such harmony and peace because we are all related by blood*" (emphasis added). Bracketing that many contested such a claim, these researchers contended that this typified regional natives' "acceptance of local pluralism and creolizing mixtures" and situated Cajuns as the white ethnic hosts of this robust interracial bonhomie.[101]

By creating a French-inflected regional society infused with a live-and-let-live ethos, these academics argued, south Louisianans had long practiced congeniality in heterogeneous circumstances. In a strife-torn nation, this constructive history of interracial harmony comprised a resource for "find[ing] instructive analogs in other culture patterns that bear on our search for quality life,"[102] the Tildenesque truth that citizens should be invited to contemplate. Alongside these other initiatives, this involved a radical shift that instigated a "regionalization of the social" and its governance.[103] It reimagined the nation as "a set of relations between regionally defined communities" that were meant to remain distinct and "be set in motion in new directions."[104] Along these lines, it proposed something else that had not previously existed: using Cajuns and their history as a positive force, agents who, materialized and mobilized in the park's representations, would help refurbish the nation's civic order.

CONCLUSION

This chapter described five distinct projects, visions for transforming and governing society, and how the history of Cajuns as the happy minority emerged from their intersections. Some of these involved the usual suspects in analyses of power—coalitions formed through electoral politics, class-based initiatives of social mobility, and efforts to preserve white dominance in the wake of civil rights reforms. But by including the efforts of a growing sphere of public historical professionals to deploy history toward citizen-making ends, I also incorporated a novel dimension into the small-*p* political analysis of this field.

This emergence implicated new, multifaceted relations of power, suggesting political dynamics that exceed conventional ways of narrating it. From Trépanier to Melançon, the story has been that the new public history emerged by and for Cajuns: The history-abetted renewal of white ethnicity in the post–civil rights era was primarily an autonomous, self-directed project. As I will explore in the next two chapters, Cajuns who promoted the need for an increased historical awareness of the Acadian past, as well as those who embraced the resulting narratives, were indeed crucial in the elaboration of the new complex. But they were far from the sole actors, and focusing on them alone obscures crucial dimensions of public history's civic politics.

An intersecting set of problematizations about the sociopolitical moment and its challenges served as a key piece of the politics that brought these varied actors into alignment. And one common feature of these problematizations was the emergent affirmation that ethnoracial differences mattered in policy and the public sphere. To be sure, such a focus was not new in electoral politics; as Jim Crow segued into its difficult aftermath, race remained prevalent as before. But in making Cajun ethnicity a factor in Louisiana's statewide elections and cultural policymaking, the political class animated a difference that was not previously salient in those spheres, opening a space for the interests of politicians, boosters, and activists to overlap with those of academics, bureaucrats, and public history practitioners. In both philosophical and practical terms, this constituted a biopolitical sea change in conceptualizing governance. Where before the weight of practice worked to diminish Cajun ethnicity and other ethnoracial modes of belonging, now a bounded realm emerged in which actors both acknowledged these differences and saw them as groups in need of support.

Thus, even if, in seeking to activate Cajun ethnicity, the aims of National Park Service officials did not fully align with those of politicians like McKeithen and Edwards, they shared a basic premise that fostered their collaboration. Cajuns' white ethnicity became a positive form of difference, a social surface on which, from various angles, the state could act. This new biopolitics—that of governing through communities—boosted the civic profile of ethnicity and race. In fields like public history and folklore, it became common to theorize relations of power from a starting point that assumed the body politic's differentiation into ethnoracial groups, and from there to imagine policies that promoted and served them. As Jacobson argues, institutionalized shifts of this kind "had vast implications . . . for the nation itself and for reigning notions of 'Americanness.'"[105] He contends that discursively, this development reinforced the predominance of whiteness and the "nation of immigrants" narrative. By stressing that the smooth integration of successive waves of European émigrés epitomized the country's past—a history that the happy minority narrative ratified—such accounts marginalized the centrality of colonization and enslavement to American nation-building. But those policy shifts also ramified into civic relations of power. Through the programmatic innovations and initiatives described in this chapter, a novel approach to *governing* citizens *as ethnic subjects* took shape.

Concerning Cajuns and their history specifically, another element predominated across these problematizations: While affirmed as crucial, knowledge and awareness of the Cajun past by all accounts barely existed. In surveying the landscape and the population, these different actors agreed that it was fictitious, flawed, absent, or fading fast. In addition to Conrad's take on Cajuns' defective historical memories, other academics claimed existing accounts of the Cajun past were "mainly of an antiquarian nature"; of the century prior to the Civil War, wrote historians Judith Gentry and John Cameron, "little is known" and despite recent efforts "the surface has only been scratched."[106] Meanwhile, practitioners agreed that the sociocultural conditions needed to support residents' awareness of the region's distinct past were dissolving. The "fabric of the whole"—the built landscape and material artifacts that sustained the state's "renowned heritage"—was "unraveling" or "in imminent danger of disappearing."[107] Because history did not signify enough to register—since "all of the [material] elements . . . [do not] interact to form an experience" of the region's past—experts deemed it necessary to create "nodes," gathering texts, images, objects, and multiple sites into assemblages that would "provide full perception" of it.[108] A similar status quo reigned in the adjacent space of folk heritage. Since forces like mass media "tended to overwhelm regional and ethnic cultures," and "there are few contemporary sources to which [the public] can turn for information" about them, folklorist Barry Ancelet conceptualized the Center for Acadian and Creole Folklore as a mechanism to "reimplant" folkways into the region, through spectacles that "recycled" the region's folklore to its natives.[109] These varied characterizations by authorities shared this premise: An accurate, substantive awareness of their past did not manifest among Cajuns themselves. It needed to be enabled, produced.

Produce it they did—or at least they sought to. Since historical awareness and the civic benefits it might engender were latent, its proponents began to imagine the infrastructure necessary to materialize them. NPS staff deemed the creation of an institutional network of professionals and laypeople (representing different sectors of society) an essential first step necessary to "bring those interests together and to unite their efforts," to "ensure enlightened public participation," to "provide coordinating direction" of the ensemble, and "to ensure quality of operations" through "adherence to standards and criteria" of interpretation.[110] All this preceded the elaborate process of designing sites and exhibits themselves, though the ultimate aim of reshaping subjectivity through history was present from the start. Paraphrasing Margaret Werry's formulation about tourism, in these schemes state policy aspired to performativity. It sought to create "microenvironments" in which history and heritage would emerge and "feedback loops" where, in the interactions between professionals and lay participants that would unfold there, the past might become an animating force in people's lives.[111]

Chapter Six

Knowing Their History for the First Time

Translation and the Civic Politics of Making the Acadian Memorial

> Cultural policy is a statement of intent, gesturing always toward new sets of relations, identifications, faculties, and forms of value and citizenship that it struggles to bring into being.
>
> Margaret Werry, *The Tourist State*

The conference hotel sat just inside the levee in downtown New Orleans, linked to a riverboat casino docked across from it in the Mississippi. Though only late April, the air-conditioning blasted as the day's humid heat intimated the direction weather would take during the coming weeks. In chilly ballrooms with names like Atchafalaya and Bienville, an annual museum conference hosted several breakout sessions featuring representatives of public and nonprofit agencies. Presenters offered endorsements of academics as potential collaborators to participants contemplating new history and heritage projects, including an Acadian Memorial board member who recommended the conference to me. At the first session I attended, Angela Turner, the director of a local history grant program for a large nonprofit, introduced a public historian from a state university. She suggested to those considering a grant application that "the best thing you [could] do" was to get in touch with "professionals like Dr. Pinkerton," who have the kind of expertise necessary to help manage the project and produce the desired results.

Justine Pinkerton proceeded to tell the fifteen or so attendees about a successful project from the previous grant cycle, one that brought organization and interpretative focus to a small-town museum of Acadian history that lacked them. She explained how the project focused on organizing the exhibit's numerous photos around themes (e.g., "Then and Now," juxtaposing older and contemporary photos of different sites to "show the progression of the town") and adding interpretive plaques to contextualize them. Turner interjected that such a grant often "raises the quality" of existing sites. This prompted Pinkerton to recall a presentation by another academic that was part of her efforts, which led locals to think historically in grounded, self-referential ways. "They're not used to thinking of their own past as being part of a history that goes back into the past few centuries," she enthused. "When a professional made these connections, lights were going off in their heads." Summing up the project's impacts, she claimed, "The public had never really had their history explained to them. Doing the exhibit the way we did made a big difference. People were captivated." While many other Louisianans did not know the remote pasts of their locales, the two seemed to assume, their initiative would address that lacuna with a historical consciousness that would invigorate their lives.

At another conference session, this focus on abetting historical remembrance extended beyond the mere diffusion of information toward the aim of shifting behaviors. At that session, Adam Sigur, project director of a state-sponsored folklore initiative, promoted a new resource guide for use in schools. The state needed such an initiative because while "folk culture is all around us. . . . we take it for granted. We don't see it. [Yet] we want people to see it. We want people to appreciate it." He then led participants in an activity to "discover how traditional arts and folklife exist in your own life" by checking boxes on a list of activities such as "have been to a Mardi Gras parade" and "ate rice last night." Sigur then previewed the guide, suggesting how it might do similar work in the classroom. The associated website contained lesson plans and activities, like one calling for students to bring family photographs to class. The goal—specified in the module's title "Discovering the Obvious: Our Lives as 'The Folk'"—would be achieved as children "work[ed] with the pictures," learning to "analyze" intimate familial experiences through a "folklife" lens. The main challenge Sigur evoked was that Louisianans didn't consider themselves heritage-carrying folk: The kind of analysis that would recast family photos as folk memories was not a given, as he admitted at the start. Precisely such "seeing" had to be formed. But the fact that folklorists were few and far between established an ancillary hurdle—and this mix of structured activity, alluring material prompts, and intervention at a distance seemed to address the latter.

In both presentations, a project was conspicuous: The state's citizens needed more historical awareness, and actors of all kinds sought to reconfigure the landscape of memory (evoked in chapter 2) to foster it. Apparently, Louisiana's memoryscape required more scaffolding—concerted efforts to stoke and orient historical remembrance in novel, widespread, public ways. To that end, these presenters were engaged in infrastructural spadework, linking academic expertise, especially the knowledge of local pasts, to the everyday interests of Louisiana residents, ostensibly for the mutual benefit of citizen and state.

A museum association; a staffer from a nonprofit institution; a consultant to a state agency; a public historian from a state university; and last but not least, civic boosters, municipal employees, and public history practitioners hailing from across the state: As the previous chapter demonstrated, an increasing number of people sought to advance public history in the region. As mentioned previously, just such a range of diverse actors designed, funded, and elaborated the Acadian Memorial. But as chapter 5 also showed, distinct groups brought varied politico-civic goals to the broad project of elaborating a new Acadian public history. In addition to Pinkerton's enthusiasm for helping people reflect historically for the first time, others centered on promoting solidarity to boost a troubled democracy, regulating ignorance and other harmful behaviors subverting social governance, and enabling the full civic status of white ethnic subjects in the body politic. As I will show, memorial supporters pursued all of these and more. These diverse aims beg the questions with which this chapter engages: Could a single site like the memorial satisfy all these actors and their varied objectives for instilling historical awareness into citizens? Did it? If so, how did their negotiations, collaborations, and differences of opinion unfold, converging to produce the site?

From one angle, these questions turn on that of how the state and its exercise of power should be seen. In both theory and everyday discourse, the state (or "the government") is often considered an undifferentiated and omnipresent force, a cold monster with a tendency to centralize and regulate everything it touches. Conceptualizations of the contemporary forms that relations of power take conventionally begin or end with the state, treating it as all-encompassing and hegemonic in its structuring effects on many (perhaps most) social relationships.[1] This is also a view that, more specifically with respect to public history, some scholars have forwarded.[2] The significant amount of public-sector support in the memorial's emergence and the presence of so many state actors at this conference could underwrite such a top-down, state-centric approach to it. Likewise, recall that in historian Glenn Conrad's polemical indictment, the truth about the regional past was necessary to admonish Cajuns and restore order by requiring them to renounce their fabricated historical memories and live by a history that would reform their unruly pride. Conrad's reproach conveyed an apparent desire for a rule of experts, a certain state-abetted vision of controlling historical speech.[3]

Yet without denying that centralizing and structural effects of state power do exist, I suggest that another view is necessary to grasp the relations of power animating those who brought the memorial and its historical narrative into existence. Consider that the problematizations and programs described in the previous chapter were just that: *theories* about sociopolitical challenges and proposals that authorities *wanted to implement*. Like Sigur, however, their centralized locations stymied them; they lacked both a technical means to relay their authoritative knowledge throughout the polity and local partners to assist them. Realizing their visions required precisely the kind of recruitment Turner, Pinkerton, and Sigur practiced: persuasion and promises aimed at generating alliances with willing accomplices. These were crucial, essential for actualizing the effects of their proposed interventions across the body politic.

Michel Foucault refers to this building of collaborative alliances as the "governmentalizing of the state,"[4] the connection of centers of political strategizing with distant spaces and relations of power, through means that align governing authorities' projects with the "personal projects of those who . . . are the subjects of government."[5] Pinkerton's implied pitch—imagine the delight of grasping, for the first time, the significance of *your* town's distant past—attempted to translate the aims of her and Turner's programs into the aspirations of potential allies in that ballroom. Through such translations between authorities and a range of other actors, a network emerged and articulated a distinctive civic politics that, as much as any other force, drove the memorial's elaboration.[6] Alongside its linkages to utilitarian dynamics, they imagined effects that were ethico-political and generative: They sought to lead citizens—all of them, but especially Cajuns—to *commit* to the truths of Acadian history, for their sake and that of a wider polity. The Acadian Memorial can thus be seen as a "technology of power," a distinct, behavior-shaping intervention animated by the broad project of guiding the conduct of a democratic citizenry through an obligation to live by historical truths.[7]

A FEDERAL-LOCAL AXIS AND ITS RACIAL BOUNDARIES

The federal policymaking featured across the previous chapter proved crucial in these efforts. As with the makers of Evangeline history earlier in the century, locals' sense that national actors gazed approvingly on the Acadian past provided them with decisive leverage for historicizing it. At this moment, too, actors forged an alliance along a federal-local axis, accelerating efforts to make historically aware Cajuns.

The inception of the National Park Service's first Acadian historic site in the town of Eunice illuminates these distinct interests and how they were translated into each other. By the early 1980s, Marc Savoy, a Cajun musician and accordion maker, had performed folk music for years in national parks outside the state and in US Information Agency–sponsored tours abroad. He recounted how these experiences confused him, raising the question of how "someone could be a cultural hero two thousand miles away from Louisiana, but on their home turf they were considered . . . a substandard citizen."[8] This recurring external recognition *as a Cajun* led Savoy to propose a national park in his hometown, one devoted to Cajun culture and history, to the Jean Lafitte National Historical Park's first director, Jim Isenogle. Significantly, Savoy assumed that an effort to promote Cajuns and their heritage would not succeed with local support alone. The derision for Cajuns that he sensed in Eunice, a large town of ten thousand in the southwestern part of the state, made him feel like a "prophet [who] goes unheeded in his own land."[9] In so many words, he grasped that federal officials were proficient in creating the "microenvironments" in which Cajuns like himself could be "heroes"; such spaces and the dispositions they engendered did not emerge organically within the local public sphere.

Though they proposed south Louisiana's ethnic diversity as Jean Lafitte's focus, National Park Service (NPS) officials were also skittish about how to implement its mandate. The implication that every ethnoracial group would want and potentially get a separate site worried them. Yet by 1983, NPS staff had operationalized the vague vision of Jean Lafitte's authorizing legislation, endorsing the "value" of "the diversity of Louisiana culture" as "representative of our diverse national heritage," diversity that the park should "put . . . visitors *into direct contact with*" (emphasis added).[10] Given this warrant, Superintendent Isenogle could not stand pat with a small space in New Orleans' French Quarter as the park's principal interpretive venue. Backed by a congressional mandate and the authoritative research overview that featured Cajuns, he surreptitiously scouted events that Savoy and his collaborators were holding in Eunice. When Savoy approached him, arguing that Cajuns were special, Isenogle and the NPS agreed.[11] Together, they then recruited a politician with clout—Eunice's mayor Curtis Joubert, for whom (unlike Edwin Edwards) "preservation of [Cajun] culture" was "exactly what [he] want[ed]"—and formed a coalition that created Jean Lafitte's Acadian Unit.[12] Their efforts culminated in a site composed of a folk music performance venue and a historical exhibit, spaces in which historians, folklorists, and docents could stimulate in visitors the positive feedback loop that Savoy first experienced elsewhere. With support from other Cajun politicians, they authorized two additional Acadian sites as well.

To achieve these intersecting aims, all the participants in this unique alliance needed to join forces. But without federal actors like Isenogle and the NPS, both the site in Eunice and the batch of Acadian historic sites that followed—including the Acadian Memorial—would not have emerged as they did. After the 1985 announcement of the Acadian Unit's launch, other actors realized that since the NPS had gone all in on representing Acadian history and heritage—creating a circuit across three municipalities and 140 miles of south Louisiana—interest in and sanction for their own efforts to represent the Acadian past would likely surge. Above all, the NPS brought unrivaled resources, expertise, and prestige, including the technical, subject-forming vision that matched Savoy's. For Cajuns to feel like heroes, material interventions that offset the forces thwarting such a reality had to be assembled. This goal formed the crux of their partnership: to produce, through instruction and promotion, ethnic subjects who could proudly embrace their Acadian history and heritage in situ.

During the park's first decade, NPS staff interpreted Jean Lafitte's mandate to focus on the region's "cultural diversity" as a charge to highlight the state's many ethnoracial groups. This public historical turn toward difference was widespread. It aligned with practitioners' wider efforts to make history relevant to varied publics and "legitimize work . . . for the purposes of particularist constituencies."[13] Organizations like the Louisiana Endowment for the Humanities (LEH) began to pursue an analogous approach in cultural policy, projecting that greater tolerance would emerge by "ensur[ing] that the many voices which have shaped this great state together are heard."[14] Such a tendency also unfolded in academic history's shift toward subaltern histories—of Blacks and other peoples of color, women, the working class, and others—a trend that, in Louisiana scholarship, produced many monographs centered on such groups. In principle, this new regime created ample room for representing the region's diversity.

But this conjuncture did not translate into inclusive practices of historical representation, particularly for Blacks. Jean Lafitte Park struggled to generate an African American site within its boundaries. Among the park's white supporters and allies, opposition to such a prospect was stiff. When staff at the park's headquarters produced an announcement featuring the image of a Black Mardi Gras Indian from New Orleans, a white member of its citizen advisory board complained, "Why the hell do we need a n***** with a flashlight on a Park Service poster?"[15] Similarly, a staff person involved in launching the Acadian Unit noted his white interlocutors' staunch opposition to Black representation in the region, regretting that "we [NPS] certainly didn't ever solve . . . the Black problem." This "problem," he explained, was that for whites "in Acadiana, . . . Blacks belong where Blacks belong, and that's in the back room." In his view, the Acadian Unit's proponents regarded representation in Jean Lafitte as a zero-sum game. Space and resources existed for a limited amount of interpretation, and they were unwilling to share them with the region's Black residents. As mentioned, NPS administrators perceived themselves to be operating in a context where elected officials held the upper hand, defining interpretive priorities and overruling NPS recommendations. In this case, NPS's deference to white political leaders' prerogatives foreclosed on the possibility of Black history within Jean Lafitte. Park insiders later acknowledged that, given its mandate, interpreting Black history ranked as a "high priority," yet they failed to materialize such a site before abandoning their plan to feature each of the region's ethnoracial groups.[16]

In addition to this marginalization of Black history, these trends favored frames of bounded identity, continuity, and "ethnogenesis"—of specifying historical moments that founded and fixed group identities—which shaped the region's public historical sphere. Their downside was a discursive regime representing each group as a kind of historical monad, following a narrow itinerary through time sans interactions with others. It produced "an abstract form of 'side-by-sideism' through which the social is mapped as a set of equivalent differences."[17] In practice, the use of this trope undercut interracial alliances and generated a skewed construal of similarities.

In St. Martinville, these weaknesses were apparent when locals paired histories of Cajuns and Blacks. On each side of the foyer in the St. Martinville Cultural Center, which houses both the Museum of the Acadian Memorial and the African American Museum, maps of the North Atlantic hang. On the right, the map is entitled "African Diaspora," with arrows signifying the traffic that brought slaves to the Americas. To the left lies a similar depiction of the "Acadian Diaspora," which emphasizes the peregrinations of Acadian refugees following their expulsion. The foyer's biracial design team intended this implied equivalence. From their perspective, comparing the histories would enable members of each group to gain deeper respect and understanding of the other.

Some white St. Martinvillers embraced this vision. A few memorial affiliates theorized that a diminished self-esteem motivated the anti-Black racism that they knew existed among Cajuns; by inviting them to appreciate similarities between their history and that of their Black neighbors, representations like the maps might attenuate that behavior. Others expected that the comparison would enable Blacks' reciprocal reevaluation of Cajuns. *As one memorial board member claimed during a meeting, seconded by nods of agreement from others, "By them learning our history and seeing how we were treated, that will make them feel closer to us."* This strategy's advocates posited a leveling effect, a decrease in asymmetries of power through increased recognition of parallel historical experiences.

But the sites instantiated a consequential disparity, undercutting such outcomes. As mentioned in chapter 3, the Black history exhibit focused on free people of color (who occupied a middling space in the three-tiered antebellum racial hierarchy), allowing it to avoid the darker aspects of enslavement and construe its African American history as a bootstrapping story of upward mobility. Meanwhile, the Acadian Memorial's narratives and imagery centered the violence of the deportation and its aftermath. In the commemorative space, the mural's celebratory depiction of Acadian arrival in Louisiana was set against the backdrop of smaller historical prints, including "Burning and Laying Waste," a depiction of British soldiers setting fire to an Acadian village. The historical exhibit's narrative also stressed the coercion and violence that Acadians endured: They were "ordered to give up their guns and boats"; "deceived and captured," "arrested, deported, and killed," "crammed into ships," and "forced to work as indentured servants."[18] This conveyed a heroic narrative about Acadians as a people—blameless targets who survived unwarranted brutality—a framing absent in the Black exhibit.

The ramifications of this discrepancy were not lost on some locals. In a focus group of Black and white residents at the African American Museum, one noted the obvious divergence, with which the others concurred. This white professional claimed, "When you leave [the Acadian Memorial], you know those people in Nova Scotia suffered. There was pain. You could see it—it was there. You can come here . . . [and conclude,] 'Gee, it wasn't all that bad after all.' And yet over there [i.e., the memorial], that's the way it should be. Here, you have this [muted representation of slavery]. . . . And you can tell the difference." The significance of citing past violence and collective suffering was hardly abstract. In many contexts—such as the controversy over town council redistricting (discussed in chapter 3)—Blacks forwarded grievances asserting continuity between past injustices and contemporary ones. Invoking the legacy of enslavement and de jure segregation grounded their claims for redress in the present.

In effect, the two exhibits achieved a remarkable transposition of a historical theme with steep political salience in postsegregation Louisiana. In narrating this new Acadian history, the memorial foregrounded their status as innocent victims of a world-historical tragedy. Meanwhile, in the African American Museum, no such dimension of Black history could be evoked.

HERITAGE TOURISM AND THE COUNTERTREND OF HISTORICAL TRUTH

The Acadian Memorial's launch could be narrated as a primarily market-driven development in the burgeoning heritage tourism landscape of late twentieth-century Louisiana.[19] Market forces certainly created the conditions for it. During the 1990s, Louisiana was awash with market-oriented public history and heritage projects. The 1984 Louisiana World Exposition opened the floodgates for these efforts, as practitioners recognized the allure that its stagings of the state's folk heritage had for tourists from across the country and the world.[20] Subsequently, public initiatives and public-private partnerships—for example, yearlong commemorative events like Louisiana Open House and Francofête (celebrating the 1999 tricentennial of the state's "discovery")—proliferated.[21] By 2000, state officials intensified this push. As a major plank in its objective to raise Louisiana's standard of living into the top ten among American states, Louisiana's economic master plan proposed leveraging the "unrivaled . . . wealth of its cultural heritage"—"attributable to [its] citizens of French Acadian and African descent"—to stoke tourism. For its authors, the economic return generated by such initiatives guaranteed their public value; they sought job creation that would "keep our citizens from leaving the state in search of employment."[22]

St. Martinville's efforts to generate heritage unfolded within this market-centered matrix.[23] One of its major inspirations came from Main Street Programs and the novel notion of regional heritage areas that they spawned.[24] Emerging from downtown revitalization and historic building preservation spaces, their advocates proposed a history-making regime that favored certain material foci centered on tourists' experience. Its stress was visual; to those strolling their sidewalks, downtowns restored to their "original look" would convey a sense of entering spaces that had (seemingly) not changed with time.[25] Given that "historic downtowns are an ideal setting for such visitor services as specialty shopping, restaurants, and lodging," its proponents intended a superficial history: well-restored facades and retro streetscapes that engendered "the past," regardless of structures' former use or local historical awareness surrounding them.[26] From the perspective of corporate interests and public officials, rehabbed main streets, connected into a trail of such downtowns, could readily manifest history in a consumable form.[27]

As leaders in St. Martinville implemented such strategies, they centered their efforts on gratifying tourists. In some respects, tourists' prerogatives trumped concerns with local history's substance. The town's Main Street Program manager led guided tours of the historic district, and *when groups expressed an interest in "the history, or the Acadians, or in Evangeline," he explained, "then I'll say more about each of them."* Yet he did not focus on imparting any historical content. Instead, he concentrated on how St. Martinville provided visitors with an engaging, convenient experience. *In targeting tour operators, he said the town had to offer them "something new" to warrant return visits; this need for novelty incited its move to generate novel sites. Another guiding principle was locating all attractions within walking distance of each other, which prompted the siting of all new initiatives within the downtown.*

This focus on tourist satisfaction dovetailed with that of tour operators. The owner of a company that frequented St. Martinville specified, *"The traveler is minimally interested in history. It's mostly older people looking for a pleasant rural experience." As such, she theorized that one key to the region's growing popularity as a destination was that it satisfied many tourists' desire for a "slow-paced feeling and a little ethnic flavor. . . . a safe and interesting ethnic experience." Her characterizations implied there was a racial dimension to this search, since "you could get [an ethnic experience] in south Los Angeles, too, but you might get blown up." In her estimation, the town's efforts were working: Although St. Martinville was formerly a "horrendous" destination, the mayor and his associates had "greatly improved" the quality of its heritage offerings.*

But concerns about economic development and tourist satisfaction were not the last word in shaping historical representation. Another group of institutional actors, loosely affiliated yet aligned, articulated a discrete approach. The relations of power these groups sought to cultivate possessed a distinct flavor, and they were suspicious of tourism as a threat to be managed. Instead, they argued that historical truth should have a larger purchase on democratic governance than market relations. As such, they insisted on transmitting truths generated through scholarship into this expanding public historical sphere, where they—and not market-driven bromides—would shape citizens' knowledge and conduct.

Even the most market-friendly among them, the Atchafalaya Heritage Trace, identified the latter as a challenge. With a mandate to create a multiparish (county) trail around the Atchafalaya Basin, a large swamp in south-central Louisiana, the trace's administrators were tasked with combining tourism-based economic development with representations based on "authentic" historical narratives. Yet Martha Shinners, its first director, took an anticommercial stance in describing market forces as a negative influence to be managed. She described stakeholders' shared sense that some narratives about Cajun culture and history had ventured toward "caricature"; influenced by tourists' tastes, they had "become real cute and quaint." To counter this tendency to "become Disney-like," she insisted that one of the project's principal goals was ensuring that residents "know the basics of who you are as a people or a town," in order to keep it "real" and "gritty." *Too much* commercialization was also a risk, one that required mitigation.

Some in St. Martinville placed an analogous stress on truth, challenging the predominance of tourists' gratification. *I was surprised when, in response to a question about what had changed at Longfellow-Evangeline State Commemorative Area (LESCA) since her arrival, a senior employee replied, "You mean since we started to tell the truth? [*Smiles*] What was here before was nothing more than common folklore. It was oriented toward appeasing the Evangeline legends."* Where some townspeople were content to maintain Evangeline-based history as part of the mix it offered to visitors, this state-run site rejected it. She explained how historical truth effected this change: *"At one point, this romantic stuff about Evangeline counted as history. Now it's not history any more. . . . Now there's a place for folklore, but that's not here. It's over there under the Evangeline Oak. There should be both [folklore and history] in a community. There's a place for* *stories about great-grandfather this and great-uncle that. Those stories should be told, and they should have their place. But the place for that is at the oak, with the Romero brothers. And it's a story. It's not history."* As mentioned before, some locals, including those linked to the town's municipal government, expressed the sentiments criticized here. One former resident thought that when, years later, the Romeros, two elderly siblings who sat underneath the oak playing folk music and spinning yarns to tourists, passed away, the region had lost something "real," not at all "fake." At Longfellow-Evangeline, however, another criterion for evaluating history dominated. While perhaps popular and entertaining, "legends" and "folklore" were excluded, failing to pass a test of truth.

Though narrated here as cut-and-dried fact, truth's triumph at LESCA was not tidy. Provoked by Carl Brasseaux's takedown of Evangeline in *In Search of Evangeline*, the site's messy transition from "story" to "history" signaled the rise of academics as powerful actors in the region (as discussed in chapter 5). From its inception to the 1970s, LESCA's main historical structure, a colonial-era plantation house, operated as an integral part of the town's Evangeline complex. The site presented it as an "Evangeline shrine" called the "Acadian House," curated as the residence of the heroine's forlorn lover.[28] When, during the 1980s, the Office of State Parks (OSP) asked professional historians to conduct archival research on the building, they established its history as the home of a white Creole planter with no past link to Cajuns. A short time later, Brasseaux's book criticized the town's decades-long commitment to perpetuating the Evangeline myth, attributing it to "merchants and . . . park personnel" who "promoted [it] to attract tourists."[29] Together, these findings gutted the site's interpretative framework, intimating the need for revision.

Yet senior OSP administrators had difficulty shifting out of that schema. When site staff submitted a plan that would "reconcile the separate histories of the house, the park, and the myth," OSP headquarters refused to acknowledge its receipt; they rejected the mere suggestion to change the structure's name from "Acadian" to "Creole House."[30] It took years before OSP administrators launched major modifications to the site. When they did, its new manager announced a comprehensive change in orientation. "We're totally changing everything that was here before," he said, because "our focus is to . . . get closer to the preservation of Louisiana's history."[31] As mentioned in chapter 2, some locals had joined OSP officials in resisting this shift. Yet their combined opposition failed to stop professionals' ascendancy.

In this light, academic historians were the most committed actors promoting empirical knowledge as a challenge to market forces in the elaboration of the region's public history. Academic institutions like the University of Louisiana at Lafayette's Center for Louisiana Studies (CLS) and historians like Glenn Conrad, its long-standing director, can be seen as motivated agents like any others in this space. They identified problems that they were well suited to solve; they developed techniques on which their influence rested; they pursued strategies against adversaries like ignorance. Furthermore, as Brasseaux's intervention against Evangeline history made clear, they positioned professional historiography as a check on the market's penchant to distort the past. While other practitioners in public history centered tourist preferences as their primary gauge for elaborating the past, they were keen to offer other criteria—those of empirical methods, the archives, and truth.

This challenge to market-centered history emerged largely because the center's history-making capacity made it pivotal, an obligatory passage point for others. It became indispensable by defining the nature of problems with historical narratives "and then suggesting that these would be resolved if [other] actors negotiated . . . [their] solution" *with it.*[32] To wit, when Melissa Keller, an architect of St. Martinville's heritage tourism expansion, began to contemplate a new Acadian history site, she contacted Conrad and Brasseaux. As one local involved in their initial discussions described it, "From the beginning, [Keller] was thinking, 'Well, given what's been written, . . . the time has come for us to tell another story. Because we can no longer continue to base our industry on local lore.'" Following his book on Evangeline, Brasseaux published two monographs, the first of which, *The Founding of New Acadia*, appealed to Keller. *"It was the kind of book I couldn't get enough of," she explained. "It was like a revelation. I'd always had the image of these people as ones who just accepted what happened to them. And it wasn't true."* Facilitated by the colonial manuscripts gathered in CLS's archives, Brasseaux's work offered a narrative about Acadian relocation to Louisiana that challenged the passivity of the Evangeline story, which proved compelling to fellow literates like Keller. In this instance of translation, expert input influenced St. Martinville's Cajun history-making, with locals accepting their input as an antidote to narratives strictly determined by the market.

As that new site, the Acadian Memorial, fleshed out its representations, another market-skeptical institution denied an initiative that it found too touristic. LEH twice rejected a proposal seeking to narrate stories of the deportation's aftermath in a filmed dramatic performance, after funding initial requests from the nonprofit foundation that Keller and her associates formed to launch and manage the site. Panelists on LEH's review committees found it a "weak mechanism for conveying the humanities," one likely to produce "little more than a tourism publicity piece."[33] Amid pressures to commercialize the past, a substantial network of actors promoted a distinct policy vision, resisting the trend. In a move echoing Freeman Tilden's prescriptions, this stance escalated an existing "truth obligation" in the region's civic politics. Adjudicating between histories that could and could not circulate, entities like LEH, CLS, and OSP went beyond promoting historical truths that citizens should *accept* as epistemically sound. Rather, extending the relationship that unfolds in, for instance, American history classrooms in high schools, they proposed that, diffused in public historical spaces, certain truths about the regional past would have positive, practical effects on citizens' conduct. However, for these effects to take hold, they had to *commit* or *submit* to those truths—to be willing, as Sigur and Conrad indicated, to have their behavior changed by them. Thus, a regime of historical truth, a systemic means of shaping conduct, intensified, in opposition to the predominance of market relations as the chief criterion for governing in matters of cultural policy.[34]

"REVERSE ENGINEERING THE GRASSROOTS SUPPORT": COMBATING ILLITERACY AND GOVERNING THE LAY PUBLIC AT A DISTANCE

Dovetailing with historians' focus on combating ignorance through historical literacy, organizations like LEH also centered knowledge's circulation in their mission. The para-statal became a major partner in St. Martinville's efforts, making two early grants to the Acadian Memorial and a third to its African American Museum. By way of explaining its goals, Keith Osborn, an LEH administrator, claimed, "We are about sharing—making information accessible, creating spaces for conversation and debates. . . . When that happens consistently and well, . . . you create citizens . . . [who] are able to engage in a democracy and sustain it." By increasing the public's literacy and its assimilation of scholarly research about the state, as well as by fostering its engagement in events that featured the exchange of ideas, LEH's premise was that it would foster citizens' informed decision-making and increase their dialogical skills. As with the historians, this challenge centered residents instead of tourists, and its politics were civic. While liberal theorists often stress legislation, electoral participation, and law enforcement as key vectors of citizen-making, practitioners in the public history space focused instead on this shaping of "custom"—cultural dispositions, moral sensibilities, local knowledges—as a crucial means of forming self-governing citizens.

For the most part, these practitioners posited that knowledge in fields like history existed on a continuum with everyday faculties of reason. *At the museum conference, an LEH project manager led a session on heritage tourism and the humanities with a participatory activity, showing the audience a World War II war bond poster with an image of Uncle Sam over the caption "Are you doing all you can?" After fielding responses to her questions about the poster's significance, she explained that the humanities were simply "a font of tools for analysis and interpretation," like those they had just employed to decode the image. She seemed to offer a demonstration that nonexperts intuitively possess the cognitive skills often imputed to be the exclusive domain of academics.* From this angle, the work of "translating scholarship for the public," as Osborn also described the organization's aim, amounted to practicing a politics of instruction. As this manager illustrated, their ideal was a relationship of teachers collaboratively guiding the skill acquisition of a less experienced yet engaged public.

The negotiation of these relations of power progressed largely inside of a liberal vision of governance, of conducting free subjects into useful knowledge as opposed to indoctrinating minds through control. Launching the Atchafalaya Trace Heritage initiative at the turn of the century, Shinners described its elaborate campaign to generate public engagement with it. This involved charrettes in the thirteen parishes comprising the project's ambit (including the one where St. Martinville is located), sessions that sought to solicit ideas and stimulate interest. In them, her team encouraged residents to reflect on their sense of the past, "to talk about the stories that make the place what it is, that make it important." She recalled that narratives emerged organically; indeed, "a lot of [the trace's stress on] authenticity and pride of place . . . came from local residents themselves. They would say, 'If more of our town members felt this way, we could do 'X.'" Echoing Bess Lomax Hawes's vision of inreach, she also cast the process as one of making manifest locals' nascent historical awareness. "It was already there in them; you just pull it up to where they can see it and act on it," she explained. These were moments of active translation, of "alignments . . . forged between the objectives of authorities wishing to govern and the personal projects of those organizations, groups, and individuals who are the subjects of government."[35]

Along these lines, practitioners were aware of a need to literally translate their civic aims into language that appealed to their interlocutors' own priorities. "I can't always go to people and say, 'Well, this is just foundational, like, why wouldn't you?,'" Osborn explained, referencing the organization's focus on citizen formation through literacy promotion. Instead, he found that speaking to potential supporters in terms of local "quality of life" more effectively evoked a response. He continued: "The reason that resonates with folks is because when you say that, then people start to think oh, right, . . . I do like to be able to go to a concert, and I do like to go to the museum, and I do like to be able to go to a festival, and buy a book at the bookstore, and they start thinking of the things that make up their quality of life, whatever it is." This effort at persuasion generated the possibility of negotiating shared interests. Osborn went on, "They start to think, 'Oh, it's about vibrant communities,' and this [their vision] is a piece of it [our mission]." Far from being an aberration, this kind of bargaining is characteristic of liberal rule, illustrating, as Nikolas Rose puts it, the indispensable creation of "relays between the calculations of authorities and the aspirations of free citizens."[36]

These interventions in the region's public historical sphere also typify a common thrust of its politics, a mode of governing at a distance—of "instrumentaliz[ing] forms of authority other than those of 'the state.'"[37] While citizen formation through knowledge diffusion was its own goal, LEH staff also recognized that, as Osborn put it, "what people love about [Louisiana] is very, very granular." This appreciation for the specificity of local interests informed an openness to support activities whose aims were not identical to their own. Some Acadian Memorial advocates, for instance, foregrounded concerns about transmitting knowledge to the next generation of Cajuns. A consultant who worked on several Acadian history projects voiced this preoccupation, insisting that, with respect to young Cajuns, "you've got to get the point across to new generations that there are things here worth preserving . . . things that set you apart, that really define your local world." While this motivated its local proponents, intergenerational transmission of ethnic identity was not LEH's focus. Yet in funding the memorial for its own purposes, LEH helped authorize that goal, empowering citizens to pursue it *and* linking it to its own citizen-forming agenda.

State-based actors commonly voiced this stance. After the Atchafalaya Trace became a National Heritage Area, a staff person explained that they had no grant-funding mechanism and thus no means to pursue its own interpretive plan. Instead, they were enabling residents "so that they can tell their own story. . . . [We] simply facilitate the voices of the heritage area," she claimed. Thus, like Keller seeking out academic historians to consult on the Acadian Memorial as she and other nonexperts launched it, the lay public could initiate projects comprising discrete, local objectives and recruit authorities into them (about which more in the following section).

At the same time, these politics of translation had limits, as amateurs were also disparaged and sidelined. As noted, actors sometimes cast the public's historical illiteracy as a nefarious nonknowledge. Like historians, LEH identified illiteracy as one of its chief challenges; in launching a major literacy initiative in the early 1990s, its executive director asserted that illiteracy helped cause "some of our most perplexing social problems."[38] As an active force of disorder, illiteracy in turn sanctioned the need to diffuse knowledge. In the memorial's first grant application to LEH, the authors wrote that "amateur historians have indulged in fanciful speculation about the Acadians and their past," fostering erroneous "popular beliefs" about it.[39] The resulting problem—"most adult Louisianans know little about the true origins of today's Cajuns"—would be solved by diffusing professionals' histories. LEH agreed, funding syntheses of scholarly research for the memorial's website. The convergence in how these actors identified the issue's root cause—an ignorance instigated by forces needing to be combated—underwrote their collaboration. Moreover, their alliance went beyond tacit agreement. LEH required that academics sponsor these local projects as a condition for civic groups like the memorial's foundation to receive its grants.

Relations of power could be less symmetrical in such formulations. Knowledge's champions situated ignorance, a common scourge under liberal governance, inside of a warped social context that produced it; its benighted agents were less peers to mentor than foes to defeat.[40] At times, proponents of this emerging regional public historical sphere described those outside it as unreasonable. Like the "fog of ethnic pride" among Cajuns that Conrad discerned, twisted beliefs distorted their grasp of the past. Meanwhile, the conditions inside the network that produced truth—skill in accessing the archives, databases that organized notes, alliances like these and the resources that flowed from them—were bracketed, such that it seemed to speak for itself.

In this era's policy guidance, amateur efforts were increasingly denigrated. One manual insisted that authorities "[owe] it to [their] . . . community" to overrule the local who lists her "dilapidated farmhouse" as a historic site, because a visitor "knows a sham when he sees it."[41] History makers also needed to rein in "endless guided tours with rabid volunteer[s]" and "'Stepford' Tour Guides," which ranked among the "worst . . . experiences" one could inflict on tourists.[42] In the *Atchafalaya Trace Heritage Area Management Plan*, its authors elevated such concerns to core principles. They elucidated multiple strategies for shaping historical speech: The trace would enable residents to "repeat a core message that [they] will remember," encourage "institutions . . . to refresh existing programs consistent with" the area's central themes, and retrain existing guides away from "contrived" histories and toward a "niche within the [trace's] interpretive themes."[43] Similarly, the trace's project manager, Shinners, also described her work during those charrettes as "reverse engineering . . . grassroots support" for the project. When legislators responded to civic groups' lobbying and funded the trace as a public effort, it had ballooned in size. Yet since residents of the sprawling region did not share an identity or historical awareness, she said, "Much of my time was spent . . . reselling it to the people who didn't know about it in the first place." This politics of "making [the trace] this larger, broader identity thing" gave her pause, as she immediately asked, "Does that sound too much [like] George Orwell['s *1984*]?"

These concerns were partly market inflected, aiming to popularize a sensitivity to tourist preferences. Yet like Conrad's preoccupation with Cajun grandmothers' flawed memories, they also extended to the merits of specific speech acts. For almost a decade, two elderly brothers, Lennis and Ophé Romero, became fixtures near the Evangeline Oak in St. Martinville, playing Cajun music to entertain tourists. Given St. Martinville's prominence in regional itineraries, a stream of travel writers transformed them into minor celebrities, as mentions of them circulated in national media. But not everyone in St. Martinville was so enamored. Retired blue-collar workers, *the two were "naively conceited," one municipal employee claimed; they chided visitors unaware of their "fame" for being uninformed. Like the staff person at Longfellow-Evangeline, some were also concerned about the accuracy of their historical accounts, going so far as to ask the mayor to chase the Romeros from their perch. Confirming that he had been approached, Mayor Eric Martin said he dismissed this proposal, joking he might need to supplement his own retirement in the same way.* The brothers stayed, though without the endorsement they would likely have received elsewhere in the region. Not every amateur merited inclusion; some were challenged and marginalized.

MOBILIZING EXTERNAL ALLIES, BRIDGING LOCAL CONSTITUENCIES

It was not only authorities whose objectives shaped the memorial. Many locals desired a new Acadian history, working to enfold others into *their* project. Attempts at translation extended in multiple directions; the aims of those "below" profoundly inflected the site's unfolding.

"We went by the book. That's the last time you'll ever see that in St. Martinville," said Alice Desjardins. She was proud of how she and her allies launched the Acadian Memorial in a town known for political shenanigans. Among other things, "the book" meant an aboveboard effort to gather endorsements from political bodies across the state as part of generating the support necessary to launch the memorial. *With respect to heritage, St. Martinville had so much, she said, but it had to be organized "in the right way." To realize that plan, they had to overcome many obstacles she characterized as "very political."* Chief among these was the possibility of competition from other towns, which were also contemplating new sites for the emerging Acadian history circuit. She perceived the contest as zero-sum; not every site would be funded and realized.

Desjardins's strategy involved mobilizing public entities as allies to ensure St. Martinville's success. This initiative began before the memorial was much more than a concept in a few people's heads. When they described it merely as a "stone marker," Desjardins and her allies succeeded in gaining the state legislature's endorsement.[44] The parish's police jury (county commission) had supported it, but this resolution—containing the kernel of a focus on "memorial[izing] all the Acadian refugees who ended their exile in Louisiana"[45]—furnished real momentum. The vague idea served as a placeholder for a detailed plan that followed; these endorsements' significance lay in how they worked to deter rivals.

Desjardins solicited support from parish governments across south Louisiana, garnering endorsements from twenty-two parish policy juries (county commissions). Elected officials were receptive to such an idea at a time when Cajun food and music had become popular nationally. John Doucet, a former politician, early memorial supporter, and self-identified

Cajun, acknowledged that the site was part of a broad heritage tourism strategy. Its authors sought to capitalize on Cajun culture's popularity, using it to entice the many tourists visiting New Orleans to extend their stays elsewhere in the state. Yet Doucet stressed that it would operate synergistically toward cultural ends. While he claimed that, by that point, "everybody want[ed] to be a Cajun," Cajuns like himself still needed the inspiration that the memorial would stir: "So this [heritage tourism scene] is all cultivating itself into getting more people to . . . instead of being embarrassed of our roots and heritage in the Cajun culture, [to] instill a new pride in the Cajun culture. And that's what I'm so happy about. Because it didn't really matter personally to me . . . what concept we would lock in to achieve our goal of making people proud of their Acadian heritage and their cultural roots. We just wanted to find the vehicles." Elected officials like Doucet readily grasped the memorial's value. Soon after the legislature's endorsement, the lieutenant governor (a St. Martin Parish native) declared a "St. Martinville Acadian Memorial Day"—years before the site opened—noting that it would "[honor] the Acadian heritage which has so richly enhanced the history of our state."[46] All ideas were good for the region's politicians, since the prospect of a pride-instilling tone mattered most. Details about specifics were secondary.

By contrast, the memorial's distinctive design was crucial in fostering another translation. The initial vagueness about the site's substance gave way to a plan incorporating multiple commemorative elements. Its backers spoke of how national sites, such as the Vietnam Veterans Memorial and Arlington National Cemetery, inspired their vision for the memorial's anchors—the wall of names, the eternal flame, and the large mural painting. The specificity of the site's materiality enabled a final alliance that bridged distinct constituencies.

As Desjardins framed it, in launching the memorial, she focused on "doing [heritage tourism] right." She was not alone. Some believed that sites designed by laypeople did not meet professional standards for alluring displays; these "undercurated" venues deterred tourists. Thus, their agenda involved designing the memorial according to expert norms; *it was imperative that it be "perfect," Keller insisted.* Alongside this stress on catering to visitors' expectations, this group professed a particular attitude toward the memorial's potential Cajun audience. When it opened, one of its sponsors asserted that it "allows [Cajuns] to have something beautiful, something nice. . . . It's the first time they are associated with something beautiful."[47] Unsurprisingly, these proponents did not identify as Cajuns.[48] As non-Cajuns concentrated on heritage tourism, the site's impact on Cajuns was secondary for them, conceived as a conventional politics of cultural uplift through aesthetic inspiration. Only once the memorial opened did Desjardins and Keller recruit self-identifying Cajuns to manage it and lead its associated nonprofit foundation.

The creators' stress on first-rate design (explored more in the next chapter) signified differently to the Cajuns who joined them. These were natives of the region—upwardly mobile, college educated, middle class, and mostly women—for whom the memorial's narrative became vital. The attention to professional-quality representations resonated viscerally with them. "For me, the Acadian Memorial . . . was like an epiphany moment," raved Susan Theriot. Explaining what she sought to accomplish once she joined the site's staff, she related how the venue transformed her self-image, displacing an ingrained sense of inferiority:

> I think that [other Cajuns] should come to the memorial and get a dose of pride. Because when you hear that those Acadians arrived before Jamestown, before the Pilgrims . . . it just makes me feel that, no, we're just not ignorant people, dumped in Louisiana. *Not.* They took those lands; they were terrific farmers. The cuisine. They were adaptable; they learned to survive; they were hard workers. They were afraid of the English, and they refused to go to school—that was their big hang-up—but they were not ignorant. . . . I mean, that is very insulting to me, and that's what I want anyone who's Acadian to realize.

Like many of these associates, Theriot arrived at the memorial with scant genealogical knowledge of her background and the sting of derogatory narratives about herself and her family. She identified with the "drama and struggle" depicted in the mural, not least because it conveyed a message negating the insults she endured. For her, this history was more than a polished tourist attraction. Instead, it became integral to a personal project of self-affirmation.

While they did not conceptualize it, these Cajuns found they could de-emphasize the memorial's touristic aims, centering its mission on helping other Cajuns get their dose of pride. "It's important to me that what we do here . . . serves as the right thing to do as far as people of Acadian descent are concerned," affirmed Jeanette Vincent, an early board member. "We're that first and tourist attraction second." They saw the mural, with its expressive depiction of Acadian immigrants, as a powerful antidote to the historical falsehoods that dogged Cajuns, especially "this whole, heavy stuff about not being wanted and not being desirable neighbors," as Vincent put it. Referencing one of the forty-plus historical Acadians featured in the mural, Theriot explained, "[Elisabeth Brasseaux] brought her two boys here [under harrowing circumstances]. So take pride. If you're a Brasseaux, you come from strong stock. You have a beautiful history. . . . If you're Brasseaux and hear that, it makes you real happy if you never knew it before." Keyed to shared concerns about Cajuns' shame, their vision was thus both psychosocial and technical. On the one hand, it posited that Cajuns' second-class status—abetted by a defective history rationalizing it—had injured their inner selves. On the other hand, it advanced that historical truth, as conveyed by the site and applied to the ethnic self, could heal those wounds. In their view, the memorial's history, expressed in compelling materiality, constituted a pastoral tool for self-care.

As Cajun advocates and non-Cajun heritage boosters shared seats on the site's board, they did not always agree. Interviewees mentioned differences of opinion over minor alterations to the memorial during the 2000s, many of which the advocates proposed to enhance the experience for other Cajun visitors. Yet similar to how broad concepts and programs (like "education") can create "mobile associations . . . between a variety of agents," the site itself accommodated each of their visions for history's uses. As such, they came "to understand their situation according to a similar language and logic, to construe their goals . . . as in some way inextricable."[49]

With respect to all those who might identify as Cajun, however, this alliance was circumscribed. As part of fundraising for the mural, the site's sponsors auctioned off the privilege of posing as models for the painting's figures. Well-heeled families purchased these opportunities, and some individual models held regional renown. Several memorial principals mentioned how residents from the immediate area were infrequent visitors, including those with ample Acadian genealogies. *In a frank assessment, one of them surmised that the mural's depiction of "les gros chiens habillés comme les ancêtres"*—"the big dogs [i.e., the wealthy and powerful] dressed like the ancestors"—contributed to this. This design feature baked a certain connotation of class hierarchy into the memorial's representations.

As mentioned, class-inflected animosity among the region's residents of Acadian descent regularly became public. Months after this comment, a debate raged in the nearby Lafayette *Daily Advertiser* over the use of the term *coonass.*

Ignited by a radio program host who used it derisively, many self-identified coonasses wrote in, claiming they were not offended and suggesting that everyone "lighten up."[50] Continuing a long-standing tradition, CODOFIL's executive director asserted that these locals were indeed "lazy and ignorant," too benighted to abandon the vulgar term and adopt *Cajun* as a self-descriptor instead.[51] But many rejected this stance. "People need to get a grip and stop worrying about the use of the word coonass," one wrote, "[They] need to realize that they too are coonasses and get over it."[52]

These dynamics ramified into history's uptake at the memorial. For its mainly middle-class supporters, the site relied on a self-identification that opened onto historical awareness; staff entitled its newsletter *Calling All Cajuns*. Linked to anti-intellectualism and predilections for base pleasures (see chapter 5), *coonass* seemed to many professionals to foreclose that possibility. Judging coonass ignorance to be insuperable, they asserted their superiority, foregoing attempts at alliance. Paraphrasing comedian Chris Rock, CODOFIL's director insisted, "There are Cajuns and there are coonasses, and the coonasses have got to go!"[53] Insofar as the memorial's images evoked such derisive positions toward blue-collar white ethnics, they shaped the site's reception (a point I return to in chapter 7).

CONCLUSION

In this chapter, I tried to elucidate a distinct civic politics that helped forge the new public history about Cajuns. To be sure, this development was overdetermined; the social power of race, to reference only one other force, was also pivotal. In his proposal to the NPS for an Acadian site within Jean Lafitte Park, Savoy wrote that, despite "200 years of storms of assimilation [*sic*] via mass media, outside influence, misunderstanding and ridicule by the outside world, [Cajuns] remain standing today . . . alive and fruitful."[54] In desegregation's wake, this idiom of past suffering had become suffused with racial overtones, largely due to Blacks' use of it in civil rights struggles—but also from a white backlash that annexed it.[55] As the NPS's reception of Savoy's petition showed, mobilizing that trope proved crucial in the effort to materialize the new history of Cajuns. Yet something not reducible to this politics of race—a robust alignment of actors, philosophies, expertise, and spatial configurations, all centered on making subjects through historical truth—also proved decisive.

Tracing the translations that brought these individuals and institutions into a momentary alliance illuminated the discrete politics of a civic axis of power.

For one, the agreements through which they joined together to make this public history entailed something besides the exercise of top-down, state-centric power. Without nonstate actors advocating for Acadian history, this new complex does not emerge, certainly not as it did. Working as citizens who established a nonprofit foundation as a node of agency to ground their efforts, Keller and Desjardins mobilized the support of a slew of state actors to join *their* initiative. Along with the academic historians at the public university–based Center for Louisiana Studies, Osborn and Louisiana Endowment for the Humanities pushed the new history away from the effects of market forces, branding those as destructive. Interventions like those of Savoy, Theriot, and Vincent bent the emergent complex toward serving Cajuns and their existential needs rather than merely providing information or touristic entertainment.

Not all these alignments were forged in harmony. Leveraging the authority generated by the archive, academic historians took the region's public historical field by storm, establishing their authority over clearly identified opponents. But most were, and in the processes of recruitment and mobilization that brought them together, everyone "got something." Individuals and groups translated the resources made available through these associations to pursue their own ends. This illuminates how authoritative institutions like the National Park Service and the Center for Louisiana Studies were able to "rule at a distance": Through these linkages, they connected their broad agenda of using history to govern, circumscribed by their centralized locations and limited resources, to the local concerns of other actors who translated it into their own projects. In the memorial's creation, a certain kind of democratic rule unfolded.

In the interconnected visions these advocates had for the memorial's anticipated citizen-forming effects, another distinctive aspect of this civic axis appeared. They were focused on specific kinds of citizen formation, accomplished in particular ways. First, this project diverged from and sidelined the prior regime, described in chapters 1, 2, and 5, whereby elites and amateurs elaborated histories for local consumption as they saw fit. Instead, the new public history relied on the circulation of authoritative knowledge. In part, these translations produced and secured that rule of experts. In Savoy's successful appeal to the National Park Service; in the Louisiana Endowment for the Humanities reliance on academics' research and sponsorship of projects to validate them; in how the memorial's Cajun advocates leveraged the archive's verity to negate the effects of previous narratives: The objective and the outcome was to ground citizen formation in professionally produced truth about the past.

In turn, their efforts shared this second quality: They promoted the notion that historical truths should have a subjective claim on citizens. The region's residents should know and speak truth about the past, not least to negate the historical ignorance and distortions now cast as threats to political order and decorum. From this perspective, one of their shared goals can be described as eliciting "truth effects" from people. They sought to produce truth as a compelling invitation to "put oneself into discourse" and "tell the truth about oneself" as an individual to whom a history "belongs."[56] Applied to this case, the memorial targeted nothing less than a new subjectivity, a way of being Cajun in the world that, as Pinkerton claimed, did not yet exist: Cajuns aware of their Acadian past, a novel condition meant to foster the various civic-political aims described across this and the previous chapter.

The combination of these elements—of political theorizing about social problems and the challenges of influencing citizens' conduct, of techno-material interventions like the memorial to deploy history to address them, and of the aim of stimulating a "subjectivity that is supposed to be 'true'"[57] *according to the truths of history*—rendered this public history a technology of power, a behavior-shaping project. They made it a distinct "mode of subject formation . . . [, of] relations to the self engendered and enjoined in specific practices," one that intersects with but is not reducible to touristic commodification, class and racial hierarchies, or other vectors of power.[58]

As a result, state agencies in Louisiana may indeed have more influence over historical discourse than before. At the same time, compared to the period described in chapter 1, there are likely *not* more state agents engaged in public history, broadly construed. Those bureaucrats, academics, and applied practitioners deployed historical discourse about Cajuns profusely in their efforts to reform them. A major difference that does exist at present is that more public-sector actors are devoted to promulgating narratives about the past in enclosures like the memorial, where historical discourse is instantiated and curated. As already stated, this represents a significant development, a novel dimension of relations of power. But crucially, it was the *outcome* of the processes described here, not their starting point. Rather than beginning from the state, these translations suggest the need to recognize the processes through which history-making alliances emerge and which, *only following their development*, become ensconced within its organs. In the case of the memorial, the influence of public agencies through historical discourse came *after* something more politically variegated occurred, not before. Conventional analyses of public history's power elide this key political moment.

Along these lines, another critical aspect they overlook pertains to how, intrinsically and on the policy implementation side, these ostensibly neutral and technical operations created asymmetries. In each of the translations I analyzed, one can discern operations that, *as a constitutive dimension of forming the network*, delineated an exterior. Illiterates, amateurs, crass entrepreneurs, working-class Cajuns, Blacks: These history-making alliances relegated them to the margins, classifying them as outsiders, citizens who, through the criteria used to elaborate this new public history's objectives and contours, could not participate on equal footing with its insiders. Conventionally, scholars locate the struggles and asymmetries that impinge upon the public historical sphere outside of it, in, for example, the efforts of outside groups like veterans or entrepreneurs to inflect its otherwise apolitical pursuit of policy goals and historical craft. In addition to the adverse effects of those "external" politics, the memorial's formation points to both the associative relations of power and the substantive exclusions that were integral to the field's emergence and "internal" operations.

From this perspective, the most compelling aspects of the political change the memorial wrought occurred before its doors opened. Through these endorsements, disputes, realignments, negotiations, and marginalizations, this network reconfigured the status quo re Cajuns, their history, and their relationship to the body politic. In the memorial, never had so many actors come together to promote the materialization of Acadian history for civic purposes, proposing that citizens be educated *and mobilized* through contact with the Acadian past. Formerly denigrated as white ethnics, Cajuns and their past became the focus of public historical exposition and thus exemplary, worthy of emulation, instructive models of agency for the future. In itself, this constituted a major shift in governance regardless of the public's reception of their efforts. As it happened, however, these efforts did succeed to a significant degree in that regard. The popular uptake of this history is the next chapter's focus.

Chapter Seven

From Cajun to Acadian

Moral Projects and Routes of Historical Remembrance

> After all, our memories are part of a landscape of action, and the broader moral and political projects and historical circumstances in which narratives are inevitably situated.
>
> Jennifer Cole, "Narratives and Moral Projects"

As dawn broke, a small group of us crossed the street from the Acadian Memorial to St. Martinville's city hall. We waited for a few others to join us, and after several minutes, the event began. As we moved into ritual mode, some asked nervous questions ("What are we gonna do?" "What song is she going to sing?"); for some this was a novel event. When a town employee raised the American flag, Jenny Dupuis began singing the "Star Spangled Banner," which she had translated into Cajun French. As this was uncommon, no one joined her. Once finished, a town councilwoman helped the worker raise an Acadian flag up a second pole while another woman sang "Ave Maris Stella," a Marian hymn. Its choice was significant relative to the occasion: August 15 was both the Feast of the Assumption and the National Day of the Acadians. This brief ceremony had launched the town's celebration of the latter.

Just after it finished, a crew from a local network television affiliate arrived, looking for the ceremony. One of the workers accompanied Dupuis back to the flagpole, where they filmed her as she sang the anthem again. The rest of us crossed the street into the memorial and sat on the cypress benches that dotted the space. When Dupuis rejoined us, she made a comment that sparked the most intense exchange of personal memories that I heard that day. Cajun *was not a word that she grew up hearing, she claimed. Once, as a young girl working in the fields with her parents, they saw an airplane pulling something like a large ball behind it.*

When Dupuis asked what it was, her mother responded, "I don't know, and we can't ask, because we're not supposed to be here." Then as now, what exactly her mother meant was opaque to her, though she had come to believe the "we" referenced their status as ethnics. We speculated about other explanations; Margaret Begnaud, a memorial docent, thought that it may have had something to do with the tenuous hold that many tenant farmers had on their land.

But then the exchange veered into other stories of discovering Cajun identity "by accident" during visits outside Louisiana. Charlene Aucoin, the city council member, recounted a childhood trip to the upper South, when her accent amazed the children she met. "Where do you come from?" they wanted to know. During the conversation that ensued, her parents used the term Cajun *to identify themselves to locals, a word they never used at home. Begnaud chimed in with a story about visiting relatives in Texas, where upon arrival, someone greeted them by saying, "The Cajuns are here." She had to ask her mother what the term meant. Remarkably, in a space devoted to giving Cajuns a history, they each recalled that their families did not use the label in everyday life. Yet all of them identified as Cajuns and counted among the event's most enthusiastic participants.*

Months later, I joined Jim Gautreaux in a parking lot a block away from the memorial. Part of a group that I knew from The Lafitte, a local bar, Gautreaux agreed to meet one-on-one to help with my research. After an exchange of greetings, he asked, "Now, tell me again what this is for." I explained my interest in the history of St. Martinville; after spending a lot of time trying to understand the historical sites, I wanted to hear how people thought about the past in their everyday lives. Despite the abstract cast to this request, Gautreaux was game and began with genealogy. Descended from the first Gautreaux who arrived in the region, he named an ancestor who is found on the memorial's mural. He also knew some details about those original immigrants, two cousins who were put on a boat by their father and uncle, the latter a war veteran who'd lost his legs in battle. But Gautreaux had never set foot in the memorial, never seen the depiction of his forebear (though he knew it was there), and had no intention of visiting it. Later that afternoon, he explained that as part of growing up in St. Martinville, he could not take that history or the people who sponsored it seriously. So instead of entering the site to connect his family memories to the memorial's public narrative, he told me to get into his Ford Crown Victoria. Off we went on a tour, during which, with the help of some friends, Gautreaux recounted what "you really *need to know" about the local past.*

These encounters raise the main empirical question I try to answer in this chapter. In the wake of the ceremony at the memorial, the moment when people began to reminisce on aspects of their lives most clearly evoked by the site's discourse produced a surprising consensus. Labeling themselves as Cajuns—a predicate for claiming Acadian history as "mine" or "ours"—was not a common practice for these women during their childhoods. Rather than an active presence in their lives, *Cajun* signified as an absence, a social category whose meaning had to be discovered—in part through engagement with the site's history. Something similar was true about the Acadian past the memorial recounted. When I asked self-identified Cajuns if, before visiting it, they knew the history the memorial represented (or prior to reading the research on which it was based), the answer was almost universally "No." The most poignant response came from Susan Theriot, a local who, after she herself learned the history as an adult, queried her grandfather about what he knew of it. Though a descendant of deportees from colonial Acadia, he knew nothing of the history; when she told him—recounting it as "our" history—it brought him to tears. Taken aback, she asked if he would have preferred that she had never mentioned it. "Mais, yeah, chère, parce que ça fait trop de la peine," he replied ("Well, yes, dear, because it hurts too much").

Meanwhile, given the chance to have his own encounter with that history, Gautreaux took a hard pass, though not from fear of being overwhelmed by its pathos. Instead, in light of his negative opinion of its local sponsors, he could not credit the narrative with veracity or significance. Rather than putting flesh on the bones of his family genealogy, the memorial's history signified as useless speech to him, bluster from people whose condescension he resented.

These moments bring into relief what is always the case with historical remembering: Its salience must be construed, made to signify in social *and* subjective terms. Indeed, they beg the question, If there is no popular memory of the Grand Dérangement and its aftermath, *how* do locals connect to this history as their own? As Geoffrey White points out, histories "have no determinate meaning and certainly no given emotive significance for individuals."[1] Thus, how do the narratives that public histories advance come to matter to people as "their own"? Do they, in fact, matter in this way? As accounts of a past that individuals have not themselves experienced, do histories come to be retold not merely as information they understand but as narratives with which they identify, from which they draw meaning and purpose? Arguing that cultural forms like the newspaper and the museum contributed greatly to the rise of nationalism, Benedict Anderson's *Imagined Communities* launched an abiding scholarly concern with histories as a potent means of generating heartfelt allegiance. Nonetheless, White claims that both the theory and the empirical focus of that work long neglected "the formation of . . . subjectivities," including remembering as such. Instead, they have focused on the "cultural-symbolic bases of shared identity and discourse structures," leaving unaddressed the question of "how . . . certain narratives gain truth value, repeatability, and emotional force."[2]

Along these lines, I suggest that, for individuals like Aucoin and Begnaud, some sort of *induction* unfolds—either individually or as part of a group—whereby Cajun-identifying selves connect historical narratives and objects to their own knowledge, experience, and recollections such that the former signify as personally meaningful.[3] Drawing on interviews with visitors, staff, and supporters, I sketch out an array of routes through which they were induced and induced themselves into remembering Acadian history.[4] Intriguingly, the site engendered multiple paths for this: via family genealogy, by historical analogies, and through autobiographical memories. I concentrate on individuals who embraced its gist but consider as well those who bypassed, rejected, or were excluded from it. As part of this, I attempt to tease out the moral projects that motivated these responses. I interweave findings from the previous chapters to do so, including those from chapter 4 on St. Martinvillers' autobiographical memories. There, individuals who could identify as Cajuns recounted their lives in different ways; here, I thread in key details about their moral positionings in those narratives to contextualize these divergent engagements with the site.

I also suggest how locals' varied encounters, these different routes and responses, aligned (or not) with the sociocivic projects described in chapters 5 and 6. As I have argued, the various initiatives that contributed to the emergence of this new Acadian history were saturated with person-making aims. These were distinct: from Freeman Tilden's vision of historic sites as existential prompts for citizen formation to the bootstrapping project of upwardly mobile Cajuns to heal the wounded subjectivity of their ethnic confreres and more. But they largely converged: In many cases, practitioners' goals in diffusing a history of the happy minority lined up with the emotion-laden motivations that visitors had for consuming it. Meanwhile, in other cases, induction was refused or blocked, and the policy goals of this new history were unrealized or subverted. In any case, historical remembrance emerged as "part of a landscape of action," and for some, historical truth became a resource for their own projects of self-fashioning.[5]

TECHNOLOGIES OF INDUCTION: THE MEMORIAL'S HISTORICAL SPACETIME

Historic sites seek to create profound impressions on visitors, heightening their perception to produce a life-altering experience. At least, one might draw that conclusion from claims made by those who designed the Acadian Memorial. Consider their public statements:

> We want an artist who could make the viewer feel the movement of a great number of people. . . . [The painter] . . . will employ this [trompe l'oeil] technique to create the illusion of figures moving through and out of the painting and into Louisiana.
>
> When descendants of Acadians visit [it], they will experience something special.
>
> Everybody is touched by it. . . . You can touch it; you can feel it. It's real to you as a person if you have Acadian descent.
>
> Now that people are able to stand in front of the painting and think about the exiles who came here . . . it will deepen the feeling about our culture.
>
> People say they feel like they are looking in a mirror.
>
> [It] will be a reserved, quiet setting so that people can remember all things close to their heart, who they are and where they have come from.[6]

Note the stress on the senses and emotions, the attention to design elements' visceral impacts (e.g., a sense of the past "moving into" the present), and the assertion of the site's exceptional significance. Without knowing the referent, one might guess that these assertions describe a liminal experience of some kind. Yet a well-defined objective shines through: to transport visitors from ordinary conditions of perception and learning into extraordinary ones, creating an entirely new dimension in the local landscape of memory.[7]

As is common in the public historical sphere, the memorial aimed to foster historical awareness by crafting such a milieu, distinct from everyday life. In her chronicle of immersive and interactive design, Allison Griffiths defines immersion as denoting spaces that announce themselves "as somehow separate from the world," departing from "conventional modes of spectatorship in favor of a more bodily participation in the experience." Designers also imbue their vision with an interactive gist, seeking to create a "special" spacetime into which "spectators insert their bodies or minds . . . and affect an outcome."[8] Illuminating how such a logic has been constitutive of the museum experience as such, Griffiths's frame can readily be applied to the memorial. As their statements make clear, its founders sought to fashion an exhibit so dramatic that Cajuns would learn to speak Acadian history as their own: that "who they are and where they come from" might become "things close to the heart."

Those comments also intimate how, as commonly practiced in the public historical sphere, the memorial's language departs from everyday discourse about the past. As Paul Ricoeur argues, representations of historical time effect two transitions from the lived experience of memory. First, they instantiate a time *extrinsic to* the remembering subject. Drawing on the calendrical system of dating, their representations erect scaffolding on which a time before memory becomes tangible in ways that do not otherwise occur. The second transition consists in a site's act of "conquer[ing] its space of . . . explanation against the speculative background . . . [of] the problems of evil, love, and death."[9] Though many notions circulate as to how it relates to ultimate questions of human existence, the meaning of history's arc, of the multimillennial unfolding of time, does not signify "objectively." To impose a lucid narrative on the remote past's multiplicity and impart an explanation of its current meaning, a site must fashion a historical "plot"—say, of progress, tragedy, salvation, and so on—to render itself intelligible. Discursively, these moves stretch understanding beyond its ordinary parameters. To "make sense" of the memorial's narrative, visitors were obliged to interweave their personal memories and expectations, their practical grasp of calendrical time, and their interpretation of the significance the site gave to the forgotten past it re-presented.

Regarding that interpretation, in the memorial—whose stated purpose lay in commemorating the eighteenth-century Acadians who immigrated to Louisiana after their deportation from colonial Acadia—visitors like Aucoin and Begnaud encountered a history possessing distinct thrusts. First, it posits Cajuns' historical continuity, contending that they have formed a cohesive, bounded group for centuries. In the exhibit next to its commemorative space, seventeen text panels narrate a continuous trajectory from seventeenth-century France to present-day Louisiana; the visitor walks a linear path along this chronology, tracing with their own movement the permanency posited by the narrative.[10] Such a gist can also be attributed to the general aim of commemorative culture. Monuments beckon from visitors a certain continuity in conduct from past to present; their warrant is to provide models of behavior that the public might emulate. "As we celebrate the strength of the people who came before us, . . . we hope that in our daily lives, [we] live up to that strength," the state's lieutenant governor intoned at one memorial ceremony.[11]

Alongside this message of continuity, the site also conveys positive qualities about the time that encompasses it. Its designers mentioned the influence of their visits to national sites, whose inspirations permeate the memorial's composition. In a garden courtyard at the venue's rear, a granite altar holds an eternal flame, an object that memorializes sacrifice in the manner of a similar device at the Tomb of the Unknown Soldier in Arlington Cemetery. Honoring "the memory of refugees who drowned at sea" and "never made it to the promised land"—referring to the hundreds of Acadians who died during and after the deportation—the eternal flame's nationalist idiom comprises one means for transforming Acadians' temporality.[12] As described earlier, Cajuns were seen as locked in a cyclical time from which they refused to exit, reproducing retrograde traditions outside modernity's trajectory. By endowing their past with heroes whose sacrifice merits reverence, the memorial suggests that Cajun temporality now mirrors that of the nation-state and its patriots. No longer maladaptive, the ethnic collective now inhabits the forward-looking temporality exemplified by those whose sacrifice serves a noble ideal (attaining "the promised land").

Arrête-toi, ami, et souviens-toi ("Pause, friend, and remember"): Inscribed in granite plates that bookend twelve bronze plaques in a wall of names, a call to remembrance specifies the action the site summons visitors to perform. Listing all the Acadian immigrants to colonial Louisiana and inspired by the Vietnam Veterans Memorial on the National Mall, the wall's material form also conveys a commemorative sense. Yet for all its emphasis on memorializing the past, the site's promoters stressed the memorial's significance as a strictly historical intervention. "We no longer have to look to a literary figure for a hero," effused Janie Bulliard, one of the cofounders, in a clear reference to the Evangeline history that historian Carl Brasseaux discredited. "The names on this wall represent true heroes."[13]

Even so, its designers presumed that many regional natives would arrive without enough genealogical knowledge to claim this truthful history. Instead, they would need assistance to "find last names like theirs . . . and then be able to trace their genealogy."[14] Thus, the memorial sought to create that awareness through a genealogical library above the commemorative space and later a digitized database on its website. This comprises another break with ordinary spacetime. Condensing scattered records within its space and endowing them with a commemorative aura, the memorial fosters not only recollection of the ancestors but also affinity with them. In this sense, it is technical, a composite of parts integrated into a machine to engender states not produced in quotidian circumstances: knowledge of distant forebears and truths about their actions, as well as identificatory remembrance of both.

These elements combine to articulate another major thrust in the site's construction of this temporality: Against a backdrop of malice, the time of Cajuns signifies as a triumph over adversaries and obstacles. The mural painting, a thirty-foot by twelve-foot canvas depicting a fictional moment of dozens of Acadians arriving in colonial Louisiana, conveys the apotheosis of this heroic quality. Many of the painting's figures, some of which are near life-size, strike valiant poses, gazing resolutely toward viewers as they take possession of an uninhabited landscape. The rest of the venue provides context for this event: A set of smaller paintings depicts idyllic moments in colonial Acadia, followed by dramatic scenes of their expulsion. Five of the exhibit's seventeen panels describe the expulsion and its aftermath, stressing its unjust character (e.g., "these exiles withstood great tragedy"). In the twentieth century, this dynamic repeats. An exhibit panel specifies that Cajuns were "punished at school . . . for speaking English" but that "the roots movement of the 1960s" spurred them to "launch activities to counter prejudice and abuse," producing a novel status quo in which "Cajun pride is everywhere today."

Designed "to convey a sense of the drama and the struggle these people experienced," the mural encapsulates the site's main message about Acadian history's meaning.[15] Both historical Acadians and contemporary Cajuns exist in a melodramatic, redemptive temporality in which, by dint of their own perseverance, they have overcome the malevolence that vexed them. If, as Carol Greenhouse argues, the construal of time "is 'about' agency and its availability as grist for political self-legitimation," the memorial's history legitimizes contemporary Cajuns in a particular way.[16] Extolling their ancestors' actions in such laudatory terms, the memorial operates to authorize their own agency in the present—to claim the full measure of citizenship previously denied them.

"WE WERE THRILLED TO SEE ALL THE NAMES WERE THERE": REMEMBRANCE VIA GENEALOGY

"Make sure to get Pierre Richard in the picture," an elderly man instructed his son, as he and his wife positioned themselves in front of the mural with their two young grandchildren. The son snapped the photo as the four of them beamed. "We have been here several times," the man explained to me when I approached them, "but our son and his family, they're visiting from out of state and have never seen it." On one side of the family, he went on, they were descended from the Richard depicted in the mural and on the other side from an Arceneaux also portrayed in it. As we chatted, the site's docent invited them to make impressions of their ancestors' names on the wall, and they accepted. The grandparents knew where their respective ancestors were listed on its bronze plaques, so they led their granddaughters to those spots. Taking sheets of paper designed for this purpose, the girls rubbed their pencils across the surface until the names appeared, angled characters in jagged blurs of graphite. Again, smiles broke out; all seemed pleased. After inquiring about the genealogical library upstairs, the grandparents mentioned that they had done work on their family tree and would like to do more. But "we'll have to come [back] when we have more time," the grandfather explained. With that, they left, concluding a brief but apparently successful visit: Now the family's younger members knew more about their ancestors.

This episode, variations of which I witnessed often during fieldwork, represents the most accessible mode through which local visitors connected with the memorial's construal of their past: through genealogy. As noted, the site's founders envisioned that the site would foster historical awareness in this way. Of the three routes into historical remembrance I outline here, designers' intentions were most aligned with visitors' uses in this path of induction.

That said, as this description intimates, "knowledge" may not be an adequate label for describing how Cajun visitors pursued this path. I wrote that the son and granddaughters "knew" more about their forebears through this outing, but that verb scarcely suffices to depict the character of this and many other visits. Their activities intimate that, in terms of its motivation, their outing was centered in the embodied pleasure of intergenerational relationships. Ostensibly, the grandparents wanted to share something they knew about the family's ancestors with their progeny, but that sharing was primarily visual, tactile, and social, not cognitive or didactic. They knew enough genealogy to connect the family to the memorial's representations of the ancestors, but they seemed focused on imbuing their offspring with the positive impression those conveyed—and of inhabiting that feeling together. Visitors like these seemed to stress enriching the bonds between living generations, not acquiring detailed information about their distant ancestors.

Along these lines, many other natives of the region voiced "feel-good" reactions to the memorial's depiction of their forebears. They found it "nice," "amazing," "great," "beautiful," "magnificent," "awesome," "a gem." They were "impressed" and professed to "love" it, saying it filled them with "pride." This emphasis on emotions suggests that in encountering the memorial, many mainly generated affective reactions, not "knowledge-based" ones. While funders and designers were focused on its capacity to diffuse knowledge, these affective superlatives intimate that for many visitors, the memorial's history was as much something they *felt* as something about which they *thought*. Researchers probing how people bear the past caution against too strong an emphasis on *consciousness* as a measure of historical awareness, since it "directs attention to cognitive process rather than to more embodied modes of engaging with the past."[17] These responses indicate that this caveat applies to public history proper. "We looked until we found every name in our family [on the wall]," enthused one woman, "and we were thrilled to see all the names were there." The most substantive takeaways were often emotional, even visceral.

Such reactions aligned with the pastoral goal pursued by many of the Cajuns who became involved in managing the memorial after its launch. Recall that they concentrated on addressing the negative effects of the long-standing denigration of Cajuns *on Cajun selves*; they sought to deploy the site to improve others' self-esteem. Many of them were convinced that the site's history could effect this kind of change. Cindy Arceneaux, a member of the memorial's board, went so far as to claim that the commercially stoked popularity of Cajun food and music was insufficient to accomplish such work; only a proper historical awareness could do this:

> But [the music and food are] not what we're about. We're going to be a caricature after a while . . . if we don't know the heart and the meat of where we started from. Why these people came to settle Acadie. Why these people struggled and ended up here and have done so well. You know, our nation of people is pretty powerful. We fought what was happening, which was a noble scheme of, you know, genocide. Wow—it's pretty powerful. And we have something to be proud of now. And we are; there's

> a lot of pride. And I'm pretty proud of what I've been able to do, as minute as it is.

As these comments intimate, it was perhaps the memorial's particular articulation of genealogical representations and historical narrative that achieved these subjective effects. That is, genealogy introduces a historical dimension to one's awareness, but in a limited chronological sense of a succession of generations. As mentioned in chapter 2, the region's elites have long promoted their genealogical ties to forebears as important, but descendance alone did not secure that significance. Instead, affirming their ancestors' distinguished historical acts procured it.

The memorial enabled its Cajun visitors to make a similar move from mere genealogy to celebrated history. Its elements allowed a visitor with Acadian ancestry to first connect themselves to immigrant forebears, then to appreciate the collective qualities that its representations imputed to those progenitors as historical actors, and then to attribute those qualities to themselves as an inheritance. Referencing the mural painting, locals often interpreted the site to convey positive traits about the Acadians, including their perseverance, religious faith, and triumph over suffering; they then extended such attributes to themselves. "To me, it's personality," one visitor commented. He said he lived his life "at full speed, whether it's work [or] play," explaining, "I think we've learned that this ancestry was like that. You know, they worked hard . . . but played as hard. . . . That's a personality trait that has transcended the generations that goes right back to that [*gestures at the mural*]." By combining the genealogical implications of inheritance with the portrayal of illustrious historical agency, the site encouraged such a connection, which many visitors made.

In the range of responses to its genealogical dimension, simple affirmations of the memorial's emotional impact comprised one end of the spectrum. At the other end, some engaged in reflexive uses of this knowledge for more elaborate acts of self-fashioning. "It was indeed a great experience for me, a great awakening to me," Sandra Mouton claimed as we sat together in the renovated opera house on the downtown square. A middle-aged housewife, Mouton began to compile a family genealogy in her spare time, which led her to the memorial. Visiting its library often, she read its texts "until [she] couldn't see straight."

Absorbing this knowledge of her family's past about which she "had no idea," she applied it to her understanding of her relatives and herself. On the Cajun side of her family, the men were "rough" and "tough," which had registered as personal flaws. "But I understand why he was a mean old coot today," she said of her grandfather, "because of what happened." Extrapolating from her acquired knowledge of the Grand Dérangement and the more recent past, she made a genealogical inference and situated their behavior in its social context. She "would often hear [her] grandpa . . . say, 'Maudits Américains' [damned Americans]," which confused her. "[Now] I know the reason why. It was tough. . . . They were not welcomed. They were not wanted." Then, in a therapeutic application of this new knowledge to her own conduct, she continued:

> **SM:** Once you understand the history and why they're that way—the bitterness, vindictiveness, the prejudice—there's a reason behind the way you feel. But if you don't get over it, it will hurt you. . . . Whatever your parents instill in you [is] something you're going to carry. You will carry it. Until you know the history and the knowledge behind what happened, then you can understand it, and then you can deal with it.
>
> **MD:** Like let go of it?
>
> **SM:** Let it go or understand and be more understanding about some people's prejudice.

This intriguing use of genealogical and historical knowledge for such extensive self-making was rare, though the remarks cited earlier hint that a similar dynamic may have been at play for others. Many Cajun-identifying interviewees were proud of their families, but some revealed domestic challenges with which they struggled, as Mouton did here. In general, authorities conceive of history's salutary effects as operating on civic relations in the body politic. Yet this suggests that it could also be used for more intimate projects. Mouton offered a compelling sense of why she interwove historical knowledge with personal memories: She used the former as tools for reshaping her grasp of family relations and her emotions surrounding them. It seems that delving deep into Acadian history had an ethical dimension, augmenting Mouton's "practical judgment in the living of a moral life."[18]

In this regard, Mouton achieved the upper bound of some of its promoters' expectations for the site. An early proponent told me that she hoped the memorial would curb the anti-Black racism she knew to be present among many Cajuns. In a rare comment along these lines, Mouton explained that her newfound grasp of history's impact on her inner life allowed her to infer the same for Blacks, saying, "I understand the bitterness of the African Americans because of what happened to them." The ideal of "the human sciences," according to Michel Foucault, has been to "constitute, positively, a new self" through "techniques of verbalization."[19] As Tilden argued, public historians often conceive of history as just this kind of prompt for self-improvement, through individuals' uptake of truths from the past. The memorial participates in this dream; with Mouton, its incitement to discourse operated expansively.

In other ways, however, many circumstances worked against such empathetic self-fashioning. There were locals of mixed racial heritage aware of their Acadian ancestry and eager to claim the memorial's history as their own. Largely, however, they did not feel welcome. Some among the memorial's administration were serious about using the site to surmount racial divisions, even hiring a biracial intern who identified as Cajun. *From working on his own family tree, he knew that an Acadian forebear married a person of color in the colonial era such that all descendants from this union were related, though most of them now identify as white. When, by chance, he greeted white visitors descended from that ancestor, he announced to them that they were relatives. They immediately left the building. About his experience as a docent, he concluded, "People are nice and everything, but I'm not always sure if they're sincere, if they really accept me."* A recurrent theme in public history proposals has been that the region's race relations are exemplary, and new sites could enhance such dynamics.[20] Yet in the mid-2010s, the site's director pulled a panel in a temporary exhibit that mentioned Acadian slave owning after some memorial board members complained that it was inaccurate. In practice, too many obstacles existed for the memorial to broadly enable such constructive effects.

"THIS IS OUR GRAND PRÉ": REMEMBRANCE BY ANALOGY

The memorial's genealogical hook was not the only way local visitors induced themselves into connecting with its history. In responding to questions about whether they felt connected to the history the memorial presented, some visitors replied in ways informed by prior experiences. "It's like the Vietnam Memorial Wall," a veteran explained, conveying his reaction to the site's wall of names. "Until you see the name of that person, 'til you know that guy died for the country, the Vietnam Wall doesn't mean anything." In professing that, through the context provided by the rest of the site, he gained a similar sense of "that wall in there of the people's names," his past visit to the war memorial in Washington served as a template, priming his impression of the memorial. In associative analogies like this, many locals generated a remembrance of Acadian history, drawing on a range of prior encounters with historical representations and knowledge about other distant pasts.

In his analysis of how intergenerational bonds form the basis for historical awareness, Maurice Halbwachs stresses that for history to become more than "so many names, dates, and formulas," individuals and groups must connect them to "currents of thought and experience within which we recover our past only because we have lived it."[21] While he described this dynamic in relation to the family, it can be applied to include other aspects of social life on which individuals draw to make historical accounts matter. While, upon arriving at the memorial, many people encountered this novel Acadian history for the first time, the notion of history, of a time beyond memory, was obviously not new to them. By virtue of their exposure to the country's expansive historical culture—history's instruction in schools, its invocation in public discourse, its instantiation in monuments like the Vietnam Veterans Memorial, and so on—many take the past's existence for granted. It should not be surprising, then, that visitors utilized such historical knowledge and experiences of historic sites to interpret the Acadian past's significance.

These extrapolations emerged from varied sources and with different degrees of intensity. While this veteran drew on an episodic memory, a recollection of a past event personally experienced, others situated their reactions to the site with respect to prior historical knowledge. "It's probably the biggest secret in the world: The Acadians were probably the most persecuted group, even more so before the Jewish people," a middle-aged man asserted, to which another person consented during a focus group inside the memorial. Responding to my query about what knowledge he gleaned from the site, he continued to assert that American Indians were the only comparable group to Acadians "because . . . the British tried to eradicate the Acadians, and the Americans tried to eradicate the Indians." In articulating their impressions, others brought similar semantic memories, or recollections of generic knowledge acquired through formal learning, to bear. Along with the previous example, these interpretations are especially intriguing. The memorial did not offer visitors an explicit comparative framework to incite such comments; these interpretations rested on their own associative efforts. As such, takeaways like these were discerned through creative, combinatory work as people made their own connections between history they acquired elsewhere and their impressions of the venue. Both responses foreground that visitors engaged in a complex compositional effort—articulating memories, emotions, and cognitive inferences—to induce themselves into a meaningful understanding of Acadian history.

Along these lines, the connections with other histories of suffering, discrimination, and violence were noteworthy. Again, the memorial did not describe what happened to the Acadians as a genocide, but as this second visitor (and Arceneaux) did, some supplied that frame themselves. As their principal takeaways from the site, many visitors cited the extreme "adversity" the Acadians faced and the resulting "misery," "hardship," and "long, arduous process of suffering." This suggests that while responding to the memorial's implicit prompts in this vein, they extended its melodramatic thrust, identifying the crux of the Acadian past as similar to that of other innocent victims in history. This stress on blameless suffering, cast with a comparative glance toward other groups, lies at the heart of the happy minority trope. Ostensibly, many visitors joined the memorial's designers in expanding it. In this regard, it bears mentioning that comparisons with Blacks (as a group whose historical hardships, like those of Jews and Native Americans, might resemble that of Cajuns) were largely absent in these interviews.[22]

Through many similar analogies, visitors conjugated past experiences of other histories with the memorial's narrative, employing them to articulate their grasp of its meaning. To be sure, for many of these interviewees—especially those who visited the site just once or with whom I had only a brief interaction—it is unclear whether their visits were memorable in any lasting sense. But among a small group of visitors, their sustained engagement did induce historical remembering through such associative dynamics, memories with which they deeply identified.

This group shared several characteristics that shaped these comparable responses. First, they numbered among the individuals who, after the memorial's launch, were recruited into leadership positions at the site, including its staff and the board of its nonprofit foundation. They also shared similar social trajectories; most rose from modest backgrounds into middle-class occupations. Yet it was travel abroad to historic sites that spurred their association with the memorial, especially in the Canadian Maritime provinces of Nova Scotia and New Brunswick. Memories of these travels featured prominently in their interpretations of the memorial and its significance to them.

For Emma Broussard, a retired bank officer, travels in the Canadian Maritimes preceded her first contact with the memorial. The daughter of parents who knew nothing of their Acadian ancestry, she began genealogical research as a favor to them, developing in the process a desire to see the places mentioned in those records. During multiple visits to the Maritimes, she and her family visited many historic sites and even met Canadians to whom they were distantly related. An emotional moment of imagination crystallized what she took away from those travels:

> [At a place in Nova Scotia], we sat out on a bench overlooking the water. It was so calm, so quiet, and it was like . . . it was just he and I that was there, you know? It was like a completeness, a completeness. It was [a feeling of] "I belong." "This is home, this is home." And when we left, we took the ferry on the last day and rode the ferry, and it was like 9:00 at night. . . . The sun was setting, and [we were] looking at the land, and my husband says, "Just imagine, pretend—let's just pretend that we were here in 1755 when all this happened. We were being deported out of here." It was awesome.

Years later, Broussard served briefly as the memorial's director. When I asked why she and others like her, people whose genealogical work and travels led them to the memorial, became so involved in it, she replied, "It's a place that they can come together and there's something there. I guess like going back [to Nova Scotia]. This is our Grand Pré. . . . Bottom line, this is our Grand Pré."

In terms of their mnemonics, something emergent and complex unfolded in these travels vis-à-vis the memorial. Through them, these individuals connected the emotional significance of their personal pasts to historical representations on foreign soil and then transferred the meaning generated by that experience to the memorial. Insofar as this led them to claim the memorial's history as their own—to mingle individual recollection and affect with historical representations so profoundly as to feel connected to (formerly) forgotten ancestors—such dynamics underscore the transformative work involved in such remembrance. Their travel memories provided a fulcrum in this process of analogous transferal of recollected historical representations in the Maritimes to Acadian history in Louisiana. As Broussard's story intimates, these individuals had learned that as Cajuns, they were not legitimate social actors in Louisiana, were not fully at "home" in the US. The information they gathered in touring Canada inspired them to avow the opposite.[23] Unlike anything in Louisiana's public historical sphere at the time of their travels, the narrative learned in Canada affirmed their life trajectories; through subsequent investment in the memorial, they transposed that message into the American context. Evoking her own travels to Grand Pré, another woman said of her commitment to the memorial, "My passion is to say, 'They were not stupid people; they were not mean people. They were quite intelligent; they were quite innovative.'" In a strict sense, she and others outlined something other than the *recovery* of a historical memory of the Acadian past. Instead, they described a complex *discovery*, an active, affective construction of "understandings of the past through encounters with people, artifacts, and landscapes."[24]

For these individuals, induction into this experience and knowledge was not only a personal matter of buttressing self-esteem. Their involvement in the memorial also provided a path for achieving the agency they sought *as Cajuns*. As details of these interviewees' lives suggest, existing interests related to their ethnic identification brought them to the memorial; many became involved in it because it sustained those passions, offering them a platform to render them social and collective. Recalling her performance of a monologue at the mural's dedication, Martha Sonnier remarked, "It was powerful because it was touching on that first day, and it grabs people." This created "the power of the memorial," she claimed, enabling her to "influence" others and "build [ethnic] consciousness." Drawing another analogy, Sonnier cast the site as the equivalent of Holocaust memorials for Jewish Americans, because the memorial allowed her "to be as militant as they have been, to keep the historical facts alive and right before people's eyes and convince them that . . . this kind of a thing [i.e., the deportation] can't happen again." To accomplish this, she and other members of le Théâtre 'Cadien, a francophone theater troupe, collaborated often with the memorial, performing at the site. For others, the memorial provided a platform to sustain all manner of similar efforts, including leadership in genealogical associations, involvement in international exchanges, artistic and literary projects, and management of the site itself through membership on its board. Given the affective investment in play, these seemed to qualify as moral projects, linking emergent passions for remembering Acadian history and ardent visions of a good life to their pastoral efforts to enroll others in the same stirring understanding.

Unsurprisingly, these interviewees counted among those who most often referenced specifics gleaned from academic histories, articulating that knowledge to their grasp of the memorial's narrative. In this regard, they could be seen as fulfilling the vision of site sponsors like the Louisiana Endowment for the Humanities, which stressed knowledge's spread as their principal aim. Yet "knowledge diffusion" hardly captures the dynamics they described. In academics' regular reminders that Americans do not know their history lies the implicit injunction that they should, as well as be able to speak it as a truth that matters. This group of memorial visitors took seriously that obligation to put themselves into historical discourse, and knowing the Acadian past put them in touch with truths about themselves, leading to a profound sense of authenticity. "It is a part of me, and it grows deeper and stronger," explained Arceneaux, the memorial board chair, of her relationship to its history. Her trajectory into the memorial tracked that of others described previously, and like Sonnier, she professed an intense satisfaction in her connection to it. "I have something special that is easy," Arceneaux claimed, "being the historian of, and being able to garner people's love for what I love." In this case, understanding the self, articulating its authentic truth and shaping its purpose, dovetailed with the site's broad civic aim of leading others into that knowledge and truth.

DIGNITY AND TRIUMPH WITH THE ANCESTORS: REMEMBRANCE THROUGH AUTOBIOGRAPHY

"I think America has finally turned its head and looked at the Cajuns themselves as some of the hardest workers and some of the most ingenious people, to get what they've got with what they've had." So responded a retiree, a man who identified as "about 50 percent" Cajun, to my question about the significance of the memorial's history. From there, however, he did not refer to the site to flesh out these thoughts. Instead, he recalled a moment from his younger days. "I knew some guys in college that worked offshore," he explained, men who were "pure Cajun," "and these guys, they worked their butts off for seven straight days." This experience apparently grounded his takeaway about Cajuns and their past, that "when the business of work comes up, . . . you're gonna sit there and work."

This may seem like a non sequitur—to respond to a question about history with a recollected anecdote from personal experience. But it was common and arguably not incongruous. Halbwachs stressed that individuals remember largely through the webs of belonging to groups, but in his analysis of the "interpenetration" of historical accounts and autobiographical memory, he observed that "we fill in these [historical] conceptions, substituting images and impressions for these ideas," and concluded that "the self-sufficient individual consciousness" serves as the "specific element" that secures historical remembering.[25] Like so many other visitors I interviewed, this man "filled in" the memorial's "condensed and schematic" narrative, drawing from the "richer portrait" of his remembered life to interpret it.[26]

In many exchanges, reactions to the site likewise segued into episodic memories of family, work, or other personal experiences. Along these lines, chapter 2 illuminated how historical remembering of St. Martinville often seemed fleeting and superficial, interspersed as those recollections were in other interests and activities. Far from being illogical, such mnemonic bricolage, the makeshift crafting of a sense of history out of experience-near recollections, characterized another substantial path into historical remembering.

Bricolage connotes the minor and the temporary, and many such responses had these qualities. But some of these efforts at self-induction were sustained and elaborate. In these statements, individuals melded their recollections and the gist of their life's trajectory with their interpretation of the memorial. "To me, when I come in here, it's kinda like, it's just a solid place to me," began Morgan Richard, a retired salesman. Gazing at the mural, he continued:

> It's something you can reflect back and think and think, what *misery* those people [*points to mural*] went through! I mean, of course, that . . . Pop, Arthur, Cindy, my son and daughter . . . we did this, we had no electricity when we were growing up as kids, and no toilets, or anything. [*Effects his child's voice*] "Y'all didn't have that?" Oh no, just couche-couche [cornpone] and cornbread, or if it wouldn't have been for that, we'd have starved to death over there, too, and the sweet potatoes we grew. I mean, things were really *backward* and all, so it . . . I guess as I get older, I'm coming into my twilight years, I've just celebrated

> eighty-two years old, and I get to appreciate this more than ever. We're proud that these people [*gestures to mural*] did all this and could really leave something to the children.

The most remarkable aspect of this response lies in the transposition that Richard effects: While beginning and ending his remarks with a clear reference to the mural and his interpretation of it, in the middle he substitutes *his* travails for those of his ancestors. Instead of describing the "misery" they endured, he replaces it with his own, including specific recollections and reported speech evoking his prior attempts to convey it to his children. And while he does not say it explicitly, his act of transposition, coupled with his gestures toward the mural figures standing confidently in the aftermath of their trials, suggests a sense that he, too, overcame great hardship. Like Julia Cormier's interpretation (described in the introduction), his sense of identification seems direct and profound: The struggle *and* triumph of historical Acadians also characterized Richard's life. Thus, when he expresses pride in their accomplishments, it appears he feels similarly about his own.

Such responses were what might be called "autohistories," an intricate interlacing of individual memories with the site's historical narrative. Richard's autohistory hints at the motivations for this enmeshing of memory and history among those who engaged it in this mode. For self-identified Cajuns, the linkage often seemed to involve an ethical affirmation of their own lives. As another member of the theater troupe, a man who also offered an autohistorical narrative, put it, the "bottom line" of the memorial's impact was that it "helps us validate ourselves." Autohistories made this connection explicit: In them, the visitor affirmed that the good, admirable traits of historical Acadians, as well as the overall arc of their lives (as conveyed by the site), manifested in one's own life as well.

As with Richard, a "memory tattoo" from childhood or early adulthood often served as the most prominent spur in autohistories, the anchor of their recollected memories transposed into the memorial's historical narrative. In the most elaborate autohistories, these searing recollections of setbacks, embarrassments, or inequities surfaced as both a reason for seeking validation and the nexus that linked remembered experiences to the Acadian narrative. Explaining her impression of the memorial, Theriot, a former social worker, asserted, "It's hard to reconcile your feelings about one human being being able to do that to another human being," referring to the deportation. While this remark indexed her ancestors' experience at the hands of the British Army, she then moved into the first-person plural, referencing events in her own lifetime. "But . . . you can make it [the burden of mistreatment as an Acadian] a thing of beauty, like, 'We're going to show you that we've survived this, that we're bigger than this,' that we're bigger than them," she explained. In this instance, she referenced herself and her generational cohort, who while previously "downtrodden" had made a "quantum leap" into social acceptance and success.

What made these sentiments so autohistorical was that before commenting on the memorial's specific resonance, Theriot recounted a litany of grievances from her life. From early on, she recalled recognizing that other white Louisianans thought she and her people were "stupid," "mean," and "riffraff"; into the present, she endured "discrimination" and "subtle prejudice" that at times "made [her] furious." In this formulation, Theriot explicitly cast her ancestors' "cross," as she put it, as parallel or continuous with her own; she mapped their struggle onto her own effort to gain respect from contemporaries. As such, the memorial's significance to someone like Theriot went beyond merely establishing historical continuity with ancestors or "accessing" one's cultural patrimony. Instead, it endorsed her sense of vindication ("we're going to show them") over antagonistic forces *in her life*. Their triumph illuminated hers, which was profoundly ethical: It comprised an adamant avowal of her own dignity, refuting so many actions that had challenged it.

After claiming that her experience of the memorial helped transform the "cross" of Acadian identity into something "beautiful," Theriot affirmed that not only she but many in her cohort had done this, that "most Acadians [went from] being downtrodden . . . to doing *really* well." In a substantive way, individuals like Theriot and Richard mapped the memorial's narrative of historical triumph onto their own story of upward mobility; the former helped illuminate and certify the latter. In this triumphant redemption arguably lies a resolution analogous to that performed by narratives of the American Dream. The plotlines are parallel: From modest beginnings, grave obstacles are encountered, yet the denouements are positive, with personal traits as a key vector enabling them.

In this regard, this case could be compared to other studies foregrounding nonelite whites who nurse resentments over the sting of social snubs, political disempowerment, and economic marginalization they endure.[27] Except that in this context, the memorial satisfied the ensuing yearning for a positive narrative about the self and its group, a story conferring respect and dignity. The memorial had the aura of a "shrine," one visitor enthusiastically claimed: Like a holy site with truths instantiated in stone, bronze, and painted canvas, it enthralled some locals, offering them a platform to discover and embrace truths about themselves. Materialized in an elaborate apparatus, its uplifting narrative quenched their desire for self-affirmation.

As such, the site helped energize an empowering circuit between the governed and the governing. Formerly, a Cajun could only dream of being included in the body politic as an ethnic subject. Now, using the site to recast their own subjectivity in positive terms, these visitors ostensibly engaged all the varied civic strategies that its proponents and designers advanced—to heal the wounded subjectivity of Cajun selves, to replace ignorance and historical myths with scholarly truths, to promote Cajuns as a model ethnic minority, to provoke profound reflection on citizenship and belonging, and to reaffirm the class and racial boundaries of Cajuns as respectable whites. In this convergence of state-sponsored policies of citizen-making, truthful discourse from the academy, and motivated individuals with projects of white ethnic self-fashioning, a novel formation of power emerged. Operative through the circulation of public history broadly construed, it illuminates how relations of power can unfold in a capillary, constructive, subject-forming way, as "a productive network that runs through the whole social body, . . . induc[ing] pleasure, form[ing] knowledge, produc[ing] discourse."[28]

OTHER ROUTES OF REMEMBRANCE: INDIFFERENCE, EVASION, REJECTION

But these paths of induction and the circuits of power they activated did not attract everyone. Indeed, there were more people without than within. In chapter 2, Austin Rodrigue lamented that many St. Martinville residents refused to participate in elaborating its historical memoryscape. Similarly, those associated with the memorial were keenly aware that others like them—individuals who could enroll themselves in its historical mode of belonging and citizenship—chose not to.

In addition to the Black locals mentioned earlier who could not easily join this project, many whites abstained from or sidestepped it. In other parts of Louisiana, people with francophone but non-Acadian roots embraced a

Cajun identity in the wake of the shifts described in chapter 5. St. Martinville was not such a place. Apart from exceptions like the memorial's founders, descendants of French immigrants kept their distance from the site in ways that were obvious to observers. "I was appalled that certain people from St. Martinville . . . that normally attend everything that goes on . . . were not present," complained one resident, noting that a highly publicized event sponsored by the memorial lacked their presence. Echoing a common opinion, he explained that "the aristocracy" (i.e., descendants of white Creole families) would not attend "Cajun functions" or "promote Cajuns."

Among those locals, there remained an unease about associating *Cajun* with activities that connoted refinement (e.g., "tennis"). For some, Cajun's signification as matter out of place endured; for all its prominence, the new public history did not fully eradicate the fear of social pollution that association with all things Cajun had long evoked. Another way of considering their avoidance is that while the ascendancy of Acadian history in the region's public sphere eclipsed their preeminence, the well-developed practices that these families had long deployed—using their family histories as means of self-fashioning and political legitimacy (described at length in chapter 2)—did not dissipate. Those alternative routes to empowered personhood through history remained effective. For their purposes, then, the memorial was unnecessary.

When it came to those who shared the sociological traits (i.e., Acadian genealogy, francophone families, working-class backgrounds, etc.) that might help induce them into the memorial's history, individuals followed multiple paths of avoidance or rejection. *Recruiting locals for interviews focused on the memorial, I decided to invite a restaurant cashier with whom I became acquainted through my frequent quests for afternoon coffee. Bridget seemed shy, but I managed to find a few things to chat about with her, like the small child whom she sometimes tended at work, about whom she would become animated. She hailed from a nearby hamlet composed of many Cajun-identifying residents; she would have provided a unique perspective, or so I thought. When I pitched participating in a focus group to her, however, she grew silent. Though the memorial was only a block away from the restaurant, Bridget had never set foot in it and intimated that she did not want to.* Others parried my requests in similar ways. Whether from the awkwardness of my invitation or the topic's otherness, they balked; talking about "history" was an acquired skill, one whose acquisition skewed up the social ladder. I made a similar point earlier (in chapter 2), which is that not a few of my interlocutors begged off from discussing "history," directing me toward the more educated as they did. Paraphrasing David Lowenthal, for many the past was a foreign country, *culturally*.[29] Unfamiliar with its specialized language and dedicated spaces—which, as the foregoing illuminates, can be seen as complicated, esoteric, even exclusive—they were uninclined to visit it.

Relatives and friends of the site's advocates constituted another group who demurred at the memorial's appeal. In principle, they were just as capable of claiming the Acadian past as these supporters were, but they were also conspicuous in their absence from the site. This nonresponse dismayed these supporters, over which they ruminated in interviews. "No, they're not [interested]," one memorial board member commented about the people she grew up with in the countryside near St. Martinville. "It's like, 'We don't know, and we don't want to know. We've moved on.'" Moving on was also explicit in the explanation offered by another native, *a passionate genealogist who claimed that his brother expressed zero interest in visiting sites like the memorial. The two were raised in modest circumstances on a small farm during the grinding poverty of the Great Depression. The historic sites evoke the old days, his brother complained, which weren't so great. Why would he want to be reminded of them?*

This suggests a desire to forget, a motivated effort to leave behind personal experiences, ones that historical narratives about a deep past of heroic ancestors, no matter how celebratory, could not rehabilitate. Such responses put into view a pragmatic approach to the memorial's history, one no less ethico-political than that of the memorial's adherents. Apparently, many could not easily discard something about the embarrassment associated with being labeled Cajun in the past. Another memorial board member articulated this sentiment, a doctor whom I asked about the relative absence of men among the site's leadership. At first, he disagreed with the question's premise, but when I pointed out that all the memorial's directors and most of its board chairs had been women, he warmed to the topic. "There was a time when it wasn't cool and nobody wanted to identify as a Cajun, because a coon's ass is lower than a Black man," he offered, referencing the epithet's use to maintain a racialized hierarchy. He implied that for men of a certain age, embracing the site's history would put their effort to escape classification as coonass or Cajun at risk. This jibes with chapter 4's analysis, which featured middle-class residents (mostly men) of Acadian descent who positioned themselves as unambiguously white. They avoided mention of Cajun ethnicity and were not associated with the memorial; instead, their stories de-emphasized their social origins, highlighted their own striving, and stressed their relationships (in both alliance and successful competition) with the town's prominent families. Moving on from memories of a Cajun childhood and young adulthood, avoiding the memorial and the open repositioning of one's self as Cajun that frequenting it would entail, might evince a "desire not to allow history . . . to define the present."[30]

Finally, some rejected the site, refusing induction outright. These working-class residents centered the venue's links to individuals and the town's social landscape, bringing memories of their social interactions to bear in their consideration of it. As mentioned, some thought that the site's representation of shared genealogical descendance reinforced their sense that all Cajuns were related, belonging to a collective that possessed a deep, active social bond. It was the opposite with Martin Johnson. In his everyday life, this carpenter experienced profound differences separating him from other Cajuns, and the memorial did not attenuate that sense. Invoking the "class distinction" that characterized St. Martinville, he explained, "Even though I'm related to half of the people in town, . . . as far as most people are concerned, we are trash, yet I'm related to them, yet I have the same blood . . . that flows in their veins." As I described in chapter 4, many like Johnson felt they were on the outside of an empowered mainstream of locals who disdained them. In different terms, they possessed a strong sense of occupying a spacetime distinct from that of other residents, including many of their putative white ethnic "cousins." As they did not experience meaningful solidarity with other Cajuns in their everyday lives, they were unwilling to invest in the memorial's representation of a unified, harmonious ethnos in the past.[31]

Gautreaux shared similar sentiments. From our first meeting at The Lafitte, he sought to extend the breadth of my inquiry. Though he knew tidbits about his genealogy going back to the colonial era, those details were relatively unimportant to him; he thought they should be less significant for me as well. Instead, his responses to my questions centered on the recent past and the skewed relations of power that impacted his life. In this focus on the practical past, he consistently evoked the social relations that Johnson referenced and their negative impacts on his well-being. *On that day near the memorial, his first story—how his grandfather was whitecapped—gave him an idea. He proposed that we visit someone who "can tell you how this town is run from experience." Off we sped to the home of a close friend, a woman in her seventies who narrated her case of similar expropriation by powerful individuals. From there, we continued on a tour, with Gautreaux stopping to introduce me to acquaintances, people whom he thought would offer me similar perspectives, who together narrated an "alternative history" of St. Martinville.*

As we concluded at a bar in the countryside, I asked him why, in response to my questions about history, he responded with such a tour. After a pause, he declared, "Truth. I wanted you to hear the truth." For Gautreaux, the narrative about the historical Acadians attempted to prettify a sordid collective past, one that, insofar as it impacted him, he found onerous and foul. Going further than Johnson, he intimated that he rejected the memorial because of the perceived disingenuity of those behind it. Significantly, his objection was not epistemological, based on criteria for verifying the history's veracity. Instead, it pertained to relations of power and sociality outside the site. "Those people, . . . they don't care about the truth," he finished, "and it hurts me to see that."

Gautreaux's vigorous rejection of the site underscores how the stakes of remembering the Acadian past varied according to social position. Together with the other reactions I outlined, these stances hint at ethical and political preoccupations motivating their rebuff: concerns with dignity and respect, commitments to fairness, and desires to maintain a long-cultivated "white" sense of self. No less than those who embraced the memorial's history, their decisions to remember otherwise intimate that remembrance is "used pragmatically to act on the present."[32] Far from operating naturally or as a kind of accessory that one easily adopts or sheds, the choice to engage with history as the memorial presented it was deeply embedded in the "moral and existential predicaments" that Cajun ethnicity presented, implicated as it was in broader material and political struggles.[33]

CONCLUSION

Across this chapter, I analyzed what might be described as the substantial yet uneven emergence of historical awareness. In processes that resembled *discovery* more than *recovery*, visitors to the Acadian Memorial drew on, among other things, memories of family life, of travels to the Canadian Maritimes, and of indignities they endured to induce themselves into a sense that a continuum spanning centuries contained their lives. In this regard, the memorial proved to be a strikingly generative resource. The site's designers intended this outcome; they envisioned an immersive, interactive space that would expand the memoryscape and induce such reactions. Still, it arguably succeeded to a remarkable degree. Drawing from the quotidian stuff of their lives, many visitors wove their recollections into their interpretation of the site's history. Much of this memory work was novel and original, motivated by and grounded in personal projects of self-fashioning and even self-transformation.

The contingency of this emergence bears emphasizing. A key condition for it peeked through much of this material—namely, the enduring effects of how many individuals and entities objectified Cajuns as problematic citizens and social "matter out of place."[34] In so many words, I discerned visitors struggling (and succeeding) to reject the negative implications of that widely affirmed dysfunction. Surfacing from childhood and early adulthood, long-embodied memories of embarrassment and marginalization became fodder for reworking self and collectivity in the memorial space. To put it bluntly, the influence of representing Cajuns as a kind of white trash operated as a precondition for the memorial's empowering impact. The fallout from an increasingly capitalist and technocratic social formation, one that vilified Cajuns and their history, constituted a key dimension of the ethico-political stakes of historical remembrance at the memorial. Feeling they were denied full personhood and citizenship, many visitors' moral project was to use the site's historical narrative to claim them. To them, history's comfort, pleasure, and empowerment were clear and palpable. Glossing Friedrich Nietzsche, Liisa Malkki summarizes this effect, claiming that "actors produce historical consciousness where they need it 'for the sake of life and actions.'"[35]

Another contingent aspect of the memorial's emergence—its relation to a set of institutions and a long, heteroclite process of policymaking—also merits emphasis. An implicit contention across the chapter has been that the self-constituting desires of many memorial visitors meshed with the subjectivizing aims of governing authorities. Simply put, the site facilitated a smooth integration of historical truth "out there" with subjective truths "in here." Memorial visitors readily used the meaning evoked by its representations of historical Acadians to redeem their memories and affirm their own emotions, goals, and sense of self. They interpreted the truths presented by the site as saying something profound, vital, and authentic *about them*. This willingness to situate their lives vis-à-vis a historical narrative underscores a basic cultural premise: that history's truths are *for* personal and collective meaning-making.

Colloquially, this is widely acknowledged. Poet Clint Smith asserts that historical narratives are intimately tied to "people's sense of who they are in the world, and their sense of how they attain meaning and a sense of personhood and a sense of value."[36] However, by situating memorial visitors' inclinations to speak history's truths about themselves in relation to the civic goals of the site's many architects, one can also gauge the profound alignment between the governed and the governing in this field. "Putting oneself in [historical] discourse"—inviting citizens to take history seriously, not simply to "know" it but also to live by it, to "tell the truth about oneself" through it—plausibly summarizes the thrust of this new public history as its advocates articulated it.[37] In this engagement with the memorial, there was no excess, no bastardization of history's "proper" purpose. Together, the region's public history practitioners and the memorial's visitors engaged this "regime of truth": to lead citizens to tell the truth about themselves *as Cajuns*, whereby they transformed their own subjectivity through the ensuing effects of the encounter. This integration arguably constitutes the obscured force of contemporary regimes of public historical discourse. In their celebratory configurations, public histories allow individuals to readily translate truths about the past into enlivening truths about themselves, contributing in turn to a range of civic, self-governing aims.

This governmental regime of historical discourse about Cajuns anchors what an academic once referred to as the "Cajun industrial complex," or the predominance of Cajun history and heritage in south Louisiana's public culture.[38] Combined with the other Acadian historic sites, the memorial instantiates Cajuns as one of the region's prime historical actors and thus the citizens whose agency its public history complex most seeks to empower.

At the same time, its limits cannot be overstated. As I have argued throughout the book, a singular and somewhat accidental inflection occurred in Louisiana beginning in the late 1960s and 1970s, whereby Cajuns became a "happy minority," usurping Black historical narratives in the process. With this chapter's findings, the full measure of this new Acadian history's configuration of historical suffering, moral innocence, and endowed citizenship can be appreciated. Through its potent emplotment of empowered agency, the memorial enabled visitors to see themselves not only as unjustly maligned but also as descendants of forebears who endured a world-historical injustice. Similar instantiations for Black citizens do not exist in Louisiana, even though their civil rights–era evocation of a similar narrative inspired this formulation. In so many words, this powerful articulation of history boosted Cajuns' status as whites at Blacks' expense. This suggests that however one might characterize the current imbrication of race in statecraft, the region remained, in the realm of public history, a racial state.[39] This unfolded in and through the public historical sphere, whose participants have allocated asymmetrical degrees of agency to groups of citizens according to their racial classifications by crafting and circulating distinct histories about them.

Meanwhile, the host of whites who, for varied reasons, abstained from claiming the memorial's history as their own also suggests that this history's reach exceeded its grasp. It did not draw all those whom decades of slights and humiliation had wounded; many found other routes into dignity, well-being, and citizenship. Embedded as it was in residents' lived circumstances, the site repelled some who found it pretentious. So while it achieved the pastoral impact intended for it, the memorial remained insufficient, an ineffectual intervention for many. Its partial success also made it something of a provocation, portending the articulation of other recollections into narratives as yet without voice—in Jim Gautreaux's formulation, of truths yet to be told.

Conclusion

The interrelated claims emerging across this book stake out a position that in the American context, history has an abiding pedigree as a discourse for *ruling and governing*: for enunciating and ranking what kinds of and whose agency counts, for ordering difference within the body politic, and for inspiring citizens to conduct themselves according to its truths. They also situate politics—grasped through Michel Foucault's expansive reformulation—deep inside the workings of memory and public history. And from this perspective, *remember* is an action verb rather than a passive state, potentially implicated in ethical practice and relations of power, and this is so whether remembrance is autobiographical and intimate, social and contested, or institutionalized and professionally curated. This reframes historical narratives and memories, casting them as widely circulating, politically generative forms of speech *and* action.

To pursue this reframing, I decentered history from the academy and the professionalized public historical sphere. Following Michel-Rolph Trouillot's warning that, to their peril, scholars have failed to take seriously how "history has many hearths and academics are not [its] sole . . . teachers," the study attempted to respond to his challenge to "examine in detail the concrete production of specific narratives."[1] I considered how accounts of Cajuns and their past circulated widely beyond the academy: in analyses of authorities and applied practitioners, historic sites based on Longfellow's *Evangeline*, assertions by white ethnic politicians and Cajun revivalists, and everyday memories of locals eager to erase harmful narratives. Reconsidered in this way, history appears as a discourse embedded in relations of power, deployed in a fractured social order where narratives about the past are motivated, contested, and laden with ethico-civic goals. By foregrounding the uses of history to "make up" citizens—at the millennium, to enable Cajun subjects who knew their Acadian past—I de-emphasized a conventional focus on history as *product* and opened expansively onto questions about *processes* through which it fosters a civic politics.

Along these lines, engaging with those who embraced the Acadian Memorial's history illuminated that historical memories are social constructions that "actors do not discover . . . before they [make] them" and that are rather "embedded in and emerge from particular, local, lived circumstances."[2] By contrast, scholars often take them for granted as products of a quasi-natural capacity that humans innately possess or ones that organically develop as peoples become more "civilized." Instead, what emerged from the foregoing were creative acts of bricolage. Cajun visitors to the memorial interwove their personal memories, interpretations of its representations, and self-fashioning aims into historical remembrance. This memory work seems even more remarkable when placed against the backdrop of an existing landscape of memory—including a prior failed attempt to activate the distant Acadian past—which underscored how much the effort to instantiate and remember a new history constituted a rupture and an innovation. History was also *for* governing the self, for shaping a person who could integrate divergent memories, affirm its dignity, and *pace* conventions insisting on the contrary, claim civic belonging as a proud white ethnic.

As such, the book offered an account of historical remembrance in the making. With respect to white ethnic revivals, scholars sometimes stress nostalgia as a motivation and a central cultural dynamic.[3] Yet that notion hardly captures the gist of the meaning-making pursued at the memorial. Distant, formative memories were present, embodied. Across the varied routes into historical remembrance, many seemed to be processing the encumbering effects of ordinary suffering in their lives. The lived past was not past. Instead of a desire for a bygone era, an ethics of using history to validate one's self *in the present* grounded much of their memory work. As visitors pursued moral projects to acquit themselves of the indictments associated with Cajuns' "faulty" conduct, I sometimes felt I witnessed the transformation of identity and historicity in real time, as the "motivations, emotions, and meanings" of their self-fashioning "vitalize[d] . . . the structures and circumstances" encompassing their lives.[4] Crucially, this underscores how the "origin" of this history and the historical consciousness it expressed cannot be situated in the "past." Among Cajuns, there was no foundational remembrance of remote Acadian history; instead, they discovered its meaning in the present.

Analyzing these visitor interviews, it occurred to me that the story they told might be undecipherable to many in the region, much less outsiders. Cajuns have been celebrated for decades as the happy minority. How could historical remembrance of the Acadian past in the twenty-first century be so emotionally fraught, so full of a lived sense of intolerance and inequities? The first chapter attempted an explanatory sketch: Into the 1960s, the vilification of Cajuns across the public sphere—buttressed by historical narratives stressing their degradation—was widespread and intense. As such, their engagement with the memorial can be seen alongside accounts of other whites who, in the nation's constant economic churn, its fraught politics of citizenship, and the struggles these entailed, accumulate subjective injuries and resentments.[5] In this sense, Cajun visitors' historical remembrance of the distant Acadian past emerged as fully American, entrenched in the country's political economy and grounded in hierarchical effects of capitalism, race, gender, and state formation.

In an ironic and unique twist, however, a slew of institutions and individuals furnished Cajuns with a public historical complex that sought to undo that disorder's harsh effects on their psyches. This volte-face, startling in its speed, was also embedded in national developments. To be sure, the multiplicity of actors who problematized the social in new ways, such that this public history emerged as a solution to the various challenges they identified, was striking in its breadth and heterogeneity. But whether it was National Park Service officials and their academic consultants situating Cajun history within interpretive grids of the nation-state, or natives like Revon Reed and Marc Savoy appealing to national actors for respect and relief, a shifting American schema of historical meaning and national belonging deeply influenced this creation. A host of forces altered a venerable tradition of state- and citizen-making through historical discourse, devising a new biopolitical mandate to govern through the bonds of Cajun ethnicity.

As Carol Greenhouse argues, one mode of wielding power within the state transpires through the management of competing histories and their claims to political prominence. Accordingly, a key strategy for those who would legitimate their power lies in crafting histories that "contain and control the public relevance of personal and group difference."[6] As conflicts over social differences threatened to tear the country apart, federal actors proposed a new narrative that the nation tell itself, in which Cajuns—precisely as white ethnics seemingly far from the mainstream—featured prominently. Reversing decades of emphasis on integration and homogeneity, they led the way in crafting a history in which Cajuns exemplified America's capacity to incorporate difference in harmony, "offering an alternative story of the compatibility between the modern [nation] and the traditional [subgroup]."[7]

As a result, this study proposes an alternative view on the operations of public history in Louisiana, situating it vis-à-vis an expanding network of historic sites, actors who promoted their elaboration and benefits, and citizens who were its (often willing) subjects. In the book's later chapters, I used the concept of a culture complex to describe and analyze the web of forces that combined to instantiate this new Acadian history. I posited a twofold value of naming this mix of persons, things, and techniques as a complex. First, such a notion helped situate many actors—from the National Park Service to the Center for Louisiana Studies, from the Louisiana Endowment for the Humanities to St. Martinville's municipal government, from Freeman Tilden and Justine Pinkerton to Melissa Keller and Devon Melançon—in the expanding space of public historical theorizing, policymaking, and site design. Through their alliances and networks that materialized the history, they elaborated a "style of reasoning, . . . an entire body of knowledge, and a toolkit of . . . original practices" in the process.[8] A distinct field not reducible to other domains, it became the consequential hub around which the history of Cajuns as the happy minority took shape. In this light, the study's most significant takeaway is that, apart from the typical focus on diffusing history as mere knowledge, the new Acadian public history's advocates tied its elaboration to various civic and political goals. Acadian history was *for* governing the region and the country, reshaping residents' relationship to the past to address a range of social problems.

Along these lines, I employed the notion of a culture complex to stress the concrete, technical character of public history's materialization in particular sites: Practitioners configured texts, objects, techniques of display, paths of circulation, and so on to reshape the understanding and behavior of those who visit the memorial—their *culture*. Barbara Kirshenblatt-Gimblett's comments about exhibitions seem relevant here, insofar as they align with public history's aim to "do for the life world what the life world cannot do for itself." Abstracting from documents, artifacts, and images, their displays purport to "show relationships that cannot otherwise be seen," specifically that of the citizen-subject to a remote past that beckons its reflection and action.[9] From this perspective, such efforts can be appreciated for what they are: discrete, techno-material interventions that seek to impact visitors' selves, to rearticulate their conduct and subjectivity. As such, they comprise a politics linked to yet distinct from other relations of power.

Truth's power operated as this complex's civic glue. Its authority and attraction for both practitioners and citizens bound them together in relations of influence, deference, and desires to access an intrinsic source of personal authenticity. For the memorial's most enthusiastic Cajun visitors, this conjunction was productive and benign. They willingly committed to the historical truth the site conveyed, embracing its implications for their own projects of self-fashioning. Consequently, the book's most provocative implication is that Foucault's notion of governmentality—whereby "the 'freedom' of subjects and the 'power' of the state are not external to each other, but constitutively related"—provides a productive lens for grasping this convergence of truth, power, and subjectivity in sites like the memorial.[10] The relations of power that unfold in them simultaneously include practitioners' efforts to form citizens *and* the ethical pursuits of citizens themselves. Accordingly, a certain circuit of veridiction unfolded: The truths of history were meant to be lived, and some did find their own living truth in those of history.

That said, the complex's boundaries and challenges, its considerable periphery and its potential risks, bear emphasizing as well. As part of its narrative, this study interwove an analysis of social class and its impacts on remembering the distant Cajun past, emphasizing that, in its elaboration and uptake, the new public history rearticulated abiding class tensions among people of Acadian descent. Not everyone desired the knowledge and empowered self-fashioning that the memorial offered. Among individuals of Acadian descent, many agnostics and skeptics sidestepped them. For some, Cajun history was a hindrance to social mobility, an embarrassment to be shed. Allowing it to define their present would have posed a problem; its salience and effects were potentially burdensome. Others were suspicious and derisive, unwilling to entertain the abstraction and artifice of historical representation. Aware of the social limitations imposed on them by authorities and the more affluent, they saw history as another obfuscating discourse that served the formers' prerogatives. Still others were apathetic; for them, history presented as a foreign country with unfamiliar terrain trod only by specialists. By comparing these "historical outsiders" to those who inducted themselves into remembering the Acadian past, this study suggests another reason why the acquisition of historical memories requires explanations grounded in the circumstances of contemporary life, not in the distant past. Acadian history presented to some as a necessary resource for living but to others as threatening, overbearing, or superfluous. What form it took depended on individuals' past experiences and current aspirations, their stances toward the fraught history of *Cajun*'s uses as a social classification, and their moral projects for inhabiting or dodging it. Refracted across class and gender locations, history was "an entirely different creature" for whites in different social positions.[11]

The racial dimensions of this new public history were equally complex and tricky, about which *Remembering the Cajun Past* offered an interpretation with several facets. Broadly speaking, I described how, through shifting public historical narratives of the past century, Cajuns became a model white ethnic minority, shedding the status of problematic not-quite-whites and achieving a fuller inclusion as whites. This reracialization was an explicit goal of many of the memorial's designers, curators, and visitors, who focused on elevating Cajuns' status. Cajuns had "triumphed twice over the English . . . and *les Américains*, who [both] tried to destroy their culture," as one site consultant described its intended message. From his perspective, the memorial served as an inclusive intervention, generating an awareness that Cajuns had escaped a "stigmatized society" and now belonged to "the mainstream"; they were eager to tell others triumphantly, "Here we are." Crucially, he cast these dynamics as unfolding *within whiteness*, describing the problem as an intra-racial struggle: He sought to negate the pernicious effects of Cajuns' relegation to a second tier of whiteness and promote the rise of all Cajuns into equal status with white adversaries. Matthew Jacobson argues that the emergence of white ethnic pride in the 1960s and '70s was in no small part linked to "self-distancing from whiteness and privilege."[12] A critical mass of Cajuns at the memorial oriented in the opposite direction. They concentrated on erasing the boundary excluding them from full-fledged whiteness; as the book shows, they stressed a profound sense of marginalization from white, middle-class belonging. As such, they largely focused up the class and racial hierarchy toward more affluent whites and much less down toward working-class whites or Blacks. By and large, they did not center their historical remembering on reinforcing the boundary between themselves and Blacks.

At the same time, Black-white relations and the enduring repercussions of the civil rights movement gave an undeniable impetus to this history-making. This manifested in several ways. In St. Martinville, these dynamics profoundly shaped how whites remembered themselves, their Black neighbors, and the interracial past. Some recent work underestimates, I believe, the degree to which a modified project of racial segregation continues to animate many whites in Louisiana.[13] Arlie Hochschild writes that her Louisiana interlocutors "were generally silent about blacks," so much so that "the [Black] man or woman standing patiently in line next to them" was "missing" from their narratives about the current moment.[14] My experience was quite the opposite. Many whites discussed their feelings toward and relationships with Blacks openly, referencing particular individuals and groups. In this sense, the negation of Blacks' "dark, miserable past" in St. Martinville rested on widespread everyday sentiments among whites that the interracial status quo most afflicted them and *not* their Black neighbors. In this sense, a structure of feeling underwrote the new Acadian history's remarkable inversion of historical victimhood—its centering of the deportation's violence as the defining event in the Cajun past, while the cruelty of slavery and Jim Crow could not be represented to any significant degree. As such, this finding does intersect with another of Hochschild's claims—namely, that whites felt strongly about meriting attention if not redress from government and the private sector. In sum, this new history reinforced the notion that, as whites, Cajuns had suffered, were disadvantaged, and did not deserve to be "strangers in their own land" when it came to their standing vis-à-vis people of color.[15]

I hasten to add that the privileging of whiteness in this public history-making was overdetermined: Structural forces were equally if not more consequential in producing it. Otherwise racially neutral practices, including a "melodramatic" mode common in public historical discourse, also fostered it.[16] The centering of oppression in the new Acadian history repeats a well-trodden trope of American history as a "nation of immigrants." In this rhetorical tradition, practically all European immigrants flee hardship or persecution and overcome great obstacles to secure their place as citizens. This figure often circulates as racially neutral. *As an academic put it in remarks at an annual Acadian Culture Day at the Vermilionville Living History Museum, a key takeaway of Acadian history was that in their relocation to Louisiana, those colonial immigrants sought not just to live out their days as exiles but rather to "create a home and a future" for themselves, their children, and their grandchildren.* What could be more fundamentally human, and thereby nonracial, than to affirm that migrants desired and made for themselves a new home?

Practically speaking, however, citizenship and its privileges turn on such discourses of belonging, of making America a home by "making a contribution" to it.[17] In principle, these themes of violence suffered and redeemed by participating in the state's progress could also be used to describe Black history in Louisiana. But in the public historical sphere, they have not been. It bears stressing that these limitations were not unique to St. Martinville. As I intimated in several chapters, the privileges that the new history accords to Cajuns—a celebratory narrative about significant contributions to the state and nation, a bespoke attention to remedying their embarrassment and exclusion, a heroizing emphasis on their historical travails—can also be found in the National Park Service's representations. Since its opening in 1994, the Jean Lafitte Park's Acadian Cultural Center in Lafayette has screened *The Cajun Way: Echoes of Acadia*, a film that graphically portrays the aggression of British soldiers against Acadians, for example, through the reenactment of a soldier rifle-butting an Acadian settler.[18] Even at Whitney Plantation, a privately funded site that narrates the history of an antebellum plantation on the Mississippi from the perspective of the enslaved, nothing so vividly evocative of domination was displayed through the end of the 2010s.

Nor did it offer anything like *The Cajun Way*'s jubilant, affirming takeaway. As it concludes with upbeat images conveying the freedom and happiness Cajuns enjoy in America, with a lively Cajun two-step as the soundtrack and joyous dancers flashing across the screen, the film features the lyrics of Bruce Daigrepont, a Cajun musician and songwriter, who sings, "On a trouvé notre pays, la Louisiane notre paradis. . . . Un grand voyage pour notre monde, pour trouver la liberté." (We found our country, Louisiana our paradise. . . . a great journey for our people, to find freedom.)[19] In the region, Black history has no public historical equivalent. By elevating Cajuns as the happy minority, enfolding them into citizenship and white racial belonging through an exclusive narrative featuring their jovial triumph over victimization, this project furthered a ranking of racial difference by enhancing whites' social power. Rather than uniting and "equalizing"—that is, enrolling citizens in a project constituting them as comembers and peers in the body politic—postsegregation public history operated to reproduce a racist hierarchy.

While this stratification through historical discourse is problematic enough, I conclude by suggesting that the most worrisome aspect of this new regime consists in how it relates truth and power to citizens' subjectivity. The analysis of the many processes surrounding this narrative's emergence suggests that the way sites like the memorial present truth and that visitors embrace it involves something perilous. For one, historical truths about Cajuns—"the story of the Acadians is one of survival against all odds"—have a static quality, an insistence on continuity and the preservation of an essence, which this study calls into question.[20] Instead, who Cajuns are and why their past mattered to the body politic were in flux. In processes that belied the maintenance of any abiding essence—as the result of diverse, intersecting forces and the spread of a professionalized, immersive regime of instantiating history—Cajuns' past as a story of the happy minority came to be. For another, sites presented these truths as a closed, finished discourse, assertions about which there was no debate. Yet such a pretense could only be secured in the manicured enclosure of venues themselves. Beyond them—in the halls of the academy and in professionals' publications, in the diverse problematizations and negotiations of the many organizations that pursued a new Acadian history, and in the local public's reception of the result—a roiling mix of persuasion, polemics, embrace, disagreement, alliance building, and refusal predominated.

Finally, the vision of truth's civic significance and utility, shared by practitioners and citizen visitors alike, unfolded within a paradigm of passive reception. Practitioners designed a site's truth statements to be digested whole; exhibited as possessing unquestioned validity, their evocative presentation privileged acquiescence. Visitors accordingly embraced these historical messages as foundational. Conveyed as a naked veracity, history appeared as discursive bedrock, sound enough *tel quel* to ground Cajuns' pursuits of dignity, self-fashioning, and authenticity. In these configurations, history's usefulness for democratic citizen formation can be doubted. An insistence on the teleological becoming of people and the state, despite their mutability; a hermetic presentation of history's truths, *pace* their piecemeal construction; and the purveyance of an aura of historical legitimacy, fostering passivity in truth's application to the self: One might reasonably ask how much these practices foster self-governance.

Admittedly, this questioning of history's politics lies in some tension with the felicitous outcome I described for many of the memorial's Cajun visitors. Given how authorities vilified Cajuns so extensively for so long—centering historical discourse to do so—a certain poetic justice, a decency and perhaps an irony, resides in the development of this public history. Yet this regime fails to fulfill the promise of historical analysis or the needs of a democratic citizenry.

The memorial's (as well as the Jean Lafitte Park Acadian Unit's) histories soothed and celebrated, a civic politics that is not in itself condemnable. But if public history's expansion has proceeded as the diffusion of truth propositions we should not merely accept but also submit to, then those sites hardly transmitted the range of skills and insights that might augment citizens' practice of freedom and self-governance.[21] They did not enable visitors' capacity to discern the contingency in how and for what purposes Cajuns and their history were objectified: to appreciate that the superseded narratives about Cajuns' troubling regression and Evangeline's heroic peregrinations, as well as the current one about the fortuitous survival of the happy minority, are productions of this world, not timeless realities. They did not create openings onto the reasoning and methods that historians use to problematize their own investigations, such that citizens might experiment with them for their own purposes. They did not connect the Acadian past to broader political challenges that prompted the new history's elaboration, enabling visitors to consider it in relation to contemporary problems and risks. Without a pedagogy that empowers citizens to problematize and act on the world and themselves, the mere diffusion of knowledge arguably amounts to a call for obedience and borders on indoctrination.[22]

The challenge evoked here is widespread, not limited to the public historical sphere in Louisiana. On the one hand, as curator Pete Daniel points out in a memoir of his long tenure at the National Museum of American History, the process of making its exhibits hardly inspires confidence in its veracity and democratic utility.[23] In Daniel's account, "visionless Smithsonian secretaries, museum directors, intrusive donors, and compliant curators dictated celebratory exhibits that minimized or ignored important scholarship" and "suggested a repository of historical clichés." As a result, the site ended staff's "traditional freedom of exploring any subject," fostering a "reluctance to confront controversial subjects . . . [that] permitted dangerous mythologies to fester."[24] On the other hand, the truth of history possesses special value, we are often told. Many actors—actors as diverse as Tilden and the National Park Service, the Center for Louisiana Studies and the Louisiana Endowment for the Humanities, and individuals like Susan Theriot and Jeanette Vincent—insisted that historical representations are verities robust enough to found and reorient our subjectivity as citizens. But therein lies a disconnect. Such a profound contradiction in the practice of history-making merits questioning.

Perhaps something more reflexive and dialogical should unfold in spaces that purport to offer us truths to live by. Otherwise, what kind of freedom, what enhancement of our capacity for self-governance, is actually on offer in the memorial and other sites—of which there are many—like it? To contribute to a practice of freedom that is more "open, inventive, and questioning," public history's instantiations will need to take a form "requiring [less] submission to . . . a truth produced by authorities."[25] Frederic Jameson's contention about science fiction also seems apropos: A politics of democratic freedom should comprise critique, to breed a "renewal of our vision such that once again, and as though for the first time, we are able to perceive [our contemporary cultures' and institutions'] historicity and their arbitrariness."[26] To foster that kind of self-governing empowerment, more experiments in a public historical practice that problematizes time's politics and humans' cultural mutability seem crucial.

Notes

INTRODUCTION

1 Michel Foucault, *Security, Territory, Population: Lectures at the Collège de France, 1977–78*, trans. Graham Burchell (Palgrave Macmillan, 2007).

2 Matt Wray, *Not Quite White: White Trash and the Boundaries of Whiteness* (Duke University Press, 2006).

3 I use "public history" in distinct ways. I employ phrases like public historical *sphere* or public history *proper* to refer to the professional field that has expanded since the 1970s. Otherwise, the conception of public history I seek to evoke is broader than that professional domain, something along the lines proposed by David William Cohen for "the production of history": "the processing of the past in societies and historical settings . . . and the struggles for control of voices and texts in innumerable settings which animate this processing." David William Cohen, *The Combing of History* (University of Chicago Press, 1994), 244–45.

4 See Sharon Macdonald, *Memorylands: Heritage and Identity in Europe Today* (Routledge, 2013), 10–17; Liisa Malkki, *Purity and Exile: Violence, Memory and National Cosmology among Hutu Refugees in Tanzania* (University of Chicago Press, 1995), 240–42; and Wulf Kansteiner, "Finding Meaning in Memory: A Methodological Critique of Collective Memory Studies," *History and Theory* 41 (2002): 179–97. On the related issue of everyday recollection of the historical past as nonexperts' unreliable "oral tradition," see Jeffrey Olick, Vered Vinitzky-Seroussi, and Daniel Levy, "Introduction," in *The Collective Memory Reader* (Oxford University Press, 2011), 43–45.

5 Cécyle Trépanier, "French Louisiana at the Threshold of the 21st Century" (PhD diss., Pennsylvania State University, 1988), 111–17; see also Gerald Gold, "The Frontier of Settlement in Louisiana: Some Observation on Cultural Change in Mamou Prairie," *Cahiers Géographiques de Québec* 23, no. 59 (1979): 273; and Jacques Henry and Carl Bankston III, *Blue Collar Bayou: Louisiana Cajuns in the New Economy of Ethnicity* (Praeger, 2002), 147–48.

6 Jennifer Cole, "Memory and Modernity," in *A Companion to Psychological Anthropology: Modernity and Psychocultural Change*, ed. Conerly Casey and

Robert Edgerton (Blackwell, 2005), 106; Maurice Halbwachs, *On Collective Memory*, trans. Lewis Coser (University of Chicago Press, 1992). See also Jan Assman, *Cultural Memory and Early Civilization: Writing, Remembrance, and Political Imagination* (Cambridge University Press, 2011); Anselma Gallinat, *Narratives in the Making: Writing the East German Past in the Democratic Present* (Berghahn, 2016); Christopher Houston, *Istanbul, City of the Fearless: Urban Activism, Coup d'état, and Memory in Turkey* (University of California Press, 2020); Christopher Nelson, *Dancing with the Dead: Memory, Performance, and Everyday Life in Postwar Okinawa* (Duke University Press, 2008); and Geoffrey White, *Memorializing Pearl Harbor: Unfinished Histories and the Work of Remembrance* (Duke University Press, 2016).

7 Jennifer Cole, *Forget Colonialism? Sacrifice and the Art of Memory in Madagascar* (University of California Press, 2001), 23.

8 Michael Lambek, "Memory in a Maussian Universe," in *Regimes of Memory*, ed. Katharine Hodgkin and Susannah Radstone (Taylor and Francis, 2003).

9 Eric Gable and Richard Handler, "Forget Culture, Remember Memory?," in *Museums and Memory*, ed. Margaret Williamson Huber (Newfound Press, 2011); Eric Gable and Richard Handler, "Public History, Private Memory: Notes from the Ethnography of Colonial Williamsburg, Virginia, USA," *Ethnos* 65, no. 2 (2000): 237–52.

10 Macdonald, *Memorylands*, 15–16.

11 Sherry Ortner, *New Jersey Dreaming: Capital, Culture, and the Class of '58* (Duke University Press, 2003), 90–91.

12 On induction into historical narratives as memories, see Charlotte Linde, *Working the Past: Narrative and Institutional Memory* (Oxford University Press, 2008).

13 Geoffrey White and Eveline Buchheim, "Traveling War: Memory Practices in Motion," *History and Memory* 27, no. 2 (2015): 7.

14 Henry and Bankston, *Blue Collar Bayou*, 185–209; cf. Shane Bernard, *The Cajuns: Americanization of a People* (University Press of Mississippi, 2003), 85–111; Matthew Frye Jacobson, *Roots, Too: White Ethnic Revival and Post-Civil Rights America* (Harvard University Press, 2006).

15 Michel Foucault, "Technologies of the Self," in *Technologies of the Self: A Seminar with Michel Foucault*, ed. Luther Martin, Huck Guttman, and Patrick Gutman (Tavistock, 1988), 16–49. On relations of power and subjectivity, see also Peter Miller and Nikolas Rose, *Governing the Present: Administering Economic, Social and Personal Life* (Polity Press, 2008); and Luisa Martin Rojo and Alfonso Del Percio, eds., *Language and Neoliberal Governmentality* (Routledge, 2020).

16 The definition of morality employed here is necessarily broad: "The human belief in the possibility of telling right from wrong and in the necessity of acting in favour of the good and against the evil." Didier Fassin, "Beyond Good and Evil? Questioning the Anthropological Discomfort with Morals," *Anthropological Theory* 8 no. 4 (2008): 334.

17 Jennifer Cole, "Narratives and Moral Projects: Generational Memories of the Malagasy 1947 Rebellion," *Ethos* 31, no. 1 (2003): 95–126. In theorizing the

intersection of morality with individual and social remembrance, I also draw on the work of Michael Lambek, who uses Charles Taylor's formulations in *Sources of the Self* to specify the ethico-moral preoccupations of the remembering self. Michael Lambek, "Past Imperfect: Remembering as Moral Practice," in *Tense Past: Cultural Essays in Trauma and Memory*, ed. Michael Lambek and Paul Antze (Routledge, 1996).

18 Cole, "Narratives and Moral Projects," 99.

19 These include historic Acadian Village in Lafayette (established in 1974); the Archive of Cajun and Creole Folklore at the University of Louisiana at Lafayette (1977); the living history site of Vermilionville in Lafayette (1990); Erath's Acadian Museum (1991); the three sites—in Eunice (1991), Thibodaux (1992), and Lafayette (1994)—that comprise Jean Lafitte National Historical Park's Acadian Unit; the Acadian Memorial and Museum (1996); and the New Acadia Project, an archaeological site in Loreauville (2003). While its nominal focus is not exclusively on Cajuns, public discourse often stresses the significance of the archive's collection of Cajun folklore and music (see, e.g., "Ancelet Recounts 40 Years of Documenting Cajun, Creole Culture," *University News*, April 23, 2025, https://louisiana.edu/news/ancelet-recounts-40-years-spent-documenting-cajun-creole-culture). As mentioned, the state launched Longfellow-Evangeline State Historic Site, a tenth site in the state devoted to Acadian history, in 1934.

20 Glenn Conrad, *The Attakapas Domesday Book: Land Grants, Claims, and Certifications in the Attakapas District, 1764–1826* (Center for Louisiana Studies, 1991), xxvi–xxvii; Nicholas Spitzer, Ray Brassieur, Michael Caron, Jeffrey Golliher, H. F. Gregory, C. Paige Gutierrez, Janice Pierce, and Robert Rathburn, *Mississippi Delta Ethnographic Overview* (National Park Service, 1979); Zachary Richard, *Against the Tide* National Endowment for the Humanities Grant Application, 8 November 1998, box 1, folder 1, Zachary Richard Papers, Acadiana Manuscripts Collection, University of Louisiana, Lafayette, LA.

21 Evoking meanings of the verb "to govern," Foucault defined power as "a way of acting upon an acting subject or acting subjects by virtue of their acting or being capable of action. . . . [To exercise power is] to structure the possible field of action of others." Michel Foucault, "Afterword: The Subject and Power," in *Michel Foucault: Beyond Structuralism and Hermeneutics*, ed. Hubert Dreyfus and Paul Rabinow (University of Chicago Press, 1982), 220, 221. On this definition of power, see also Thomas Lemke, *Foucault's Analysis of Modern Governmentality: A Critique of Political Reason* (Verso, 2019), 18–27; and Nikolas Rose, *Powers of Freedom: Reframing Political Thought* (Cambridge University Press, 1999), 94–97.

22 Jonathan Xavier Inda, *Anthropologies of Modernity: Foucault, Governmentality, and Life Politics* (Blackwell, 2005), 1.

23 Though see Denise Meringolo, *Museums, Monuments, and National Parks: Toward a New Genealogy of Public History* (University of Massachusetts Press, 2012). Ranjan notes that when philosophers like Hegel and Kant made historical narratives central to the development of the nation-state, they conceived of it as a moral discourse of citizen formation. Ritwik Ranjan, "Postcoloniality and the Two Sites of Historicity," *History and Theory* 56, no. 1 (2017): 38–53. On

the fundamentally political character of all narratives of social time, see Carol Greenhouse, *A Moment's Notice: Time Politics across Cultures* (Cornell University Press, 1996).

24 John Hope Franklin and the National Park System Advisory Board, *Rethinking the National Parks for the Twenty-First Century* (National Geographic Society, 2001), 6.

25 See, e.g., Lynne Cheney, "The End of History," *Wall Street Journal*, October 20, 1994, A22; Gary Nash, Charlotte Crabtree, and Ross Dunn, *History on Trial: Culture Wars and the Teaching of the Past* (Alfred A. Knopf, 1997); and Social Studies Review and Development Committee, *One Nation, Many Peoples: A Declaration of Cultural Interdependence* (New York State Education Department, 1991). Cf. Terrie Epstein, *Interpreting National History: Race, Identity, and Pedagogy in Classrooms and Communities* (Routledge, 2009).

26 Teresa Bergman, *Exhibiting Patriotism: Creating and Contesting Interpretations of American Historic Sites* (Routledge, 2013); James Oliver Horton and Lois E. Horton, *Slavery and Public History: The Tough Stuff of American Memory* (University of North Carolina Press, 2008); James Loewen, *Lies My Teacher Told Me: Everything Your American History Textbook Got Wrong* (Simon and Schuster, 1995); Ian Tyrrell, *Historians in Public: The Practice of American History, 1890–1970* (University of Chicago Press, 2005).

27 Karaca Banu, "Governance *of* or *through* Culture? Cultural Policy and the Politics of Culture in Europe," *Focaal—European Journal of Anthropology* 55 (2009): 27–40; Ghassan Hage, *White Nation: Fantasies of White Supremacy in a Multicultural Society* (Routledge, 2000).

28 Marita Sturken, *Tourists of History: Memory, Kitsch, and Consumerism from Oklahoma City to Ground Zero* (Duke University Press, 2007); Mike Wallace, *Mickey Mouse History and Other Essays on American Memory* (Temple University Press, 1996). Cf. Alison Landsberg, *Prosthetic Memory: The Transformation of American Remembrance in the Age of Mass Culture* (Columbia University Press, 2006); and Cathy Stanton, *The Lowell Experiment: Public History in a Postindustrial City* (University of Massachusetts Press, 2006).

29 Margaret Werry, *The Tourist State: Performing Leisure, Liberalism, and Race* (University of Minnesota Press, 2011), xx.

30 See, e.g., Brittney Lewer, *Reimagining American History Education* (Woodrow Wilson National Fellowship Foundation, 2019); *Putting the Teaching of American History and Civics Back in the Classroom: Hearing of the U.S. Senate Committee on Health, Education, Labor, and Pensions*, 108th Congress (Government Printing Office, 2003); Diane Ravitch and Chester E. Finn Jr., *What Do Our 17-Year-Olds Know? A Report on the First National Assessment of History and Literature* (Harper and Row, 1987); Henry Steele Commager, "The Search for a Usable Past," *American Heritage* 16, no. 2 (1965); and Edgar Wesley, ed., *The Report of the Committee on American History in Schools and Colleges of the American Historical Association, the Mississippi Valley Historical Association, and the National Council for the Social Studies* (Macmillan, 1944).

31 See Alison Griffiths, *Shivers Down Your Spine: Cinema, Museums, and the Immersive View* (Columbia University Press, 2008).

32 Tony Bennett, *Making Culture, Changing Society* (Routledge, 2013), 49–69.

33 Jacobson, *Roots, Too*, 19–22.

34 Shane Bernard, "Acadian Pride, Anglo-Conformism: The Acadian Bicentennial Celebration of 1955," *Louisiana History* 41, no. 2 (2000): 161–74.

35 Bennett, *Making Culture, Changing Society*, 13–17.

36 See Rose, *Powers of Freedom*, 167–96.

37 Freeman Tilden, *Interpreting Our Heritage* (University of North Carolina Press, 1957), 32–33. Tilden's influential text outlined six principles of interpretation, which were widely adopted across the public history field. See, e.g., Patricia Mooney-Melvin, "Beyond the Book: Historians and the Interpretive Challenge," *The Public Historian* 17, no. 4 (1995): 75–82; and Richard Handler and Eric Gable, *The New History in an Old Museum: Creating the Past at Colonial Williamsburg* (Duke University Press, 1997), 174–76.

38 Stephen Collier, *Post-Soviet Social: Neoliberalism, Social Modernity, Biopolitics* (Princeton University Press, 2011), 24.

39 Cf. Ian Hacking, "Making Up People," in *Reconstructing Individualism: Autonomy, Individuality, and the Self in Western Thought*, ed. Thomas Heller, Morton Sosna, and David Wellbery (Stanford University Press, 1986), 222–36.

40 Carl Brasseaux, *In Search of Evangeline: Birth and Evolution of the Evangeline Myth* (Blue Heron Press, 1988).

41 Paul Rabinow, *Reflections on Fieldwork in Morocco* (University of California Press, 1977), 38.

42 Barry Ancelet, "The Cajun Who Went to Harvard: Identity in the Oral Tradition of South Louisiana," *Journal of Popular Culture* 23, no. 1 (1989): 101–15; Ron Emoff, "A Cajun Poetics of Loss and Longing," *Ethnomusicology* 42, no. 2 (1998): 283–301; Shana Walton, "Louisiana's Coonasses: Choosing Race and Class over Ethnicity," in *Signifying Serpents and Mardi Gras Runners: Representing Identity in Selected Souths*, ed. Celeste Ray and Luke Lassiter (University of Georgia Press, 2003).

43 Bernard, "Acadian Pride, Anglo-Conformism"; Sylvie Dubois and Megan Melancon, "Cajun Is Dead, Long Live Cajun: Shifting from a Linguistic to a Cultural Community," *Journal of Sociolinguistics* 1, no. 1 (1997): 63–93; Patricia Rickels, "The Folklore of the Acadians," in *The Cajuns: Essays on Their History and Culture*, ed. Glenn Conrad (Center for Louisiana Studies, 1978), 240–54.

44 As Ortner points out, upward mobility often comprises an element of negation, of "drawing negative lines between one's own group and those below it" (*New Jersey Dreaming*, 52). Cf. Michèle Lamont, *The Dignity of Working Men: Morality and the Boundaries of Race, Class, and Immigration* (Harvard University Press, 2000).

45 Virginia Domínguez, *White by Definition: Social Classification in Creole Louisiana* (Rutgers University Press, 1986), 149–51, 189; Henry and Bankston, *Blue Collar Bayou*, 36–39; Bonnie James Shaker, *Coloring Locals: Racial Formation in Kate Chopin's* Youth's Companion *Stories* (University of Iowa Press, 2003), 49, 75.

46 Mary Frances Berry, *Five Dollars and a Pork Chop Sandwich: Vote Buying and the Corruption of Democracy* (Beacon Press, 2016).

47 John Hartigan Jr., *Racial Situations: Class Predicaments of Whiteness in Detroit* (Princeton University Press, 1999), 8.

48 See John Hartigan Jr., *Odd Tribes: Toward a Cultural Analysis of White People* (Duke University Press, 2005); and Arlene Dàvila, *Latinos, Inc.: The Marketing and Making of a People* (University of California Press, 2012). This formulation also engages studies that track the gradual redefinition of white ethnics as more normatively white yet not through the labor-centered route that often predominates; e.g., see David Roediger, *Working toward Whiteness: How America's Immigrants Became White* (Basic Books, 2018).

49 Cf. Ortner, *New Jersey Dreaming*, 41–48.

50 See Sara Le Menestrel, *La voie des Cadiens: Tourisme et identité en Louisiane* (Belin, 1999).

51 Instead, I follow those who, in their scan of US scholarship, see ethnicity often operating as a superficial "stand-in" for class positions: see Phyllis Pease Chock, "The Irony of Stereotypes: Toward an Anthropology of Ethnicity," *Cultural Anthropology* 2, no. 3 (1987): 348; and Ortner, *New Jersey Dreaming*, 51–53; cf. Micaela Di Leonardo, *The Varieties of Ethnic Experience: Kinship, Class, and Gender among California Italian-Americans* (Cornell University Press, 1984); and Henry and Bankston, *Blue Collar Bayou*.

52 Across the book, I sometimes use the term *social project* or simply *project* in a technical sense, referring to "relatively coherent bundles of ideas and practices as realized in particular times and places." Anna Tsing, "The Global Situation," *Cultural Anthropology* 15, no. 3 (2000): 347.

CHAPTER ONE

1 C. M. Ulrich to J. F. McIndoe, May 11, 1906, box 1, folder 13, Rice Irrigation and Mill Company Records, Acadiana Manuscripts Collection, University of Louisiana at Lafayette (hereafter ULL).

2 The State Board of Engineers determined that the Mermentau River dam did not cause the flooding. But when its proponents rebuilt it after the explosion, the structure was again dynamited in 1907. Despite Ulrich's protestations, authorities never charged anyone for either of those actions. See James Wright to Abrom Kaplan, May 7, 1906, box 1, folder 13, Rice Irrigation Company Records, ULL; Tom Watson, *Green House Report* (Lacassane, 2005), https://www.lacassane.com/Greenhouse/Tom%20Watson%20Greenhouse%20Report.pdf.

3 Alvin Bertrand and Calvin Beale, *The French and Non-French in Rural Louisiana: A Study of the Relevance of Ethnic Factors to Rural Development* (LSU Agricultural Experiment Station, 1965), 41.

4 Bertrand and Beale, *French and Non-French in Rural Louisiana*, 9.

5 Jacques Henry and Carl Bankston III, *Blue Collar Bayou: Louisiana Cajuns in the New Economy of Ethnicity* (Praeger, 2002); Shane Bernard, *The Cajuns: Americanization of a People* (University Press of Mississippi, 2003).

6 Thomas Lemke, *Foucault's Analysis of Modern Governmentality: A Critique of Political Reason* (Verso, 2019), 73.
7 Stephen Collier, *Post-Soviet Social: Neoliberalism, Social Modernity, Biopolitics* (Princeton University Press, 2011), 3.
8 Robert Harrison and Walter Kollmorgen, "The Place of French-Speaking Farmers of Southern Louisiana in Future Land Development and Reclamation Projects," *The Journal of Land and Public Utility Economics* 22, no. 2 (1946): 227.
9 See Jean Ann Scarpaci, *Italian Immigrants in Louisiana's Sugar Parishes: Recruitment, Labor Conditions and Community* (Arno Press, 1980); Rocky Sexton, "Iowans in Cajun Country: An Overview and a Request," *The Palimpsest* 72, no. 1 (1991): 34–37.
10 Harrison and Kollmorgen, "Place of French-Speaking Farmers," 230.
11 Walter Kollmorgen and Robert Harrison, "French-Speaking Farmers of Southern Louisiana," *Economic Geography* 22, no. 3 (1946): 160.
12 Kollmorgen and Harrison, "French-Speaking Farmers," 159.
13 Kollmorgen and Harrison, 159. To be sure, not everyone viewed Cajuns' cultural practices in this way. For alternate views, see, e.g., Lauren Post, *Cajun Sketches: From the Prairies of Southwest Louisiana* (Louisiana State University Press, 1974); and T. Lynn Smith and Lauren Post, "The Country Butchery: A Co-operative Institution," *Rural Sociology* 2, no. 3 (1937): 335–37. But such stances were in the minority. The consensus was that Cajuns' antimodern dispositions—"a provincial outlook, a resistance to social change, and a devotion to time-honored customs"—were obstacles to economic progress. Harlan Gilmore, "Social Isolation of the French Speaking People of Rural Louisiana," *Social Forces* 12, no. 1 (1933): 82.
14 Kollmorgen and Harrison, "French-Speaking Farmers," 159.
15 See, e.g., Deborah Brandt, *Literacy in American Lives* (Cambridge University Press, 2001).
16 Ruth Landes, "Gentlemen of the Bayous," 1945, p. 12, box 13, Ruth Landes Papers, National Anthropological Archives, Suitland, MD. On Cajuns' resistance to education, see also James Dormon, *The People Called Cajuns: An Introduction to an Ethnohistory* (Center for Louisiana Studies, 1983), 70.
17 Rose, *Powers of Freedom*, 123.
18 Marguerite Roman, "Les Acadiens au XXe siècle," *Comptes rendus de l'Athénée Louisianais*, May 1924, 13.
19 Roman, "Les Acadiens au XXe siècle," 15.
20 Louisiana authorities were embarrassed by statistics showing that, as the local newspaper editor put it, "St. Martin Parish is the most illiterate Parish in the United States." Marcel "Blackie" Bienvenu, "This and That," *Weekly Messenger* (St. Martinville, LA), August 10, 1945, 1.
21 L. H. Boulet, "Visiting Teacher Work Explained," *Weekly Messenger* (St. Martinville, LA), September 7, 1945, 1.
22 Paul Young, "Can They Read?," *Weekly Messenger* (St. Martinville, LA), August 10, 1945, 3.
23 Landes, "Gentlemen of the Bayous," 13.

24 Landes, 15–16.

25 Landes, 16, 13.

26 Packer summarizes the normalizing thrust of the moment: "This was a time of great domestic uniformity, if not empirically, then as an ideal. Suburbanization, the baby boom, and economic prosperity all demanded domestic security, economic reliability, and social normalization." Jeremy Packer, *Mobility without Mayhem: Safety, Cars, and Citizenship* (Duke University Press, 2008), 118.

27 Two consecutive presidents of Southwestern Louisiana Institute (now the University of Louisiana at Lafayette), Edwin Stephens and Joel Fletcher, dissented from the predominant view. Edwin Stephens, "The Story of Acadian Education in Louisiana," *Louisiana Historical Quarterly* 18, no. 2 (1935): 397–406; Joel Fletcher, "The Acadians of Today," *The Boardman: Official Journal of the Louisiana School Boards Association*, January 1948, 3–6, 44–48.

28 T. Lynn Smith and Homer Hitt, *The People of Louisiana* (Louisiana State University Press, 1952), 107.

29 Smith and Hitt, *People of Louisiana*, 107.

30 Grace McKinstry, "With the Hospitable Acadians," *Catholic World* 122 (1926): 19, 24; Dean Tevis, *Land of Evangeline: Stories of St. Martinville and the Teche Country* (Bienvenu, 1935), 13.

31 Homer Borst, "Social Work in Acadia," *The Survey* 44, no. 1 (1920): 9.

32 Frederick Williamson, "The Acadians in Louisiana," *Kiwanis Magazine* 22, no. 5 (1937): 316. The first-cousin marriages that so exercised these critics were first outlawed at the turn of the twentieth century. This move proved largely unsuccessful, and such unions remained a common practice long after, though ostensibly among well-heeled families (not Cajuns) who evaded the law by marrying outside the state. Virginia Domínguez, *White by Definition: Social Classification in Creole Louisiana* (Rutgers University Press, 1986), 60–61.

33 Borst, "Social Work in Acadia," 11.

34 Landes, "Gentlemen of the Bayous," 6.

35 Edward Kammer, *A Socio-economic Survey of the Marshdwellers of Four Southeastern Louisiana Parishes* (Catholic University of America Press, 1941), 62.

36 Kammer, *Socio-economic Survey*, 92–93, 153–54.

37 In 1945, for instance, the local newspaper published "letters" from "correspondents" who mocked Cajuns (e.g., for attempting to drive long distances in a car without purchasing gas). See, e.g., Charles Fuselier, "Moe Bon Vieux Podna, Alphae," *Weekly Messenger* (St. Martinville, LA), September 14, 1945.

38 Marguerite Pecot, "The Cajun" (master's thesis, Louisiana State University, 1932), 32, 34.

39 T. Lynn Smith and Vernon Parenton, "Acculturation among the Louisiana French," *American Journal of Sociology* 44 (1938): 364.

40 Pecot, "Cajun," iii.

41 Kollmorgen and Harrison, "French-Speaking Farmers," 159.

42 See, e.g., Adam Fairclough, *Race and Democracy: The Civil Rights Struggle in Louisiana, 1915–1972* (University of Georgia Press, 1995), 36–38, 164–95; cf. Lee Baker, *Anthropology and the Racial Politics of Culture* (Duke University Press, 2010).

43 Borst, "Social Work in Acadia," 9, 11.

44 Smith and Hitt, *People of Louisiana*, 106–7.

45 Michel Foucault, *Society Must Be Defended: Lectures at the Collège de France, 1975–76*, trans. David Macey (Picador Press, 2003), 239–64.

46 See Nikolas Rose, *Powers of Freedom: Reframing Political Thought* (Cambridge University Press, 1999), 98–136.

47 Felix Voorhies, *Acadian Reminiscences: The True Story of Evangeline* (Rivas, 1907).

48 Brasseaux, *In Search of Evangeline*, 8.

49 Wilbur Blackman diary entry, November 27, 1892, unpublished manuscript in author's possession.

50 In late 1901, unidentified vandals hacked the tree on Bayou Teche that boosters identified as the Evangeline Oak, and some in Lafayette were trying to compete with St. Martinville and establish it as Evangeline's final resting place. Weekly Messenger, "Shockingly Mutilated," *Weekly Messenger* (St. Martinville, LA), January 4, 1902, 1; Lafayette Gazette, "Evangeline's Grave," *Weekly Messenger* (St. Martinville, LA), May 24, 1902, 1.

51 Mrs. A. A Anding, "Gentlemen of the Legislature," address to the Louisiana House of Representatives (?), June 30, 1930, folder 9, Mrs. A. A. (Susan) Anding Collection, Opelousas Museum and Interpretive Center, Opelousas, LA.

52 Photograph of Andre Olivier, folder 14, Anding Collection, Opelousas Museum.

53 Mrs. A. A. Anding, "The Spirit of Evangeline Appeals to You," folder 8, Anding Collection, Opelousas Museum.

54 W. Fitzhugh Brundage, "Le Reveil de la Louisiane: Memory and Acadian Identity, 1920–1960," in *Where These Memories Grow: History, Memory, and Southern Identity*, ed. W. Fitzhugh Brundage (University of North Carolina Press, 1999), 280.

55 Louisiana State Museum, *Biennial Report of the Board of Curators for 1936–1937* (Louisiana State Museum, 1938), 14–15.

56 Tony Bennett, *Pasts Beyond Memory: Evolution, Museums, Colonialism* (Routledge, 2004), 532.

57 N. E. Simoneaux, *Second Biennial Report of the State Parks Commission of Louisiana, 1936–1937* (State Parks Commission, 1938), 65.

58 Carroll Wood Jr., "Purpose of Commission," in *Fourth Biennial Report of the State Parks Commission of Louisiana, 1940–41*, ed. Carroll Wood Jr. (State Parks Commission, 1942), 28.

59 Shields McIlwaine, *The Southern Poor-White from Lubberland to Tobacco Road* (University of Oklahoma Press, 1939), 141, 143.

60 Bonnie James Shaker, *Coloring Locals: Racial Formation in Kate Chopin's* Youth's Companion *Stories* (University of Iowa Press, 2003), xiii.

61 Shaker, *Coloring Locals*, 49.

62 Times-Picayune, "Acadian Girls Visit City on Way to Teche Country," *Times-Picayune* (New Orleans), October 12, 1946, 7.

63 Brundage, "Le Reveil de la Louisiane," 286.

64 Paul Hardy, "Cajun Capital Title Brings Letters," *Teche News* (St. Martinville, LA), November 21, 1968, 4.

65 As Marjorie Esman notes, the different emphases in Breaux Bridge's Crawfish Festival also split along class lines, between "Acadians" and "coonasses." "The Celebration of Cajun Identity: Ethnic Unity and the Crawfish Festival" (PhD diss., Tulane University, 1981), 56–73, 153–70.

66 See Mrs. Ed Bulliard, "Letter to the Editor," *Teche News* (St. Martinville, LA), December 12, 1968, 2.

67 Hal Pen, "Cajun Controversy Highlights City Council Meeting Tuesday," *Teche News* (St. Martinville, LA), March 6, 1969, 1; Hal Pen, "City Council Notes," *Teche News* (St. Martinville, LA), March 20, 1969, 1.

68 Mrs. Ed Bulliard, "Cajun Capital Title Brings Letters," *Teche News* (St. Martinville, LA), November 21, 1968, 4; Verne Maraist Bienvenu, "Cajun Capital Title Brings Letters," *Teche News* (St. Martinville, LA), November 21, 1968, 4; St. Martinville Garden Club, "Cajun Capital Title Brings Letters," *Teche News* (St. Martinville, LA), November 21, 1968, 4; Club Français du Petit Paris d'Amérique, "Letter to the Editor," *Teche News* (St. Martinville, LA), October 24, 1968, 8.

69 Bulliard, "Letter to the Editor," 4.

70 In his work on the social use of the label white trash, Matt Wray also notes that a moralizing stress on behaviors has historically been central to the making of boundaries within whiteness. Matt Wray, *Not Quite White: White Trash and the Boundaries of Whiteness* (Duke University Press, 2006), 16.

71 Andre Mouton, "Letter to the Editor," *Teche News* (St. Martinville, LA), December 12, 1968, 2.

72 John Kasson, *Rudeness and Civility: Manners in Nineteenth-Century Urban America* (Hill and Wang, 1990), x.

73 Mikhail Bakhtin, "Forms of Time and of the Chronotope in the Novel," in *The Dialogic Imagination: Four Essays by M. M. Bakhtin*, ed. Michael Holquist (University of Texas Press, 1981), 84–259.

74 Peter Novick, *That Noble Dream: The "Objectivity Question" and the American Historical Profession* (Cambridge University Press, 1988).

75 Michel-Rolph Trouillot, *Silencing the Past: Power and the Production of History* (Beacon Press, 2015), 19, 20.

76 Greenhouse, *Moment's Notice*, 7.

77 Carolyn Ramsey, *Cajuns on the Bayous* (Hastings House, 1956), 19.

78 Ramsey, 293, 294, 296.

79 Ramsey, xv.

80 Indeed, others warned Ramsey to "never to their faces call them 'Cajun'" (*Cajuns on the Bayous*, 4). On the label's use as an epithet, see also Gilmore, "Social Isolation of the French Speaking People," 82; and Bern Keating, "Cajunland: Louisiana's French-Speaking Coast," *National Geographic* 129, no. 1 (1966), 355.

81 Wray, *Not Quite White*, 141.

CHAPTER TWO

1 Henri Bienvenu, "Pense Donc!," *Teche News* (St. Martinville, LA), November 22, 2000.
2 Maurice Halbwachs, *On Collective Memory*, trans. Lewis Coser (University of Chicago Press, 1992), 50–87.
3 Paul Ricoeur, *Memory, History, Forgetting*, trans. Kathleen Blamey and David Pellauer (University of Chicago Press, 2004), 397.
4 Laurence Kirmayer, "Landscapes of Memory: Trauma, Narrative, and Dissociation," in *Tense Past: Cultural Essays in Trauma and Memory*, ed. Michael Lambek and Paul Antze (Routledge, 1996).
5 Jennifer Cole, *Forget Colonialism? Sacrifice and the Art of Memory in Madagascar* (University of California Press, 2001), 289.
6 See, e.g., Geoffrey White, "Epilogue: Memory Moments," *Ethos* 34, no. 2 (2006): 325–41.
7 Marjorie Esman, "The Celebration of Cajun Identity: Ethnic Unity and the Crawfish Festival" (PhD diss., Tulane University, 1981), 129–39.
8 Bruno Latour, *Science in Action: How to Follow Scientists and Engineers through Society* (Open University Press, 1986).
9 See, e.g., Marian Barras and Jane Bulliard, "*There Was a Time . . .": The Mercy Order in St. Martinville, 1881–1981* (self-published, 1981); Amy Chatham, *La Maison Duchamp: The History of a St. Martinville Landmark* (Friends of the La Maison Duchamp, 2000); Leona Martin Guirard, *St. Martinville: The Land of Evangeline in Picture Story* (self-published, 1950); Charles Larroque, *Memories of St. Martinville* (Pelican, 1999); Dean Tevis, *Land of Evangeline: Stories of St. Martinville and the Teche Country* (Bienvenu, 1935); and Edwin Willis, *Notes for a History of St. Martin Parish* (Library of Congress, 1957).
10 As Marjorie Esman puts it, "St. Martinville embraces the Acadians but not the Cajuns . . . denying the influence of Evangeline's 'descendants'" ("Celebration of Cajun Identity," 214n2).
11 Cécyle Trépanier, "The Cajunization of French Louisiana: The Forging of a Regional Identity," *Geographic Journal* 157, no. 2 (1991): 161–71; see also Virginia Domínguez, *White by Definition: Social Classification in Creole Louisiana* (Rutgers University Press, 1986), 194–95; and Sara Le Menestrel, *La voie des Cadiens: Tourisme et identité en Louisiane* (Belin, 1999), 162–63.
12 Esman, "Celebration of Cajun Identity," 116–20; Louis Jacques Dorais, *Les francophones des Avoyelles: des Cadjins comme les autres?* Projet Louisiane document de travail no. 9 (Université Laval, 1980); Gerald Gold, "The Frontier of Settlement in Louisiana: Some Observation on Cultural Change in Mamou Prairie," *Cahiers Géographiques de Québec* 23, no. 59 (1979): 263–80.
13 See Alcée Fortier, *Louisiana Studies: Literature, Customs, and Dialects, History and Education* (F. F. Hansell and Bro., 1894), 170–86; and George Lane, "Notes on Louisiana-French I: Spoken Standard French of St. Martinville," *Language* 10 (1934): 323–33.

14 This tracks the trajectory of Domínguez's white Creole informants (*White by Definition*, 176–81).

15 Esman noted a similar dynamic, whereby "many residents claim descent exclusively from aristocrats and emphatically deny any affiliation with Cajuns" ("Celebration of Cajun Identity," 214n2).

16 See, e.g., entries for Emile Edouard Simon, James Dudley Simon, and Wade O. Martin Jr., in *A Dictionary of Louisiana Biography*, vol. 2, ed. Glenn Conrad (Center for Louisiana Studies, 1988).

17 Chatham, *La Maison Duchamp*.

18 Barbara Dumesnil de la Houssaye, "Tribute to Louis le Pelletier de la Houssaye" (1975), OoCities, http://www.oocities.org/heartland/meadows/6534/tribute .html.

19 Harnett Kane, *Deep Delta Country* (Duell, Sloan, and Pearce, 1944), 243–56.

20 John Kasson, *Rudeness and Civility: Manners in Nineteenth-Century Urban America* (Hill and Wang, 1990), 63.

21 Joseph Tregle Jr., "Creoles and Americans," in *Creole New Orleans: Race and Americanization*, ed. Arnold Hirsch and Joseph Logsdon (Louisiana State University Press, 1992).

22 Le Menestrel, *La voie des Cadiens*, 247.

23 This aligns with art historian Randolph Delehanty's claim that the state's museums have had an exclusive slant, "enshrin[ing] the tastes and values of one small segment of the population." Randolph Delehanty, "Louisiana's Museums: Traditions, Realities, and Hopes for the Future," in *Treasure Houses: Louisiana Museums for a New Millennium*, ed. Randolph Delehanty, Herman Mhire, and Erin O'Donnell (Louisiana Association of Museums, 2000), 14.

24 Dorson in Carl Brasseaux, *In Search of Evangeline: Birth and Evolution of the Evangeline Myth* (Blue Heron Press, 1988), 7.

25 Brasseaux, *In Search of Evangeline*, 52.

26 Geoffrey White, "Emotional Remembering: The Pragmatics of National Memory," *Ethos* 27, no. 4 (2000): 519.

27 Though apparently embellished, the unexpected existence of Old-World sophistication at the state's periphery anchored the narrative of St. Martinville as *le Petit Paris d'Amérique*. See George Washington Cable, *Strange True Stories of Louisiana* (C. Scribner's Sons, 1889), 92; William Henry Perrin, *Southwest Louisiana Biographical and Historical* (Gulf Publishing, 1891), 71; and Kane, *Deep Delta Country*, 260–61.

28 Cf. Randall Mason and Max Page, *Giving Preservation a History: Histories of Historic Preservation in the United States*, 2nd ed. (Routledge, 2019).

29 Cf. Martin Heidegger, *Being and Time*, trans. J. Stambaugh (State University of New York Press, 1996), 344–45.

30 Cf. Edward Said, *Beginnings: Intention and Method* (Columbia University Press, 1985).

31 Cf. James Ferguson, *Expectations of Modernity: Myths and Meanings of Urban Life on the Zambian Copperbelt* (University of California Press, 1999).

32 MDC, *The State of the South: Shadows of the Sunbelt Revisited* (MDC Inc., 2002), 13.

33 Louisiana Economic Development Council, *Louisiana Vision 2020: Master Plan for Economic Development* (Louisiana Economic Development Council, 1999).

34 Jacques Henry and Carl Bankston III, *Blue Collar Bayou: Louisiana Cajuns in the New Economy of Ethnicity* (Praeger, 2002), 87–95; Ian Rutledge, "Profitability and Supply Price in the U.S. Domestic Oil Industry: Implications for the Political Economy of Oil in the 21st Century," *Cambridge Journal of Economics* 27 (2003): 3–5; Council for a Better Louisiana, *Fighting Poverty, Building Community: A Report on Poverty in Louisiana* (CABL Futures Institute, 1999).

35 Henri Bienvenu, Chère Doiron, Jackie Courville, and Marc Allemond, *Vision St. Martinville: A Community Development Project* (Vision Plan Commission, 1996), 17.

36 Bienvenu et al., 16.

37 Bienvenu et al., 31.

38 Bureau of Governmental Research, *Plan and Program for the Preservation of the Vieux Carré* (City of New Orleans, 1968), 2.

39 Preserving a town center's core of historic buildings, for instance, might evoke residents' memories and thereby "elicit positive emotional responses . . . that contribute to [citizens'] enjoyment of life." Divisions of Archaeology and Historic Preservation, *Louisiana Comprehensive Statewide Historic Preservation Plan* (State Library of Louisiana for the Division of Historic Preservation, 2001), 4.

40 Felicia Landry, "Prospects Favorable for Historic District Growth," *Teche News* (St. Martinville, LA), January 31, 1996; Marc Allemond in Felicia Landry, "Historic District Board OKs House," *Teche News* (St. Martinville, LA), December 11, 1996.

41 Both disputes centered on the introduction of structures into the historic district that its proponents claimed would undermine its integrity. One case involved a twentieth-century shotgun house whose style clashed with the nineteenth-century aesthetic that predominated in the downtown core (Landry, "Historic District Board OKs House," A8). The other unfolded over a trailer home moved into a residential backyard (Steven Landry, "Owners Resent Restrictions," *Teche News* [St. Martinville, LA], December 25, 1996, A1, A8).

42 Zerben Champagne in Steven Landry, "SM Historic District Area Reduced by Half," *Teche News* (St. Martinville, LA), December 25, 1996.

43 Michel-Rolph Trouillot, *Silencing the Past: Power and the Production of History* (Beacon Press, 2015), 6–8.

44 Roy Rosenzweig and David Thelen, *The Presence of the Past: Popular Uses of History in American Life* (Columbia University Press, 2000).

45 Cf. Nikolas Rose, *Powers of Freedom: Reframing Political Thought* (Cambridge University Press, 1999), 177.

46 See Jeffrey Olick, Vered Vinitzky-Seroussi, and Daniel Levy, "Introduction," in *The Collective Memory Reader* (Oxford University Press, 2011), 43–45. As

one example, entries on "Memory and History," "Oral History," and "Oral Tradition" in *A Global Encyclopedia of Historical Writing* explicitly convey such views. Daniel Woolf, ed., *A Global Encyclopedia of Historical Writing* (Garland Publishing, 1998).

47 Glenn Conrad, *The Attakapas Domesday Book: Land Grants, Claims, and Certifications in the Attakapas District, 1764–1826* (Center for Louisiana Studies, 1991), xxvi–xxvii.

48 White, "Epilogue," 331.

49 Maurice Bloch, *How We Think They Think: Anthropological Approaches to Cognition, Memory, and Literacy* (Westview Press, 1998), 117.

CHAPTER THREE

1 During this period, locals also recounted the curse to other outsiders. See Nathan Stubbs, "Council Controversy," *Independent Weekly* (Lafayette, LA), April 13, 2005. http://theind.com/article-753-Council-Controversy.html; and Gilbert King, *The Execution of Willie Francis: Race, Murder, and the Search for Justice in the American South* (Basic Civitas, 2008).

2 On high mortality and low birth rates among the enslaved in Louisiana's sugar belt, see Michael Tadman, "The Demographic Cost of Sugar: Debates on Slave Societies and Natural Increase in the Americas," *American Historical Review* 105 (2000): 1534–75.

3 Carl Brasseaux, Keith P. Fontenot, and Claude F. Oubre, *Creoles of Color in the Bayou Country* (University Press of Mississippi, 1994); Sybil Kein, *Creole: The History and Legacy of Louisiana's Free People of Color* (Louisiana State University Press, 2000); Shirley Elizabeth Thompson, *Exiles at Home: The Struggle to Become American in Creole New Orleans* (Harvard University Press, 2009).

4 Two suppressions of insurrections occurred, one of a feared uprising and another of an actual one. See Junius Rodriguez, "'We'll Hang Jeff Davis on the Sour Apple Tree': Civil War Era Slave Resistance in Louisiana," *Gulf Coast Historical Review* 10, no. 2 (1995): 9–10; Enrico Dal Lago, *Civil War and Agrarian Unrest: The Confederate South and Southern Italy* (Cambridge University Press, 2018), 325–27; Peyton McCrary, *Abraham Lincoln and Reconstruction: The Louisiana Experiment* (Princeton University Press, 1978), 145–46; and C. Peter Ripley, *Slaves and Freedmen in Civil War Louisiana* (Louisiana State University Press, 1976), 98–99.

5 Suzy Shea, "A Man for the People: Alcibiade DeBlanc and the St. Martinville Insurrection of 1873," *Attakapas Gazette* 14, no. 1 (1979): 3–10; James Dauphine, "The Knights of the White Camelia and the Election of 1868: Louisiana's White Terrorists; A Benighting Legacy," *Louisiana History* 30, no. 2 (1989): 173–90; Jonathan Obert, *The Six-Shooter State: Public and Private Violence in American Politics* (Cambridge University Press, 2018), 184–85; Gilles Vandal, *Rethinking Southern Violence: Homicides in Post-Civil War Louisiana, 1866–1884* (Ohio State University Press, 2000), 141–43.

6 Adam Fairclough, *Race and Democracy: The Civil Rights Struggle in Louisiana, 1915–1972* (University of Georgia Press, 1995), 36; King, *Execution of Willie Francis*; Arthur Miller and Jeffrey Bowman, *Death by Installments: The Ordeal of Willie Francis* (Greenwood Press, 1988).

7 Richard Baudouin, "Politics as Usual in St. Martinville," *Times of Acadiana* (Lafayette, LA), March 23, 1994, 20–22, 24–26; Mary Frances Berry, *Five Dollars and a Pork Chop Sandwich: Vote Buying and the Corruption of Democracy* (Beacon Press, 2016); Steven Landry, "The City That Democracy Forgot," *Southern Exposure* 30 (2002): 4–7. On the settlement and court order that resolved *Thomas v. St. Martin Parish School Board*, see Legal Defense Fund, "Thomas v. St. Martin Parish School Board," National Association for the Advancement of Colored People Legal Defense and Education Fund, 2023. https://www.naacpldf.org/case-issue/thomas-v-school-board-st-martin-parish/.

8 On the dynamics of forgetting, see Marc Augé, *Oblivion*, trans. Marjolijn de Jager (University of Minnesota Press, 2004); and Paul Connerton, "Seven Types of Forgetting," *Memory Studies* 1 (2008): 59–71.

9 The Greigs—Errol, his spouse Sue, and his brother Eddy—were particularly active in challenging the political status quo during this time (Berry, *Five Dollars and a Pork Chop Sandwich*, 61, 67, 72–73).

10 See Robert Maguire, "Hustling to Survive: Social and Economic Change in a South Louisiana Black Creole Community" (PhD diss., McGill University, 1987).

11 Such moral assessment has arguably been at the heart of racial classification. See John Hartigan Jr., *What Can You Say? America's National Conversation on Race* (Stanford University Press, 2010); and Jennifer Harvey, *Whiteness and Morality: Pursuing Racial Justice through Reparations and Sovereignty* (Palgrave Macmillan, 2007).

12 Pamela Perry offers evidence that whites' prejudice increases with social distance and attenuates through proximity to racial others; *Shades of White: White Kids and Racial Identities in High School* (Duke University Press, 2002).

13 Michèle Lamont also found that working-class whites explain Black poverty as a consequence of their moral failings (*The Dignity of Working Men: Morality and the Boundaries of Race, Class, and Immigration* [Harvard University Press, 2000], 55–72) and that upper-middle class whites conflate socioeconomic and moral measures of success, such that the presence of the former attests to that of the latter (*Money, Morals, and Manners: The Culture of the French and the American Upper-Middle Class* [University of Chicago Press, 1992], 85).

14 E.g., on the inequitable allocation of GI Bill benefits to ex-soldiers during the postwar period, see Ira Katznelson, "White Veterans Only," in *When Affirmative Action Was White: An Untold History of Racial Inequality in Twentieth-Century America* (W. W. Norton, 2006), 113–41.

15 The parallel with the sentiments that historian Jason Sokol describes is striking. See *There Goes My Everything: White Southerners in the Age of Civil Rights, 1945–1975* (Alfred A. Knopf, 2006).

16 In the mid-1990s, white residents on the majority-Black south side petitioned for a zoning change near their homes, arguing they required a "buffer zone"

between themselves and nearby Black residents. See Errol Greig, "Resident Reflects on Implications of Zoning Issue," *Teche News* (St. Martinville, LA), April 10, 1996, A5; and Felicia Landry, "Council Denies Zoning Change," *Teche News* (St. Martinville, LA), April 3, 1996, A2.

17 In interviews, some whites mentioned similar reactions to other spatial shifts, including the renaming of College Street to Martin Luther King Drive. See Gail Garcia, "St. Martinville Sticks to Plan to Name Street," *Daily Advertiser* (Lafayette, LA), September 20, 1988, 6.

18 Jennifer Cole, *Forget Colonialism? Sacrifice and the Art of Memory in Madagascar* (University of California Press, 2001), 290.

19 Berry, *Five Dollars and a Pork Chop Sandwich*, 62–65, 67–68.

20 On the charges related to the election and their fallout, see Ken Grissom, "Pam Thibodeaux Pleads Not Guilty: Election Fraud Trial Set March 1," *Teche News* (St. Martinville, LA), January 21, 2004, A1, A8; and Berry, *Five Dollars and a Pork Chop Sandwich*, 68–83.

21 Councilman Mike Fuselier in Joseph Rich, Robert Kengle, and Michael Zwibelman, "Plaintiff United States' Memorandum of Law on the Proper Benchmark under Section 5 of the Voting Rights Act," Greig et al. v. City of St. Martinville, Case 6:00-CV-00603, June 16, 2000 (Western District of Louisiana, 2000), 8.

22 Since the Voting Rights Act construed white bloc voting—which the Department of Justice claimed was endemic in St. Martinville—as an obstacle to fair elections, it rejected this position. Bill Lann Lee to George W. McHugh, October 19, 1998, Attachment 3 to Joseph Rich, Robert Kengle, and Michael Zwibelman, "Defendant United States' Memorandum in Support of Motion for Dismissal as Defendant and Realignment as Plaintiff," Greig et al. v. City of St. Martinville, Case 6:00-CV-00603, June 2, 2000 (Western District of Louisiana, 2000), 4.

23 See Rich et al., "Plaintiff United States' Memorandum of Law," 6–8; Berry, *Five Dollars and a Pork Chop Sandwich*, 65–66; and Kent Davidson, "Council Members View Proposal as Personal Attacks," *Daily Iberian* (New Iberia, LA), February 21, 1989, 9.

24 Berry, *Five Dollars and a Pork Chop Sandwich*, 83.

25 Henri Bienvenu, "Pense Donc!," *Teche News* (St. Martinville, LA), February 18, 1999, A4. The editor folded a convenient omission into this scolding. Acadian Memorial insiders acknowledged that Charles's support was crucial to its realization. The memorial received municipal funding because Charles and fellow Black councilman Douglas François voted for it, while two of the three white council members consistently did not. Sara Le Menestrel quotes "Mayor Michot" as saying local Blacks did not support his heritage initiatives (*La voie des Cadiens: Tourisme et identité en Louisiane* [Belin, 1999]). While many of them were unconvinced of heritage tourism's effectiveness for economic development, it was also true that, ironically, St. Martinville's emergence as the "Birthplace of Acadiana" relied on backing from Black politicians.

26 Reinhart Koselleck, *Futures Past: On the Semantics of Historical Time*, trans. Keith Tribe (Columbia University Press, 2004), 266–67.

27 Daily Advertiser Editorial Board, "Church Documents Need to be Easily Available," *Daily Advertiser* (Lafayette, LA), July 29, 2000, 2D; Steven Landry, "Priest Wary of Plan to Open Church Records," *Baton Rouge Advocate*, July 21, 2000, 1B, 2B.

28 Virginia Domínguez, *White by Definition: Social Classification in Creole Louisiana* (Rutgers University Press, 1986), 56–89. Locally, marriages between Blacks and whites were rare: less than 1 percent of all unions in 2000 and 2010. See Tallese Johnson and Rose Kreider, "Mapping the Geographic Distribution of Interracial/Interethnic Married Couples in the U.S.: 2010," paper presented at the Annual Meeting of the Population Association of America, New Orleans, LA, April 11–13, 2013, https://www.census.gov/content/dam/Census/library/working-papers/2013/demo/2013-19.pdf. The relatively more frequent occurrence of various forms of interracial relationships during the eighteenth and nineteenth centuries is well documented (see Brasseaux et al., *Creoles of Color in the Bayou Country*).

29 To gauge this sharing of patronyms and perceptions of it, I invited two locals known for their genealogical skills to review a list of the town's most common family names. I asked them to check names used by members of both races, currently and historically. Responses ranged from 60 percent (from a young Black teacher, who also claimed the mixed-raced ancestry of over a third of those families could be documented) to 30 percent (from a white repairman in his sixties, who insisted that both of the former's estimates were too high and could not be substantiated).

30 On the Willie Francis case, during which the state electrocuted Francis twice in the mid-1940s, see King, *Execution of Willie Francis*; and Miller and Bowman, *Death by Installments*. On the execution of Louis Michel, who was falsely convicted of murder in 1893, see Weekly Messenger, "The Noose! Louis Michel Paid the Penalty of His Crime on the Gallows," *Weekly Messenger* (St. Martinville, LA), March 25, 1893, 1; and King, *Execution of Willie Francis*, xii–xiv, 252–59.

31 See Silvan Niedermeier, *The Color of the Third Degree: Racism, Police Torture, and Civil Rights in the American South, 1930–1955* (University of North Carolina Press, 2019).

32 E.g., Gladys de Villier offers an account that belittles the curse's significance and stresses the executee's depravity. "Does 'Johnson's Curse' Haunt St. Martinville?," *Teche News* Centennial Edition (St. Martinville, LA), April 2, 1986, 26C–27C.

33 Frank Tannenbaum, *Slave and Citizen: The Negro in the Americas* (Alfred A. Knopf, 1963).

34 Fairclough insists that, historically, relations between Blacks and whites in the state "followed the ugly pattern of the region," while acknowledging the claim that Catholicism and French culture shared across the color line in south Louisiana gave racial relationships "an underlying feeling . . . of some kind of comradeship" (*Race and Democracy*, 7, xx).

35 Transcribed from the video recording of the municipal council meeting on August 17, 1998. Videocassette in St. Martinville City Hall Council meeting collection.

36 See Allan Durand, dir., *Willie Francis Must Die Again* (Cote Blanche Productions, 2006).

37 Ron Delhomme, "Museum to Highlight African-American Experience," *Sunday Advertiser* (Lafayette, LA), September 5, 1999, 12A.

38 Following the release of her compilation of slave and free people of color records, historian Gwendolyn Hall suggested that Blacks elsewhere in Louisiana held similar views. Littice Bacon-Blood, "Database Offers Slave History in Louisiana: Identities Thought Lost Have Been Set Free by Diligent Historian," *Times-Picayune* (New Orleans), August 6, 2000, A1.

39 Cf. Arlie Hochschild, "Emotion Work, Feeling Rules, and Social Structure," *American Journal of Sociology* 85, no. 3 (1979): 551–75.

40 "Managing the self" registers as one common tactic African Americans pursue in the face of stigmatizing behavior from others. See Crystal Fleming, Michèle Lamont, and Jessica Welburn, "African Americans Respond to Stigmatization: The Meanings and Salience of Confronting, Deflecting Conflict, Educating the Ignorant and 'Managing the Self,'" *Ethnic and Racial Studies* 35, no. 3 (2012): 400–417.

41 City of St. Martinville, "Louisiana Municipal Association Community Achievement Awards Entry Form: The St. Martinville Cultural Heritage Center" (unpublished manuscript, 2002), 3, 9.

42 Trevis Badeaux, "History Without Sugarcoating: African American Museum Opens in St. Martinville," *Daily Advertiser* (Lafayette, LA), June 24, 2000, 1A; Charles Larroque, "Fraternité Brothers from Way Back," *Daily Advertiser* (Lafayette, LA), November 20, 2001, 5C; Associated Press, "Museum Notes Black Life in Louisiana: Slavery Is Included, But Not Emphasized," *Times-Picayune* (New Orleans), June 24, 2001, B4.

43 Antoine claimed that on the sugar cane farm where he grew up—one of the area's largest antebellum plantations and a farm that continued operating into the twenty-first century—80 percent of employees' wages were paid in scrip for use at a company store.

44 In addition to texts referenced in notes 1–5, see, e.g., Alexandre Barde, *The Vigilante Committees of the Attakapas: An Eyewitness Account of Banditry and Backlash*, ed. David Edmonds (Acadiana Press, 1981); and W. E. B. Du Bois, *Black Reconstruction in America, 1860–1880* (Free Press, 1998).

45 See, e.g., Steven Landry and Shannon Chataignier, "Sharpton Hears Stories of Unfair Racial Tactics," *Teche News* (St. Martinville, LA), June 28, 2000, A1, A10; and Steven Landry, "Judicial System Scorned: Blacks Stage Demonstration at Courthouse," *Teche News* (St. Martinville, LA), July 1, 1999, A1, A6.

46 Johannes Fabian, *Memory against Culture: Arguments and Reminders* (Duke University Press, 2007), 78.

47 Designing a National Heritage Area that includes two former plantations in northwest Louisiana, National Park Service (NPS) staffer Muriel Crespi found that among both Black and white residents, "slavery [was] a nearly tabu subject." "Local Pasts in National Programs," *CRM Magazine* 21, no. 4 (1998): 28. Ultimately, NPS followed locals' preferences and avoided making slavery the site's focus.

48 Cf. Linda Williams, *Playing the Race Card: Melodramas of Black and White from Uncle Tom to O.J. Simpson* (Princeton University Press, 2001).

49 Geoffrey White, "Museum/Memorial/Shrine: National Narrative in National Spaces," *Museum Anthropology* 21, no. 1 (1997): 24.

CHAPTER FOUR

1 See Marita Sturken, *Tourists of History: Memory, Kitsch, and Consumerism from Oklahoma City to Ground Zero* (Duke University Press, 2007); Kirk Savage, *Monument Wars, Washington, D.C., the National Mall, and the Transformation of the Memorial Landscape* (University of California Press, 2011); and Harriet Senie, *Memorials to Shattered Myths: Vietnam to 9/11* (Oxford University Press, 2016).

2 Jennifer Cole, "Memory and Modernity," in *A Companion to Psychological Anthropology: Modernity and Psychocultural Change*, ed. Conerly Casey and Robert Edgerton (Blackwell, 2005), 109.

3 Jennifer Cole, *Forget Colonialism? Sacrifice and the Art of Memory in Madagascar* (University of California Press, 2001), 23.

4 See, e.g., Katharine Hodgkin and Susannah Radstone, eds., *Contested Pasts: The Politics of Memory* (Routledge, 2003); Christopher Houston, *Istanbul, City of the Fearless: Urban Activism, Coup d'état, and Memory in Turkey* (University of California Press, 2020); and Jon Berndt Olsen, *Tailoring Truth: Politicizing the Past and Negotiating Memory in East Germany, 1945–1990* (Berghahn, 2015).

5 In addition to Jennifer Cole's work (referenced earlier), see also Michael Lambek, "Past Imperfect: Remembering as Moral Practice," in *Tense Past: Cultural Essays in Trauma and Memory*, ed. Michael Lambek and Paul Antze (Routledge, 1996); and Charlotte Linde, *Life Histories: The Creation of Coherence* (Oxford University Press, 1993).

6 Maurice Bloch, *How We Think They Think: Anthropological Approaches to Cognition, Memory, and Literacy* (Westview Press, 1998), 123.

7 Bloch, *How We Think They Think*, 122.

8 Methodologically, the moral grid I use is, in a certain sense, narrow. I follow Charles Taylor's assertion that among the most basic moral questions for individuals are issues of respect, dignity, and conceptions of what constitutes a good or "full life"; see *Sources of the Self: The Making of Modern Identity* (Harvard University Press, 1989), 15–16. I draw on this notion heuristically, without seeking to affirm or challenge it through the research. Yet given the gist of interviewees' responses, it seems appropriate: Issues of respect, dignity, and a good life figured prominently in them, with individuals positioning themselves relative to the social world in terms of others' beneficence, indifference, malevolence, fairness and injustice, and so on.

9 The three cohorts presented in this chapter do not compose an exhaustive representation of the social landscape; more fieldwork would likely produce a more variegated sketch. At the same time, I contextualize the twenty-four interviews analyzed here vis-à-vis the rest of my fieldwork among whites in St. Martinville, including more than eighty interviews.

10 Sherry Ortner, *New Jersey Dreaming: Capital, Culture, and the Class of '58* (Duke University Press, 2003), 90–91.

11 Ortner, *New Jersey Dreaming*, 91.

12 On the wounds associated with class, see Michèle Lamont, *The Dignity of Working Men: Morality and the Boundaries of Race, Class, and Immigration* (Harvard University Press, 2000); and Richard Sennett and Jonathan Cobb, *The Hidden Injuries of Class* (Knopf, 1972).

13 In its simplest form, the indictment was not ethnicized per se; it referenced a matter of social provenance, of being from the "country." Yet in her response—"I know very well where I come from, and I'm not embarrassed. As a matter of fact, I am truly blessed that I have the love of parents who worked hard . . . for what we had and what we have, and I'm proud of that"—Chiasson interpreted the insult in familial terms. As Barriot's remarks indicate, this symbolic terrain was linked to ethnoracial categories.

14 See Mark McDaniel and Gilles Einstein, *Prospective Memory: An Overview and Synthesis of an Emerging Field* (Sage, 2007).

15 Carolyn Ware, *Cajun Women and Mardi Gras: Reading the Rules Backward* (University of Illinois Press, 2006), 178.

16 Cf. Glenn Conrad, *The Attakapas Domesday Book: Land Grants, Claims, and Certifications in the Attakapas District, 1764–1826* (Center for Louisiana Studies, 1991), xxvi; and Jacques Henry and Carl Bankston III, *Blue Collar Bayou: Louisiana Cajuns in the New Economy of Ethnicity* (Praeger, 2002), 119.

17 Liisa Malkki, *Purity and Exile: Violence, Memory and National Cosmology among Hutu Refugees in Tanzania* (University of Chicago Press, 1995), 194.

18 Henry and Bankston, *Blue Collar Bayou*, 88–100.

19 Rotary Clubs began to admit female members only in 1987, after a successful court challenge.

20 Sylvie Dubois and Megan Melancon, "Cajun Is Dead, Long Live Cajun: Shifting from a Linguistic to a Cultural Community," *Journal of Sociolinguistics* 1, no. 1 (1997): 82.

21 Virginia Domínguez, *White by Definition: Social Classification in Creole Louisiana* (Rutgers University Press, 1986), 149–51.

22 For an example of such a narrative in everyday discourse, see Phyllis Pease Chock, "The Landscape of Enchantment: Redaction in a Theory of Ethnicity," *Cultural Anthropology* 4, no. 2 (1989): 163–81.

23 See, e.g., J. Minos Simon and David Leon Chandler, *Law in the Cajun Nation* (Prescott Press, 1993).

24 Kathleen Stewart, *A Place on the Side of the Road: Cultural Poetics in an "Other" America* (Princeton University Press, 1996), 61.

25 Henry and Bankston, *Blue Collar Bayou*, 111. See Barry Ancelet, "The Cajun Who Went to Harvard: Identity in the Oral Tradition of South Louisiana," *Journal of Popular Culture* 23, no. 1 (1989): 101–15; and Ware, *Cajun Women and Mardi Gras*.

26 See Dorice Tentchoff, "Speech in a Louisiana Cajun Community" (PhD diss., Case Western Reserve University, 1977); and Charles Ray Brassieur, "A

Preliminary Ethnographic Survey of the Atchafalaya Basin Area" (master's thesis, Louisiana State University, 1980), 37–38.

27 Peggy King, "The Effects of Displacement on Levee Dwellers, Atchafalaya Basin, Louisiana" (master's thesis, Louisiana State University, 1977); Steven Landry, "Basin Access Generating Heat," *Teche News* (St. Martinville, LA), March 14, 2001, A1, A8.

28 Johannes Fabian, *Remembering the Present: Painting and Popular History in Zaire* (University of California Press, 1996), 198.

29 Julie Lindquist, *A Place to Stand: Politics and Persuasion in a Working-Class Bar* (Oxford University Press, 2002).

30 Carol Greenhouse, *A Moment's Notice: Time Politics across Cultures* (Cornell University Press, 1996), 7.

CHAPTER FIVE

1 See Gerald Gold, "The Cajun French Debate in Louisiana," in *Issues in International Bilingual Education: The Role of the Vernacular*, ed. Beverly Hartford, Albert Valdman, and Charles Foster (Plenum, 1982). In a script provided to the memorial, Brasseaux wrote that when CODOFIL "impose[d] standard French" as the language taught in Louisiana public schools, the move "did much to alienate grassroots Cajuns" (70–71). Carl Brasseaux, "Exhibit Script for the Museum of the Acadian Memorial," February 2000, Acadian Memorial administrative files, St. Martinville, LA.

2 On the lack of correspondence between subject position, lived experience, and identity, see, e.g., Joan W. Scott, "The Evidence of Experience," *Critical Inquiry* 17, no. 4 (1991): 773–97. Throughout this research, Louisiana's rates of poverty and unequal income distribution were among the highest in the country. See Elizabeth McNichol, Doug Hall, David Cooper, and Vincent Palacios, *Pulling Apart: A State-by-State Analysis of Income Trends* (Center for Budget and Policy Priorities and Economic Policy Institute, 2012).

3 See Michel Foucault, *Security, Territory, Population: Lectures at the Collège de France, 1977–78*, trans. Graham Burchell (Palgrave Macmillan, 2007), 116–20; and Thomas Lemke, *Foucault's Analysis of Modern Governmentality: A Critique of Political Reason* (Verso, 2019), 145–52.

4 Cécyle Trépanier, "The Cajunization of French Louisiana: The Forging of a Regional Identity." *Geographic Journal* 157, no. 2 (1991): 164; Warren Perrin, "The Cajuns in Louisiana," in *Acadie Then and Now: A People's History*, ed. Warren Perrin, Mary Broussard Perrin, and Phil Comeau (Andrepont Publishing, 2014).

5 Into the twenty-first century, some viewed Cajuns as a distinct voting bloc in statewide races. See Richard Skinner and Philip Klinkner, "Black, White, Brown, and Cajun: The Racial Dynamics of the 2003 Louisiana Gubernatorial Election," *The Forum* 2, no. 1 (2004): 1–8. Kathleen Babineaux Blanco, a lieutenant governor and governor who identified as Cajun, made multiple visits to St. Martinville's

historic sites during a ten-year stretch, including two dedications at the Acadian Memorial.

6 Shane Bernard, *The Cajuns: Americanization of a People* (University Press of Mississippi, 2003), 87–111.

7 Adam Fairclough, "A Political *Coup d'état*? How the Enemies of Earl Long Overwhelmed Racial Moderation in Louisiana," in *Massive Resistance: Southern Opposition to the Second Reconstruction*, ed. Clive Webb (Oxford University Press, 2005), 70.

8 Adam Fairclough, *Race and Democracy: The Civil Rights Struggle in Louisiana, 1915–1972* (University of Georgia Press, 1995), 339.

9 See Bernard, *Cajuns*, 88–89, 98–99.

10 Raymond Rodgers to John McKeithen, October 18, 1967, box 1, folder 13, Raymond S. Rodgers Collection, Acadiana Manuscript Collection, University of Louisiana, Lafayette, LA.

11 Raymond Rodgers to John Rarick, October 21, 1967, box 1, folder 11, Rodgers Collection, University of Louisiana, Lafayette (hereafter ULL).

12 Raymond Rodgers to Russell Long, Edwin Willis, and Edwin Edwards, October 21, 1967, box 1, folder 12, Rodgers Collection, ULL.

13 Teche News, "French Fete Draws Large Crowd, Governor Attends," *Teche News* (St. Martinville, LA), October 24, 1968, 1, 12.

14 Aihwa Ong, *Buddha Is Hiding: Refugees, Citizenship, the New America* (University of California Press, 2003), 11.

15 Roy Reed, "Louisiana's Cajuns, a Minority with Power," *New York Times*, May 9, 1972, 42.

16 Revon Reed, *Lâche pas la patate: Portrait des Acadiens de la Louisiane* (Éditions du parti pris, 1976), 19, 20 (emphases added; my translation).

17 Shane Bernard, "Acadian Pride, Anglo-Conformism: The Acadian Bicentennial Celebration of 1955," *Louisiana History* 41, no. 2 (2000): 163–64.

18 Matthew Frye Jacobson, *Roots, Too: White Ethnic Revival and Post-Civil Rights America* (Harvard University Press, 2006), 19.

19 Lalonde in Lisa Belkin, "A Legislator's Bayou Boyhood Is at Root of a Bill to Aid Cajuns," *New York Times*, June 14, 1988, A16; Barry Ancelet, "Ragin' Cajuns: What's in a Name?," *Creole Magazine* 3, no. 12 (1992): 42; Bernard, *Cajuns*, 142; Pat Mire, dir., *Against the Tide* (Action Cadienne and Louisiana Educational Television Authority, 2000); Ron Thibodeaux, "Royal Regrets Offered for Acadian Expulsion," *Times-Picayune* (New Orleans), December 11, 2003, A1.

20 Ron Thibodeaux, *Hell or High Water: How Cajun Fortitude Withstood Hurricanes Rita and Ike* (University of Louisiana at Lafayette Press, 2012), 4.

21 Sara Le Menestrel and Jacques Henry, "Figure du 'survivor': Gestion de la catastrophe et mémoire en Louisiane après les ouragans Katrina et Rita," *Ethnologie française* 40, no. 3 (2010): 502.

22 Karen Fields and Barbara Fields, *Racecraft: The Soul of Inequality in American Life* (Verso, 2012).

23 F. Edward Hébert, "The New Louisiana Story," March 5, 1974, 93rd Cong., 2nd sess., *Congressional Record* 120, pt. 4: 5417–22.

24 Carol Greenhouse, *A Moment's Notice: Time Politics across Cultures* (Cornell University Press, 1996), 3.

25 Since Louisiana had marginalized French language education in public schools, Cajuns and speakers of other French vernaculars were generally illiterate in them. On these media challenges, see David Wetsel, "Le CODOFIL et la langue française en Louisiane: Cajun ou standard?," in *Les acadiens: État de la recherche*, ed. Jacques Lapointe and André Leclerc (Conseil de la vie française en Amérique, 1987), 161–68; and John Smith-Thibodeaux, *Les francophones de Louisiane* (Éditions Entente, 1978), 78, 80–81.

26 See Gold, "Cajun French Debate in Louisiana."

27 See Bernard, *Cajuns*, 99–101; Wetsel, "Le CODOFIL et la langue française en Louisiane," 151–60; and Dorice Tentchoff, "Speech in a Louisiana Cajun Community" (PhD diss., Case Western Reserve University, 1977), 112.

28 Seminar for Constitutional Convention Delegates and Academic Humanists, *Gateway to Tomorrow: A New Constitution for Louisiana's People* (League of Women Voters of Louisiana, 1973), 10.

29 Edwards offered only lukewarm endorsements to speak French (Bernard, *Cajuns*, 105). The revised 1974 state constitution, whose passage Edwards oversaw, does not "afford [French] any real status or special protection." Roger Ward, "The French Language in Louisiana Law and Education: A Requiem," *Louisiana Law Review* 57, no. 4 (1997): 1301.

30 Cf. Jacques Henry and Carl Bankston III, *Blue Collar Bayou: Louisiana Cajuns in the New Economy of Ethnicity* (Praeger, 2002), 87–113.

31 Reed, "Louisiana's Cajuns," 42. Others echoed such language. See, e.g., Bernard, *Cajuns*, 94; Becky Tillson, "A Celebration of Family Reunion," *Daily Advertiser* (Lafayette, LA), July 28, 1999; and J. Minos Simon and David Leon Chandler, *Law in the Cajun Nation* (Prescott Press, 1993), 16.

32 Bernard, *Cajuns*, 137.

33 Sherry Ortner, *New Jersey Dreaming: Capital, Culture, and the Class of '58* (Duke University Press, 2003), 207.

34 Myron Tassin, *We Are Acadians: Nous Sommes Acadiens* (Pelican, 1976), 90–91.

35 Reed, *Lâche pas la patate*, 9.

36 Walton, "Louisiana's Coonasses," 42.

37 Warren Perrin, "Use of Slang Word Is Offensive to Acadians," *Times-Picayune* (New Orleans), January 27, 1990, B6; Perrin in Herman Fuselier, "Musicians, Attorney Spar over Patois," *Daily Advertiser* (Lafayette, LA), September 6, 2017. Similar complaints have been common; see Barry Ancelet, "A Perspective on Teaching the 'Problem Language' in Louisiana," *French Review* 61, no. 3 (1988): 354n5; and Ron Thibodeaux, "'Coonass' Carries Baggage That Some Would Prefer to Leave Behind," *Times-Picayune* (New Orleans), July 17, 2001.

38 Ron Emoff, "A Cajun Poetics of Loss and Longing," *Ethnomusicology* 42, no. 2 (1998): 285.

39 Moreau in Walton, "Louisiana's Coonasses," 43; James Dormon, *The People Called Cajuns: An Introduction to an Ethnohistory* (Center for Louisiana Studies, 1983), 87–88.

40 Shana Walton, "Louisiana's Coonasses: Choosing Race and Class over Ethnicity," in *Signifying Serpents and Mardi Gras Runners: Representing Identity in Selected Souths*, ed. Celeste Ray and Luke Lassiter (University of Georgia Press, 2003), 47.

41 Perrin in Richard Burgess, "Epithet Foe, 84, Dead: Cajun Sued Firm for Derogatory Term," *Baton Rouge Advocate*, March 26, 2010, 1B.

42 Perrin in Fuselier, "Musicians, Attorney Spar over Patois."

43 U.S. Congress, Senate, Committee on Interior and Insular Affairs, Subcommittee on Parks and Recreation, *Establishment of the Jean Lafitte National Park in the State of Louisiana*, 94th Cong., 2nd sess., 1976, 39–41.

44 Lieber in Carroll Wood Jr., "Purpose of Commission," in *Fourth Biennial Report of the State Parks Commission of Louisiana, 1940–41*, ed. Carroll Wood Jr. (State Parks Commission, 1942), 13; William Wells, "Future Needs," in *Tenth Biennial Report of the State Parks Commission of Louisiana, 1952–60*, ed. William Wells (State Parks and Recreation Commission, 1960), 51–52.

45 One exception is a brief passage from a report during World War II, stating, "We feel it is important to preserve certain heritages of the past, especially in the ways of living." E. Herman Guillory, "Introduction," in *Fifth Biennial Report of the State Parks Commission, 1942–1943*, ed. Williams Wells (State Parks Commission, 1943), 15.

46 Robert Blythe, *Administrative History of Jean Lafitte National Historical Park and Preserve* (National Park Service Southeast Regional Office, 2012), 94.

47 Handwritten note to Harry (Pfanz?), December 2, 1976; Erwin Thompson to Harry Pfanz, January 17, 1973; Harry Pfanz to Associate Director, Preservation of Historic Properties, January 7, 1977; Folder "Jean Lafitte National Historical Park correspondence, 1970–," Jean Lafitte National Historical Park Planning Division files, National Park Service Headquarters, Washington, DC.

48 Joe Frantz to Linden Pettys, March 25, 1977, folder "Jean Lafitte Task Force—December 1976," Planning Division files, National Park Service (hereafter NPS) HQ.

49 As Jean Lafitte's authorizing legislation neared passage, NPS Assistant Secretary Robert Herbst told the House Interior Committee that the Park's Advisory Board "believe[d] that a case can be made for a park honoring Cajun culture." See U.S. Congress, House, Miscellaneous Reports on Public Bills, *Establish Jean Lafitte National Park and Preserve in Louisiana*, 95th Congress, 2nd sess., 1978, H. Rep. 1544, serial 13201, 8.

50 U.S. Congress, *National Parks and Recreation Act of 1978: Title IX Jean Lafitte National Historical Park*, Pub. L. No. 95-625, § 901, 92 Stat. 3534–35.

51 Blythe, *Administrative History of Jean Lafitte*, 98.

52 Ronald Foresta, *America's National Parks and Their Keepers* (Resources for the Future, 1984), 151. In one sense, the NPS ultimately prevailed. Its staff never made Lafitte the overarching theme of its historical interpretation. Links between his history and that of Acadians in the park sites are "extremely tenuous to nonexistent" (Blythe, *Administrative History of Jean Lafitte*, 197).

53 Foresta, *America's National Parks and Their Keepers*, 129–48.

54 See Peter Novick, *That Noble Dream: The "Objectivity Question" and the American Historical Profession* (Cambridge University Press, 1988), 469–521.

55 Denise Meringolo, *Museums, Monuments, and National Parks: Toward a New Genealogy of Public History* (University of Massachusetts Press, 2012), xxi, xx.

56 Ian Tyrrell, *Historians in Public: The Practice of American History, 1890–1970* (University of Chicago Press, 2005); Randall Mason and Max Page, *Giving Preservation a History: Histories of Historic Preservation in the United States*, 2nd ed. (Routledge, 2019); Meringolo, *Museums, Monuments, and National Parks.*

57 The NPS has remained committed to following Tilden's vision, though it is not without its critics (e.g., Anne Mitchell Whisnant, "Case Statement," in *Interpreting Our Heritage in the 21st Century Working Group*, 2019 National Council on Public History Annual Meeting, 2019, https://interpretingourheritage.com/case-statements/anne-mitchell-whisnant-case-statement/).

58 Freeman Tilden, *Who Am I? Reflections on the Meanings of Parks on the Occasion of the Nation's Bicentennial* (Department of the Interior, 1976), 21–22; first emphasis added, subsequent emphases in original.

59 Tilden, *Who Am I?*, 24.

60 Michel Foucault, *On the Government of the Living: Lectures at the Collège de France, 1979–80*, trans. Graham Burchell (Picador, 2012), 311.

61 Marc Malik, William Jones, Bonnie Campbell, L. Clifford Soubier, and Arthur Hehr, "Suitability/Feasibility Study: Proposed Jean Lafitte National Cultural Park," 1973, p. 1, Planning Division files, NPS HQ.

62 Malik et al., "Suitability/Feasibility Study," 2.

63 In this case, the authors explicitly intended this modeling to generate such an effect. While Louisiana advocates wanted a park that qualified as a natural site, NPS rejected this and proposed a historical/cultural one. This study was the service's first attempt to convince them to adopt its position (Blythe, *Administrative History of Jean Lafitte*, 96–97).

64 Tim Radford and Cecile Chevrier, dirs., *The Cajun Way: Echoes of Acadia* (National Park Service and Les Productions du Phare-Est Canada, 1995).

65 Rose, *Powers of Freedom*, 42.

66 Freeman Tilden, *Interpreting Our Heritage* (University of North Carolina Press, 1957), 33, 44.

67 Louisiana Historical Association, *An Invitation to Join the Louisiana Historical Association* (Louisiana Historical Association, 1958), 10. See Kenneth Urquhart, "Seventy Years of the Louisiana Historical Association," *Louisiana History* 1, no. 1 (1960): 5–25.

68 For the first series of newsletters, see Louisiana Historical Association, *Newsletter* (Louisiana Historical Association, 1958–60); for the second, see Louisiana Historical Association, *Louisiana History Newsletter* (University of Southwestern Louisiana and Louisiana Historical Association, 1975–).

69 Membership Meeting, May 30, 1966, box 1, folder 3, "Minutes, General Meetings, 1966," Attakapas Historical Association Records, Acadiana Manuscript Collection, University of Louisiana at Lafayette, Lafayette, LA.

70 Mrs. T. P. Saizin, Minutes, Attakapas Historical Association Meeting in Franklin, p. 3, box 3, folder 11, "Minutes, General Meetings, 1968," Attakapas Historical Association (hereafter AHA) Records, ULL.

71 Board Meeting, March 16, 1970, box 3, folder 5, "Minutes, Board of Directors, 1970," AHA Records, ULL.

72 Set in their broader context (which extends beyond this book's focus), activities like involvement in the AHA and launching the Center for Louisiana Studies can be seen as typical strategies among administrators and faculty at regional state universities during this moment, when responding to local cultural and civic needs, adopting roles as anchor institutions, and becoming more comprehensive to compete with public flagships were common objectives. See, e.g., E. Alden Dunham, *Colleges of the Forgotten Americans: A Profile of State Colleges and Universities* (McGraw-Hill, 1969).

73 Vaughn Baker, Minutes, Attakapas Historical Association, Publications Committee Meeting, February 20, 1976, 2, box 3, folder 8, "Minutes, Board of Directors, 1976," AHA Records, ULL.

74 On this Colonial Records Collection at the Center for Louisiana Studies and Conrad's role in it, see Carl Brasseaux, "The Colonial Record Collection of the Center for Louisiana Studies," *Louisiana History* 25, no. 2 (1984): 181–88.

75 Mrs. T. P. Saizin, Minutes, Attakapas Historical Association Meeting in Franklin, p. 3, box 3, folder 11, "Minutes, General Meetings, 1968," AHA Records, ULL.

76 States-Item, "Fighting the Myths of Cajun Heritage," *States-Item* (New Orleans), November 10, 1975, 27; Glenn Conrad, ed., "The Acadians: Myths and Realities," in *The Cajuns: Essays on Their History and Culture* (Center for Louisiana Studies, 1978), 1.

77 Conrad, "Acadians," 2.

78 States-Item, "Fighting the Myths," 26.

79 Thomas Osborne, "The Ordinariness of the Archive," *History of the Human Sciences* 12, no. 2 (1999): 52.

80 Bruno Latour, *Science in Action: How to Follow Scientists and Engineers through Society* (Open University Press, 1986), 150, 182. Among other effects, such a politics "escalates the proof race" among competing interpreters (232).

81 Osborne, "Ordinariness of the Archive," 53–54.

82 See Bernard, "Acadian Pride, Anglo-Conformism"; and W. Fitzhugh Brundage, "Le Reveil de la Louisiane: Memory and Acadian Identity, 1920–1960," in *Where These Memories Grow: History, Memory, and Southern Identity*, ed. W. Fitzhugh Brundage (University of North Carolina Press, 1999).

83 Thomas Clausen, "Foreword," in *Acadians of Louisiana: Curriculum Guide. Grade 8. Bulletin 1780* (Louisiana State Department of Education, 1987), iii.

84 See Malcolm Comeaux, *Atchafalaya Swamp Life: Settlement and Folk Occupations* (LSU School of Geoscience, 1972).

85 Glenn Conrad, *The Attakapas Domesday Book: Land Grants, Claims, and Certifications in the Attakapas District, 1764–1826* (Center for Louisiana Studies, 1991), xxvi, xxvii.

86 Tony Bennett, *Making Culture, Changing Society* (Routledge, 2013), 52.

87 Acadian Memorial grant proposal draft, 1992, Acadian Memorial administrative files.

88 This initial proposal featured a multimedia presentation for which Brasseaux advocated. It was not funded, so memorial designers never realized that aspect

of the design. But they reused Brasseaux's framing "for many other successful endeavors" (personal communication from Janie Bulliard, July 26, 2001).

89 The National Museum of American History's Bicentennial exhibit *A Nation of Nations*, which foregrounded a range of immigrant experiences in representing the nation's past, nonetheless concluded by stressing the shared experiences of public schooling and military training that forged a common American identity. William Walker, *A Living Exhibition: The Smithsonian and the Transformation of the Universal Museum* (University of Massachusetts Press, 2013), 163–81.

90 See John Szwed, *Alan Lomax: The Man Who Recorded the World* (Penguin, 2011).

91 U.S. Congress, Senate, Committee on Labor and Public Welfare, Subcommittee on Education, *Hearing on the American Folklife Foundation Act*, 91st Cong., 2nd sess., 1970, 28.

92 Toby Miller and George Yúdice, *Cultural Policy* (Sage, 2002), 49. Nonprofits like the Rockefeller Foundation shared this diagnosis, envisioning "arts infrastructure as an alternative to the grave peril of 'leisure'" in troubled regions of the country (50).

93 Jacobson, *Roots, Too*, 23.

94 Charles Hosmer interview with George Hartzog, August 5, 1981, box 1, Subsubseries 2, Subseries B, Series V, National Park Service Oral History Collection, Harpers Ferry Center Archives, Harpers Ferry, WV.

95 Alan Lomax to Joseph Duffy, February 28, 1979, with attached proposal "Toward a Presidential Commission on Grass Roots Culture," box 34, folder E16(a) "Folklife—Federal Council on the Arts and Humanities," Records of the National Foundation on the Arts and the Humanities, Record Group 288, National Archives, College Park, MD.

96 Rose, *Powers of Freedom*, 168. Other calls to govern through communities were arguably neoliberal; e.g., Peter Berger and Richard John Neuhaus, *To Empower People: The Role of Mediating Structures in Public Policy* (American Enterprise Institute, 1977).

97 Bess Lomax Hawes to Larry Kubota, planning document draft, July 25, 1980, box 7, folder 5, Louisiana Folklife Program Project Files, Louisiana and Lower Mississippi Valley Collections, Louisiana State University, Baton Rouge, LA.

98 From the beginning, NPS consultants described the region as culturally unique, where peoples from all over the Atlantic world "have been fused into a whole while retaining the best features of each." "The Delta Strategy: A Concept," n.d., p. 1, Planning Division files, NPS HQ.

99 Nicholas Spitzer, Ray Brassieur, Michael Caron, Jeffrey Golliher, H. F. Gregory, C. Paige Gutierrez, Janice Pierce, and Robert Rathburn, *Mississippi Delta Ethnographic Overview* (National Park Service, 1979), 394.

100 During the early 1970s, the NPS created a cultural park category that it initially used to conceptualize Jean Lafitte. The mandate for such parks was to "preserve folkways of the past as well as establishing sites for contemporary programs" (Malik et al., "Suitability/Feasibility Study," 71). Ultimately, the new site launched as a historical park, but a stress on the region's folklife remained.

101 Spitzer et al., *Mississippi Delta Ethnographic Overview*, 395.

102 Malik et al., "Suitability/Feasibility Study," 71.

103 Dominique Poulot, "Identity as Self-Discovery: The Eco-Museum in France," in *Museum Culture: Histories, Discourses, Spectacles*, ed. Daniel Sherman and Irit Rogoff (University of Minnesota Press, 1994).
104 Bennett, *Making Culture, Changing Society*, 61, 55.
105 Jacobson, *Roots, Too*, 4.
106 Judith Gentry and John Cameron, "A Social and Economic History of Colonial and Antebellum Acadian Louisiana," NEH Research Grant proposal, February 22, 1979, n.p., box 3, folder 13, "Faculty grant proposals 1970s," University Archives, Department of History, Acadiana Manuscripts Collection, ULL.
107 "Delta Strategy," 1, 2.
108 "Delta Strategy," 10, 4.
109 Barry Ancelet and Mathé Allain, "Center for Acadian and Creole Folklore: A Progress and Status Report," March 27, 1979, box 8, folder 18, "Center for Acadian and Creole Folklore (1979–1981)"; "The USL Center for Louisiana Studies: A Proposal," July 24, 1973, box 9, folder 12, "Folklore and Folklife Programs—Center for Louisiana Studies," Glenn Conrad Papers, Acadiana Manuscripts Collection, University of Louisiana at Lafayette, Lafayette, LA.
110 Malik et al., "Suitability/Feasibility Study," 226–27.
111 Margaret Werry, *The Tourist State: Performing Leisure, Liberalism, and Race* (University of Minnesota Press, 2011), 150.

CHAPTER SIX

1 See Bob Jessop, *The State: Past, Present, Future* (Polity Press, 2016).
2 See, e.g., James Loewen, *Lies My Teacher Told Me: Everything Your American History Textbook Got Wrong* (Simon and Schuster, 1995).
3 Timothy Mitchell, *Rule of Experts: Egypt, Techno-politics, Modernity* (University of California Press, 2002).
4 Michel Foucault, *Security, Territory, Population: Lectures at the Collège de France, 1977–78*, trans. Graham Burchell (Palgrave Macmillan, 2007), 109.
5 Nikolas Rose, *Powers of Freedom: Reframing Political Thought* (Cambridge University Press, 1999), 48.
6 Michel Callon, "Some Elements of a Sociology of Translation: Domestication of the Scallops and the Fisherman of St. Brieuc Bay," in *Power, Action and Belief: A New Sociology of Knowledge?*, ed. John Law (Routledge, 1986).
7 On technologies of power as one dimension of his "microphysics of power," see Foucault, *Security, Territory, Population*, 116–19.
8 Marc Savoy, *Made in Louisiana: The Story of the Acadian Accordion* (University of Louisiana at Lafayette Press, 2021), 52.
9 Savoy, *Made in Louisiana*, 58.
10 Denver Service Center, "Interpretive Prospectus: Jean Lafitte National Historical Park," August 1983, box 12, folder 4593, Jean Lafitte National Historical Park Collection, University of New Orleans, New Orleans, LA.

11 Savoy led a nonprofit whose acronym was SPECIAL, the Society for the Preservation of Ethnic Culture in Acadian Louisiana. Marc Savoy, "Eunice: Center of Cajun Culture," n.d., box 3, folder 4510, Jean Lafitte National Historical Park Collection, University of New Orleans.

12 Robert Blythe interview with Curtis Joubert, November 26, 2008, Jean Lafitte National Historical Park Headquarters Archives files, New Orleans.

13 Peter Novick, *That Noble Dream: The "Objectivity Question" and the American Historical Profession* (Cambridge University Press, 1988), 472.

14 Louisiana Endowment for the Humanities, *A Report to the People* (Louisiana Endowment for the Humanities, 1994), 2.

15 Robert Blythe, *Administrative History of Jean Lafitte National Historical Park and Preserve* (National Park Service Southeast Regional Office, 2012), 189.

16 Blythe, *Administrative History of Jean Lafitte National Historical Park*, 191, 192.

17 Tony Bennett, *Making Culture, Changing Society* (Routledge, 2013), 67.

18 Excerpts from text panels in the Museum of the Acadian Memorial, St. Martinville, LA.

19 Marita Sturken argues compellingly that because "authorities speak to Americans in the language of consumerism more than the language of citizenship," national identity and the historical commemorations that buttress it convey "a deep alliance between the practices of consumerism and the practices of patriotism." Marita Sturken, *Tourists of History: Memory, Kitsch, and Consumerism from Oklahoma City to Ground Zero* (Duke University Press, 2007), 15, 40. On dynamics of the commodification and consumption of heritage elsewhere, see Sharon Macdonald, *Memorylands: Heritage and Identity in Europe Today* (Routledge, 2013), chaps. 5 and 6; and John L. Comaroff and Jean Comaroff, *Ethnicity, Inc.* (University of Chicago Press, 2009).

20 Kevin Fox Gotham, *Authentic New Orleans: Tourism, Culture, and Race in the Big Easy* (New York University Press, 2007), 120–23.

21 Louisiana Office of Tourism, *Louisiana Open House Manual: Louisiana Tourism: A Grassroots Guide to Success* (Louisiana Office of Tourism, 1989); Allyson Fertitta, "*Bienvenue en Louisiane*: A Case Study of the Louisiana Public Relations Campaign to Promote Francophone Tourism for Francofête '99, the Louisiana Tricentennial" (master's thesis, Louisiana State University, 2000).

22 Louisiana Economic Development Council, *Louisiana Vision 2020: Action Plan 2001* (Louisiana Economic Development Council, 2001), D-34.

23 Others have noted the effect that a media-inflected craze for Cajun food and music had on such developments during the 1980s. See Sara Le Menestrel, *La voie des Cadiens: Tourisme et identité en Louisiane* (Belin, 1999), 191–207; and Jacques Henry and Carl Bankston III, *Blue Collar Bayou: Louisiana Cajuns in the New Economy of Ethnicity* (Praeger, 2002), 185–209.

24 Both were present in St. Martinville: the former through a public-sector position devoted to the program and the latter from its participation in the state-sponsored Atchafalaya Heritage Trace.

25 Cf. Henri Lefebvre, *The Production of Space*, trans. Donald Nicholson-Smith (Blackwell, 1991), 98–99, 127–28.

26 Mary Means, "Heritage Areas as an Approach to Regional Planning," in *Time-Saver Standards for Urban Design*, ed. Donald Watson, Alan Plattus, and Robert Shibley (McGraw-Hill, 2003), 5.6-4.

27 In the late 1990s, the state contracted with Mary Means and Associates, a consulting firm specializing in heritage area conceptualization, to craft a management plan for what later became the Atchafalaya National Heritage Area. Atchafalaya Trace Commission, *The Atchafalaya Trace Heritage Area Management Plan* (Louisiana Department of Culture, Recreation, and Tourism and Atchafalaya Trace Commission, 2002).

28 Susan Ditto, "Maison Olivier: The Public and Private Life of a Creole Raised Cottage in the Longfellow-Evangeline Park, St. Martinville, Louisiana" (master's thesis, University of Southwestern Louisiana, 1990), 111.

29 Carl Brasseaux, *In Search of Evangeline: Birth and Evolution of the Evangeline Myth* (Blue Heron Press, 1988), 52, 45.

30 Ditto, "Maison Olivier," 127, 123, 124.

31 Ron Delhomme, "Longfellow-Evangeline State Commemorative Area," *Daily Advertiser* (Lafayette, LA), January 11, 1992, B1.

32 Callon, "Some Elements of a Sociology of Translation," 196.

33 Jennifer Mitchell, summary of grant panel reviews of "You Were There: Day of Sorrow at Grand Pre" submissions from the Acadian Memorial Foundation to the Louisiana Endowment from the Humanities. Personal communication with the author, n.d.

34 On truth obligations and regimes of truth, see Daniele Lorenzini, *The Force of Truth: Critique, Genealogy, and Truth-Telling in Michel Foucault* (University of Chicago Press, 2023), 33–41.

35 Rose, *Powers of Freedom*, 48.

36 Rose, 49.

37 Rose, 49.

38 Michael Sartisky, "Illiteracy Affects Us All," *Cultural Vistas* 1, no. 2 (1990): 1.

39 Acadian Memorial Foundation, "Ensemble Encore: The Acadian Memorial Multimedia Archive," General Grant Application to the Louisiana Endowment for the Humanities, October 31, 1997, Louisiana Endowment for the Humanities files, New Orleans.

40 Thomas Kirsch and Roy Dilley, "Regimes of Ignorance: An Introduction," in *Regimes of Ignorance: Anthropological Perspectives on the Production and Reproduction of Non-knowledge* (Berghahn, 2015), 22–23.

41 Louisiana Office of Tourism, *Louisiana Open House Manual*, 3.

42 Mary Means and Elaine Carmichael, "Old Wine, New Bottles: Rethinking How Culture and History Are Marketed," summary of workshop presentation, Governor's Conference on Travel and Tourism, April 2–4, 2001, Hyannis, Massachusetts, 4.

43 Atchafalaya Trace Commission, *The Atchafalaya Trace Heritage Area Management Plan* (Louisiana Department of Culture, Recreation, and Tourism and Atchafalaya Trace Commission, 2002), 27.

44 Louisiana House of Representatives, *House Concurrent Resolution no. 13*, Regular Session 1991, Attachment to letter from Alfred Speer, House Clerk, to

St. Martinville City Council, June 24, 1991, 2, Acadian Memorial administrative files, St. Martinville, LA.

45 Louisiana House of Representatives, *House Concurrent Resolution no. 13*, 1.

46 Office of Lieutenant Governor Paul Hardy, "Proclamation of St. Martinville Acadian Memorial Day," July 16, 1991, Acadian Memorial administrative files.

47 Le Menestrel, *La voie des Cadiens*, 247.

48 Le Menestrel, 162.

49 Rose, *Powers of Freedom*, 50.

50 J. Conrad Miller, "Thanks for Telling Me When to Be Offended," *Daily Advertiser* (Lafayette, LA), April 4, 2001, A9.

51 Ron Thibodeaux, "'Coonass' Carries Baggage That Some Would Prefer to Leave Behind," *Times-Picayune* (New Orleans), July 17, 2001.

52 S. R. Greene, "Need to Get a Grip about Use of Word, 'Coona—,'" *Daily Advertiser* (Lafayette, LA), April 4, 2001, A9.

53 Thibodeaux, "'Coonass' Carries Baggage."

54 Savoy, "Eunice: Center of Cajun Culture," 2.

55 Matthew Frye Jacobson, *Roots, Too: White Ethnic Revival and Post-Civil Rights America* (Harvard University Press, 2006), 187–97.

56 Michel Foucault, *On the Government of the Living: Lectures at the Collège de France, 1979–80*, trans. Graham Burchell (Picador, 2012), 311.

57 Thomas Lemke, *Foucault's Analysis of Modern Governmentality: A Critique of Political Reason* (Verso, 2019), 26.

58 Peter Miller and Nikolas Rose, *Governing the Present: Administering Economic, Social and Personal Life* (Polity Press, 2008), 4.

CHAPTER SEVEN

1 Geoffrey White, "Emotional Remembering: The Pragmatics of National Memory," *Ethos* 27, no. 4 (2000): 506.

2 White, "Emotional Remembering," 506.

3 Charlotte Linde, *Working the Past: Narrative and Institutional Memory* (Oxford University Press, 2008).

4 For this chapter, I interviewed forty-nine individuals in three different settings: (1) I conducted brief interviews with nineteen randomly selected individuals immediately following their visits to the memorial; (2) I invited eighteen individuals—residents of the region who had visited the site—to participate in five focus groups; and (3) I conducted extended interviews with twelve others, all of whom had served as memorial staff or members of its nonprofit board.

5 Jennifer Cole, "Narratives and Moral Projects: Generational Memories of the Malagasy 1947 Rebellion," *Ethos* 31, no. 1 (2003): 98.

6 Carol Lancon quoted in "Dafford Making Progress on Acadian Memorial Mural," *Teche News* (St. Martinville, LA), February 23, 1994, A-1; memorial cofounder Janie Bulliard in Jonas Breaux, "Acadian Memorial: A Dream Come True," *Daily Advertiser* (Lafayette, LA), August 13, 1995, A-13; Mayor Eric Martin in Pam

Boyd Brownlee, "Acadian Memorial's Strength Will Be That It Names Names," *Times of the Teche* (Lafayette, LA), August 10, 1995, 13; muralist Robert Dafford in Jacqueline Cochran, "Memorial Opening Draws Special Guest," *Advertiser* (Lafayette, LA), April 30, 1996, A-7; memorial cofounder Pat Resweber in "About the Mural," *Acadiana LifeStyle* (New Iberia, LA), December 1995, 33; Pat Resweber in Gladys de Villier, "Acadian Memorial Opens," *Teche News*, May 1, 1996, A-2.

7 Such statements were not the result of hyperbole that only small-town boosterism could generate. For instance, academics whom the National Park Service (NPS) consulted on exhibit design for the Acadian Unit in its Jean Lafitte Park urged NPS to use "sensory-oriented" exhibits to "[insert] the visitor directly into the sensory world of Cajun life" and create "a more direct perceptive (and hopefully emotional) contact" with it. Jay Edwards, "Recommendations for Organization of Cajun Culture Centers," in *The Cajuns: Their History and Culture*, ed. Hamilton and Associates (Hamilton and Associates, 1987), 203–4. The NPS employed this strategy.

8 Alison Griffiths, *Shivers Down Your Spine: Cinema, Museums, and the Immersive View* (Columbia University Press, 2008), 2, 3.

9 Paul Ricoeur, *Memory, History, Forgetting*, trans. Kathleen Blamey and David Pellauer (University of Chicago Press, 2004), 155.

10 As mentioned in chapter 5, the memorial's designers chose to foreground group cohesion over the stress on class fissures that recent scholarship featured.

11 Kathleen Blanco in Don Shoopman, "Wall of Names Salutes Acadians Who Settled Here," *Daily Iberian* (New Iberia, LA), June 4, 1998.

12 Diane Moore, "Stepping Out of the Past," *Acadiana LifeStyle* (New Iberia, LA), April 1994, 44; Breaux, "Acadian Memorial," A-13.

13 Janie Bulliard quoted first by Ron Delhomme, "Wall of Names Unveiled," *Daily Advertiser* (Lafayette, LA), June 1, 1998, 1A; then by Henri Bienvenu, "Wall of Names Unveiled," *Teche News*, June 3, 1998, A-1.

14 Breaux, "Acadian Memorial," A-13.

15 "Artist Commissioned for Acadian Mural," *Teche News*, January 22, 1992, 1A.

16 Carol Greenhouse, *A Moment's Notice: Time Politics across Cultures* (Cornell University Press, 1996), 7.

17 Sharon Macdonald, *Memorylands: Heritage and Identity in Europe Today* (Routledge, 2013), 15.

18 Michael Lambek, "Memory in a Maussian Universe," in *Regimes of Memory*, ed. Katharine Hodgkin and Susannah Radstone (Taylor and Francis, 2003), 213.

19 Michel Foucault, "Technologies of the Self," in *Technologies of the Self: A Seminar with Michel Foucault*, ed. Luther Martin, Huck Guttman, and Patrick Gutman (Tavistock, 1988), 49.

20 Similar to the NPS's *Mississippi Delta Ethnographic Overview* decades earlier, the Atchafalaya Trace Heritage Area's Management Plan claimed that the region's "long legacy of multiculturalism presents interesting opportunities to examine how so many distinct cultures have survived in relative harmony." Atchafalaya Trace Commission, *Atchafalaya Trace Heritage Area Management Plan*, 5.

21 Maurice Halbwachs, *On Collective Memory*, trans. Lewis Coser (University of Chicago Press, 1992), 64.

22 In addition to Sandra Mouton's comment, one other exception occurred when another member of the focus group mentioned earlier in the chapter ranked Cajuns higher than Blacks in a hierarchy of discrimination, as it were. He claimed, "We're one of the last minorities where it's allowed and acceptable to portray us as, I don't know, savages or half-breeds or whatever, and nobody says anything about it. They couldn't do it to Black people."

23 Cf. Bayo Holsey, *Routes of Remembrance: Refashioning the Slave Trade in Ghana* (University of Chicago Press, 2008).

24 Geoffrey White and Eveline Buchheim, "Traveling War: Memory Practices in Motion," *History and Memory* 27, no. 2 (2015): 5.

25 Maurice Halbwachs, *The Collective Memory*, trans. Francis Ditter Jr. and Vida Yazdi Ditter (Harper and Row, 1980), 56, 59.

26 Halbwachs, 52.

27 See, e.g., Thomas Gorman, *Growing Up Working Class: Hidden Injuries and the Development of Angry White Men and Women* (Palgrave Macmillan, 2017); John Hartigan Jr., *Racial Situations: Class Predicaments of Whiteness in Detroit* (Princeton University Press, 1999); and Michèle Lamont, *The Dignity of Working Men: Morality and the Boundaries of Race, Class, and Immigration* (Harvard University Press, 2000).

28 Michel Foucault, "Truth and Power," in *Michel Foucault: Power*, trans. Robert Hurley, ed. James Faubion (New Press, 2000), 120.

29 David Lowenthal, *The Past Is a Foreign Country* (Cambridge University Press, 1985).

30 Liisa Malkki, *Purity and Exile: Violence, Memory and National Cosmology among Hutu Refugees in Tanzania* (University of Chicago Press, 1995), 223.

31 See Ron Emoff, "A Cajun Poetics of Loss and Longing," *Ethnomusicology* 42, no. 2 (1998): 285.

32 Geoffrey White, "Epilogue: Memory Moments," *Ethos* 34, no. 2 (2006): 331.

33 Cole, "Narratives and Moral Projects," 122.

34 Mary Douglas, *Purity and Danger: An Analysis of Concepts of Pollution and Taboo* (Praeger, 1966).

35 Malkki, *Purity and Exile*, 242.

36 Chris Hayes, "*How the Word Is Passed* with Clint Smith," *Why Is This Happening?*, June 3, 2021, podcast transcript, https://www.msnbc.com/msnbc-podcast/how-word-passed-clint-smith-podcast-transcript-n1269544.

37 Michel Foucault, *On the Government of the Living: Lectures at the Collège de France, 1979–80*, trans. Graham Burchell (Picador, 2012), 331.

38 Cf. Alexandra Giancarlo, "'Don't Call Me a Cajun!': Race and Representation in Louisiana's Acadiana Region," *Journal of Cultural Geography* 36, no. 1 (2018): 23–48; Christophe Landry, "Francophone Louisiana: More Than Cajun," *Louisiana Cultural Vistas*, Summer 2010, 50–54.

39 David Theo Goldberg, *The Racial State* (Wiley-Blackwell, 2001).

CONCLUSION

1 Michel-Rolph Trouillot, *Silencing the Past: Power and the Production of History* (Beacon Press, 2015), 20, 22.
2 Liisa Malkki, *Purity and Exile: Violence, Memory and National Cosmology among Hutu Refugees in Tanzania* (University of Chicago Press, 1995), 240, 241.
3 See Matthew Frye Jacobson, *Roots, Too: White Ethnic Revival and Post-Civil Rights America* (Harvard University Press, 2006); and Jacques Henry and Carl Bankston III, *Blue Collar Bayou: Louisiana Cajuns in the New Economy of Ethnicity* (Praeger, 2002).
4 Jeannette Mageo and Bruce Knauft, "Introduction: Theorizing Power and the Self," in *Power and the Self* (Cambridge University Press, 2002), 1.
5 E.g., Katherine Cramer, *The Politics of Resentment: Rural Consciousness in Wisconsin and the Rise of Scott Walker* (University of Chicago Press, 2016); Arlie Hochschild, *Strangers in Their Own Land: Anger and Mourning on the American Right* (New Press, 2016); cf. Aihwa Ong, *Buddha Is Hiding: Refugees, Citizenship, the New America* (University of California Press, 2003).
6 Carol Greenhouse, *A Moment's Notice: Time Politics across Cultures* (Cornell University Press, 1996), 220.
7 Premesh Lalu, "In the Event of History," *Kronos* 47 (2021): 97.
8 Stephen Collier, *Post-Soviet Social: Neoliberalism, Social Modernity, Biopolitics* (Princeton University Press, 2011), 24.
9 Barbara Kirshenblatt-Gimblett, *Destination Culture: Tourism, Museums, Heritage* (University of California Press, 1998), 3.
10 Thomas Lemke, *Foucault's Analysis of Modern Governmentality: A Critique of Political Reason* (Verso, 2019), 154.
11 Malkki, *Purity and Exile*, 233.
12 Jacobson, *Roots, Too*, 22.
13 See, e.g., Carl Bankston III and Stephen J. Caldas, *A Troubled Dream: The Promise and Failure of School Desegregation in Louisiana* (Vanderbilt University Press, 2002).
14 Hochschild, *Strangers in Their Own Land*, 146, 147.
15 Hochschild, 135–40.
16 Cf. Linda Williams, *Playing the Race Card: Melodramas of Black and White from Uncle Tom to O.J. Simpson* (Princeton University Press, 2001).
17 Robert Fleegler, *Ellis Island Nation: Immigration Policy and American Identity in the Twentieth Century* (University of Pennsylvania Press, 2015).
18 Tim Radford and Cecile Chevrier, dirs., *The Cajun Way: Echoes of Acadia* (National Park Service and Les Productions du Phare-Est Canada, 1995).
19 Bruce Daigrepont, "Acadie à la Louisiane," *Coeur des Cajuns* (Rounder Records, 1989).
20 Carl Brasseaux, *French, Cajun, Creole, Houma: A Primer on Francophone Louisiana* (Louisiana State University Press, 2005), 39–40.
21 Daniele Lorenzini, *The Force of Truth: Critique, Genealogy, and Truth-Telling in Michel Foucault* (University of Chicago Press, 2023), 36–41.

22 See, e.g., James Loewen, *Lies across America: What Our Historic Sites Get Wrong*, 2nd ed. (New Press, 2019); cf. Edward Said, *Culture and Imperialism* (Knopf, 1993), xxvi.

23 Daniel is not alone in raising these issues. See Robert Post, *Who Owns America? The Smithsonian and the Problem of History* (Johns Hopkins University Press, 2017); and Lonnie Bunch III, *A Fool's Errand: Creating the National Museum of African American History and Culture in the Age of Bush, Obama, and Trump* (Smithsonian Books, 2019).

24 Pete Daniel, *Curating the American Past: A Memoir of a Quarter Century at the Smithsonian National Museum of American History* (University of Arkansas Press, 2022), 8, 9, 102, 142.

25 Nikolas Rose, *Powers of Freedom: Reframing Political Thought* (Cambridge University Press, 1999), 97.

26 Frederic Jameson, *Archaeologies of the Future: The Desire Called Utopia and Other Science Fictions* (Verso, 2005), 255.

Index